THE NORMS OF ANSWERABILITY

THE NORMS OF ANSWERABILITY

SOCIAL THEORY BETWEEN BAKHTIN AND HABERMAS

୧ଛ

GREG MARC NIELSEN

FOREWORD BY
CARYL EMERSON

STATE UNIVERSITY OF NEW YORK PRESS

For information, address State University of New York Press,
90 State Street, Suite 700, Albany, NY 12207

Production by Kelli M. Williams
Marketing by Anne M. Valentine

Library of Congress Cataloging-in-Publication Data

Nielsen, Greg Marc, 1953–
    The norms of answerability : social theory between Bakhtin and
Habermas / Greg Marc Nielsen.
        p. cm.
    Includes bibliographical references and index.
    ISBN 0-7914-5227-1 (alk. paper) -- ISBN 0-7914-5228-X (pbk. :
alk. paper)
    1. Social norms.   2. Sociology--History.   I. Title.

HM676 .N54 2002
306--dc21   2001049306

10 9 8 7 6 5 4 3 2 1

Contents

FOREWORD

In his early ruminations on moral philosophy, published only posthumously, Bakhtin announced as part of his work plan for the 1920s an ambitious four-part project.[1] It would begin with the architectonic of the answerable act, that is, with "the world actually experienced, and not merely the thinkable world"; its subsequent parts would discuss aesthetic activity as a performed act or deed (the ethics of artistic creation), the ethics of politics, and the ethics of religion. As it happened, Bakhtin devoted the rest of his life to exploring the first two domains. Neither religion nor politics were appropriate theoretical interests for an independent scholar to pursue in Stalinist Russia. But later scholars have found it hard not to speculate on this unfulfilled agenda. Since Bakhtin's death in 1975, and even more since the death of Soviet Communism in 1992, the fourth area, "Bakhtin and religion," has become a fertile (if much contested) field of study.[2] And the ethics of politics? For a long time now, a sort of politics has been extracted from Bakhtin's carnival idea—although this has not been politics of a durable institutional variety, emphasizing as it does the ecstatic revolutionary moment over patterns of everyday behavior or civic procedures. Only quite recently, with Ken Hirschkop's *Mikhail Bakhtin: An Aesthetic for Democracy* (1999),[3] has this final "unwritten" part of Bakhtin's visionary plan begun to receive serious, systematic, nonutopian attention.

Greg Nielsen is part of this recent movement. He views politics not as a philosopher or political scientist, however, but as a sociologist. Accordingly, he begins by asking a number of professional questions:

where should sociologists look for a history of their young discipline? Since the foundational thinkers of sociology emerged out of nine-teenth-century socioeconomics, political and moral philosophy, and psychology (or, more accurately, they pursued their critiques through a reconsideration and statistical refinement of those more established fields), and since several of those thinkers were also of importance to Bakhtin, perhaps a Bakhtinian "ethics of politics" could be assembled at their points of intersection? Nielsen himself locates the prehistory of sociology in philosophies of consciousness and the self—selves that are linked, one self at a time, into local commitments, larger commu-nities, then ultimately sociopolitical units. His primary anchors are Kant (at the beginning) and Habermas (at the end). Again, in what has become for Bakhtin researchers a somewhat mournful exercise, Nielsen demonstrates Bakhtin's heavy and uncredited debt to several luminaries of German social thought, especially Georg Simmel.[4]

At the end of his first chapter, Nielsen makes a general comment about moral philosophy that might serve to orient readers of his book. One side of philosophy, he writes, has taught that the "best way to live ethically" is by "reminding each other about the transcendence of the norm"; the other has affirmed "that the only way to live ethically is to first be true to oneself." Is it possible to combine the advantages of each side? For a select group of neo- (and revisionist) Kantians in the late nineteenth century, as well as for several of the great European minds that founded sociology, it most definitely was; in fact, to over-come the arbitrary, a priori division between self-subject and society-object was for them the central task of the day. In subjecting this question to a specifically sociological resolution, Nielsen accomplishes a number of highly useful things in several interrelated disciplines.

The first order of business, as the provocative title of this book makes clear, is to rehabilitate the *norm* and attach it firmly to individ-ual moral judgment. In Nielsen's view, the concept of normativity has fallen into undeserved disregard among those who use Bakhtin. In *To-ward a Philosophy of the Act,* Bakhtin focuses on the "once-occurrent act," lamenting the Platonic bias in philosophy against transitory phe-nomena. Since in his view we become ethical agents to the extent that we can answer for one event in its own unrepeatable time and space, Bakhtin even comes close to suggesting that the best test of a true thing is whether or not it *can* change. This Heraclitian insight creates obvious problems for the Categorical Imperative, which Nielsen deftly examines in his discussions of Bakhtin's revisioning of Kant. More central to his methodological inquiry, however, is the fact that a radically individualist answerability has worked to reduce the relevance of this Russian thinker for the sociological disciplines. Nielsen is correct to sense that Bakhtin had a keen sense not only of a subject's singular answerability to another singular subject but also of norm-governed social responsibility. Getting at this position, however, is difficult. In the notoriously socialized, standardized Soviet epoch, Bakhtin was famous—and admired—for his dislike of institutions and personal disdain of officially bestowed honors and recognition. Only in the 1950s does he address norm-governed speech behavior in a complex way; in his earlier work on genres, what is routinely valued is the rebellious, unexpected "outgrowing" of every category or precedent, in a word, everything that is "novel."

To be sure, in these contexts "normative" sounds constrictive, epic, unfree. But Nielsen shows how an analysis of "consummated, but not finished" acts need not in any sense be hostile to normative treatment. In fact, individual creativity can only be measured by the presence of norms, whose task it is to discipline subjectivity, to enable it to communicate both with others and with options untaken within its own self. A norm both resembles, and differs from, a transcendental imperative. As Bakhtin wrote in *Toward a Philosophy of the Act,* a norm is "a special form of free volition of one person in relation to others." Once codified, it becomes prominent in the formal spheres of law and religion. But "in the process of its creation" for each of us, a norm functions as simply a "verbal form for conveying the adaptation of certain theoretical propositions to a particular end" (24)—that is, as the most routine "If I want x, then I must do y" sorts of hypothetical reasoning. "The whole system," Bakhtin insists, "is open." To be open does not mean to be arbitrary or autonomous. While possessing perspectival uniqueness, each of us is coordinated with others at the level of the "transgredient"; we "cross over" to other normative positions as we become ourselves. As Nielsen explains patiently in his gloss on such passages, just because an ethical event recognizes no categorical imperative or universally valid law does not mean that it rejects normative thinking.

Once a continuum is acknowledged between (at one end) law, religion, and social practices and (at the other) my own microlevel "what if" decision making, new questions and new heroes arise. In his first chapter, Nielsen sets out to recuperate some aspects of the idiosyncratic, personalist Bakhtin for the more systemic social sciences. But he is also interested in defending Habermas, celebrated for his discourse ethics, from the charge of too much system, that is, from what some critics have considered his unrealistic assumption that agreement can always, in principle, be reached. Nielsen will demonstrate some surprising things. For example, the question at the base of Bakhtin's dialogism—"What should I do when faced with someone who can answer back?"—is revealed as considerably more reflexive, self-absorbed, and indifferent to instantiating the good than is the equivalent recurrent question for Habermas: "How can I reach understanding with another?" Bakhtin ultimately grounds himself in "eventness" and individual creation; Habermas, in "metanorms" that promise to govern relations among lifeworlds in a reasonable way. Appreciating how these poles might be inclined toward one another, and perhaps even complement one another, is at the center of Nielsen's project. Although discussions of Bakhtin's self-other constructs have become highly sophisticated over the past decade, most have adopted one of two popular orientations: either the conservative liberal view, in which the individual self with its duties and rights is the ultimate value, or the more radical carnival view, in which liberated bodies collectively possess exciting, destabilizing political potential. In this book Nielsen is attempting a more difficult thing. He de-emphasizes the banner-waving politics implicit on both sides and traces, as a historian of his profession, the long history of correctives and checks-and-balances devised by social thinkers who refuse to sacrifice either self to society, or society to the self. Indeed: the sociology that matters to him must confront, as its highest priority, the problem of proper balance, literally face-to-face.

To this end, much of Nielsen's discussion centers around Bakhtin's debts to, or parallels with, such neo-Kantians as Alexander Vvedenskij (philosophy professor at Petrograd University while the young Bahktin was an auditor there) and Hermann Cohen (Marburg teacher of Bakhtin's best friend Matvei Kagan); the sociologists Georg Simmel, Max Weber, and Max Scheler; and the American social psychologist and pragmatist George Herbert Mead. These chapters are the meat of the book. All the above thinkers were critical of Kant's ethical formalism, and each devised modifications that built on the richness of the Kantian framework while profoundly adjusting its emphases. Take, for example, the matter of Kant's three postulates for enabling ethical action: the possibility of immortality, of the existence of God, and free will. In his lectures on Kant's moral philosophy to his study circle in the mid-1920s Bakhtin alluded to these postulates,[5] but for his own evolving *phronesis* of practical behavior, their importance came to be dwarfed by Vvedenskij's neo-Kantian amendment, the so-called

"Fourth Postulate": an a priori belief in the objective existence of other egos. These other egos, inaccessible in their entirety but nevertheless authentic, must be accepted on faith, as things-in-themselves. Such an act of faith is possible for Bakhtin because, unlike Kant, he argues that we *can* know the other—only partially, to be sure, and "transgradiently," but this, after all, is how we know our own selves too. Knowledge of selectively internalized parts of others is our primary means for gaining access to the self of our own consciousness.

Here Hermann Cohen's community ethics, with its calibrated "degrees of stranger-ness" and its careful attention to the obligations we assume at each degree, becomes intensely interesting (chapter 4). As Nielsen notes, Bakhtin shared with the German Romantics the belief that moral subjectivity has the force of law. A "free" self versus a "law-bound" society is a fiction. Any meaningful continuum must consider the binding, step-by-step transition from autonomy to intimacy, from intrusion to community, which was the burden of Hermann Cohen's "sociology" inspired by Old Testament models. According to Cohen, the self's relation to the *Nebenmensch* or "merely the next man" is in principle indifferent; toward the "stranger" however, it is potentially hostile, toward the "guest-friend" it is obligated, and finally toward the *Mitmensch*, or "fellowman," the self is lovingly engaged. Answerability is variously defined at different points along this path; as a matter of course, heterogeneous moral norms are generated. To the growing list of wholesale borrowings from German philosophy that Bakhtin is now known to have permitted himself, Nielsen adds Georg Simmel's potent notion of the Ought as a category of the individual—not the transcendental—act.

In an illustrative aside on "Action and Eros" (chapter 5), Nielsen considers Bakhtin's and Kant's attitude toward carnal love and sexual appetite. Sex is something of a touchstone relation, for—notoriously—it can combine the most self-centering impulses with the most other-inspired sensitivities. In Kant, bodies in their sexual aspect have above all else *duties*. Parallels are drawn between Bakhtin's infrequent, awkwardly clinical remarks on the nature of the sexual act and the Kantian celebration of the marriage contract. Both are wary of consummation solely on behalf of the hypersensate inner body, and both would agree that in this unreliable realm it is the dutiful body that reaps the long-term pleasure. Indeed, it would seem that pleasure, in Kant, is not related to transgression. And in Bakhtin? Nielsen does not speculate, but we immediately sense a dialogue-in-the-making between the body valued as transgressor (a staple in Bakhtin's image of both carnival and the modern novel) and the body as our most valuable instrument of social cohesion, Hermann Cohen's *Mitmensch*. Subsequent chapters are rich in such stressed moments, which hint at unresolvable juxtapositions.

One such moment is the doubled reading that Nielsen provides, in his chapter 6, of what might well be Dostoevsky's most uncrackable moral paradox (more challenging even than his "Grand Inquisitor"): the episode of the "Mysterious Visitor" from the Elder Zosima's "Life" in *The Brothers Karamazov*.[6] Nielsen's reading is the culminating point of his comparison between Bakhtin's "reflexive subjectivity"—the sense of self that is produced by looking back at past actions of the "I" from an outside position—and that of George Herbert Mead. The Bakhtin-Mead juxtaposition is a fascinating one, for which Dostoevsky's episode is the perfect foil. For both Bakhtin and Mead, the "I" is an entity in flux, unrecordable and fleeting. But as regards the Other, Bakhtin's category (his so-called "I-for-another"/"the-other-for-me") is quite different from Mead's "generalized other." Mead's other is more syntactically static and one-way: "I" am "I" until the community turns me into "Me," a unitary and stabilizing gesture that provides me with rules and a sense of belonging. The generalized other is also more law-abiding. As a social theorist Mead prefers the category of "Me," unabashedly an object-self and the sum of society's projections: thoughtful, conventional, accessible to reason, the repository of memory, a game player in the "good citizen" sense. Community solidarity and mutual understanding among members of the group are prime values for the practical, pragmatic Mead, as they will be for Habermas. In comparison, Bakhtin's more unstable and noncumulative model ("I" am as many different "Me's" as there are others to gaze on me) appears chaotic and "aesthetic." Bakhtin asks only, "What should I do in the presence of another's responsive consciousness?" and not, as does Mead, "How do the I and the Me think through an act so that we might come to agreement?" In an instructive paradox, Bakhtin—resident of the collectivized and regimented Soviet Union—permits far more privacy, eccentricity, and noncooperation than does Mead, raised on North American values of self-reliance and individual expression.

Nielsen's hypothetical response on behalf of Bakhtin and Mead to the "Mysterious Visitor" episode from *The Brothers Karamazov* will unfold in its own time. But for this Preface, in my capacity as Russianist, let me provide some background for it—and suggest why "reflexive subjectivity" in Nielsen's sense is such an excruciating investigatory tool. The "Life of the Elder Zosima," recorded by the youngest Kara-

mazov brother Alyosha, is a self-enclosed inserted narrative, framed
off from the present-tense time of the novel. Its task is to "look back
on a self from the outside." Essentially a placid, "consummated" series
of biographical recollections and maxims, the "Life" does contain one
recollection with more than its share of anger, cruelty, crime, doubt,
awful suffering and unresolvable moral confusion: the tale of the confession and death of Mikhail, Zosima's "Mysterious Visitor." Nielsen
means us to read this tale as more than a personal confession, in an
extra-personal, "sociological" way, with larger family and societal imperatives in mind. After a series of visits to his new friend, Mikhail reveals his long past perfect crime, the murder of a woman who did not
return his love, in which no suspects survived. Mikhail proceeded to
live a virtuous life, untroubled by conscience, becoming a benefactor to
society. Then his torment began. Having acquired a beloved wife and
children, Mikhail felt unworthy of caressing them: "What if they
knew?" Withdrawing his caress, however, would hurt them even more.
Seeking to break this paralysis, he discloses the murder to Zosima,
who urges him to confess. This advice only sharpens the conflict.
Mikhail keeps delaying the terrible moment, returning with ever
stronger arguments for transcending the murder for the sake of those
living now (all legitimate, loving, dialogically sensitive arguments).
Zosima stands behind his initial counsel to confess publicly. "But is
there any need?" Mikhail exclaims (309). "Is there any necessity? . . . .
I am ready to suffer still, all my life, for the blood I have shed, only so
as not to strike at my wife and children. Would it be just to ruin them
along with myself?"

Dostoevsky draws the battle lines here with exquisite impartiality.
On the one side the Holy Spirit, moving through Zosima, assures
Mikhail that he first must confess and then "all will pass, the truth
alone will remain" (308). And on the other side, human beings, who
in Mikhail's judgment also represent a living truth and whose "passing"
was for him no cavalier matter, those beloved members of his family
who, as an inseparable part of his life, have potent claims upon it.
Mikhail makes a final visit to his confessor, where, driven to despera-
tion by these contradictory mandates, he is on the edge of murdering
him with a knife. But looking into his host's face, suddenly he smiles,
rises, departs, and confesses the next day—thereby causing universal
confusion, pain, disbelief, the predicted diagnosis of madness, the ruin
of his family, his own death, and an aftermath of resentment on the
part of the aggrieved wife and stunned townsfolk against Zosima, who
endures the calumny and then leaves town. What indeed *had* been

gained by this act, in the real world of loving human beings? Absolutely the only thing in its favor is that it was the truth. It is a portrayal of the innerly "right and necessary thing" accomplished, but where all outer parties to the event are guaranteed to lose in the present—and only the criminal, at the last minute before his death, selfishly reaps relief.

The tale is perfect for Nielsen's purposes. Self and society each have its rights, its own truth, its own sort of memory and answerability, its particular investments in future and past. In his writings on Dostoevsky, Bakhtin makes only minor passing references to the episode; as far as we know, Mead (who lectured more enduringly than he wrote) made none at all. And yet we see in Mikhail, the "Mysterious Visitor," something like an exemplarily failed "Me," an "I" whom the community failed to shape, from the moment of the crime to the criminal's final confession of it. Mead is not especially good with deviance. For him, as Nielsen explains, "understanding and explaining moral crisis and crime are not fundamentally different, because the ethical self is not a neutral self but social and even political." Bakhtin, in contrast, resists the elevation of interpersonal obligations into social mandates and from there into political duty. At one point in *Toward a Philosophy of the Act,* he even remarks that religious and political rituals, where we "represent" some larger unit rather than present ourselves in person, run a serious risk of turning us into "imposters or pretenders" (52). Bakhtin is drawn to Dostoevsky not only because that great novelist heard many voices where others sought only one, but also because Dostoevsky considered deviance and alienation—the endless rebellion of the "I-for-myself" against others who would define it—to be quite normal. "Reflexive subjectivity" fragments us as agents as often as it consolidates us. Bakhtin hardly sees, or hears, the authoritative community that might discipline a "Me" and align object-selves in a politically reliable way.

This distinction between the political consciousness of Mead and the far less socialized scenarios of Bakhtin leads us to Nielsen's final chapters. There he returns to political sociology, to Habermas, and to vexed contemporary debates over appropriate norms for national identity. His case study is Quebec—whose separatist movement, on a world scale, has surely been among the most law-abiding and patient of recent years. Nielsen is sympathetic to the distinction Habermas draws between *ethnos* and *demos;* the cultural traditions and lifeworlds of the former, he argues, need not be threatened by the "purely civic sense of belonging to a political community" (chapter 7). But he acknowledges the difficulty of realizing Habermas's dictum that "a nation should be subjectless." A more commonsensical goal would be some form of "two-sided answerability" between ethnos and demos. Here Nielsen urges social theorists to seek out more subtle, nuanced options as they move into macrolevels of interaction. Pluralist societies need not treat all groups the same for all purposes. How I behave—and am expected to behave—toward a person who is committing an evil act should be different from how I am expected to behave toward a person who is simply different from me. In some situations, judgments are universally binding; in others, "associational sovereignty" can provide more flexibility of interpretation. For not only are we all different; we are *differently* different.

This, perhaps, is the simplest way to understand the impress of Bakhtin on Nielsen's project. In his Foreword to the English translation of *Toward a Philosophy of the Act*, Michael Holquist defines that early text on practical ethics as "an attempt to detranscendentalize Kant . . . to think beyond Kant's formulation of the ethical imperative" (ix). Nielsen, it appears, would marshal the sociologists who parallel Bakhtin in this "differentiating" direction and detranscendentalize political thought. The challenge is immense. For every concretization is a delimitation; every freshly delimited difference must struggle to reestablish its authority and authenticity. Absolute poles no longer hold. Matter falls toward the middle. "Although Bakhtin is not a sociologist," Nielsen remarks appreciatively in chapter 6, "his theory of culture, and of the self, provides a potentially important support to sociologists who seek to continue an in-between kind of theorizing." The chapters that follow are a tribute to the achievements and trials of the in-between.

Caryl Emerson

AKNOWLEDGMENTS

The idea for this book began several years ago in conversations about Bakhtin and critical theory with graduate students at York University in Toronto. It travelled to Mexico, Europe and the United States before finally settling in Montreal. Along the way I picked up a long list of debts. First, I would like to thank my friend Brian Singer for sharing his considerable erudition over the years and for showing me the limitations of my arguments with imagination, care, and force. The book's "tone" originates in our conversations and the fruits of Brian's insights are evident throughout. Tapani Laine, Bakhtin's Finish translator, and I have had an ongoing discussion about the problems of reconstructing Bakhtin's thought and I would like to thank him for lending me his very sensitive "touch" with the texts, teaching me how to look at concepts in terms of local context, and for keeping me abreast with new Russian literature on the subject. Many years ago, and again more recently while working on this project, Fred Evans helped give me the "taste" for travel in philosophy (and other places!), however ill prepared I may be for such a voyage, and I thank him warmly.

I am very grateful to Caryl Emerson for her Foreword and for dropping in from cyber space a couple of years ago to offer encouragement and support at a time when it was most needed. Thanks to Louis Jacob who played an important editorial role at the beginning of the project. I learned a lot about social theory from my colleagues at the monthly meetings of the "Montreal School" of sociology *(Le groupe interuniversitaire d'étude de la Postmodernité)* and about Bakhtin and social theory through exchanges with Michael Gardiner and Craig Brandeis.

At International Bakhtin conferences, I was most inspired by the generosity and good humour of Anthony Wall, Vitaly Makhlin, Nicolai Nicolaev and David Shepard. Thanks also to Brian Poole who was always willing to share his unpublished materials and research. Hans Joas offered very valuable advice on an earlier version of the chapter on Mead and Bakhtin, and Wolgang Knöbl, Frederick Vandenbergh and the late Cary Bocock each provided me with thoughtful commentary and criticisms of an earlier draft of the manuscript. Regina Wenzel provided the brief translations of Simmel from the German in Chapter Four and Christine Swartz helped me through a reading of the German version of Simmel's text. I am responsible for any translations from the French that appear unless otherwise indicated.

I have a very personal sense of gratitude to offer *ma copine de vie* and collaborator Marie Cusson, not just for her emotional support but for her exemplary intellectual courage and creative talent. Other very special freinds, Chantal Collard, Jean-François Côté, John Jackson, and Domminique Legros, each challenged me in their own way to reach for higher levels (however much we may disagree on the details!). In the end, this work would not have been possible without the students who always encouraged my uneven attempts to introduce Bakhtin's work into the world of social theory. In particular, I would like to thank Shanna Braden, Christine Ramsey, and Kathy White whose own work on Bakhtin helped shape my thinking. Thanks to Mark Lajoie and Sandra Song who helped correct an earlier draft of the manuscript and Kathy White who edited the second draft and offered pertinent advice on the book's conceptual development. Finally, thanks to Kathy Allen and Michael Craig for preparing the index and especially for the warmth and good humour of their company.

This book draws on parts of previously published essays in which I attempt to think through a variety of theoretical, cultural and political issues against the foil of Bahktin's and Habermas's core ideas. The fragments from these essays have been extensively rewritten, extended and reorganized for the book. I achnowledge the following publishers for their permission to include parts of these texts: "Bakhtin and Habermas: Toward A Transcultural Ethics," *Theory and Society: Renewal and Critique* (Vol.24/6, 1995); "Action and Eros in the Creative Zone;" *Dialogism: An International Journal of Bakhtin Studies* (Issue 4, 2 000) "Looking Back on the Subject: Bakhtin and Mead on Reflexivity and the Political" in Craig Brandist and Galin Tihanov's *Materializing Bakhtin: The Bahktin Circle and Social Theory* (Macmillan, 2000); and "The Norms of Answerabilituy: Bakhtin and the Fourth Postulate," in Michael Gardiner and Michael Bell. *Bakhtin and the Human Sciences: No Last Words* (Sage, 1998); "The Frankfurt School." *Encyclopedia of Contemporary Literary Theory*. Edited by Irene Makaryk (University of Toronto Press, 1993). Much earlier versions of the last two chapters were presented in a series of talks in 1999 and the summer of 2000. I would like to thank all those who offered comments and advice at these occasions: a lecture to the PhD seminar in sociology at the John F. Kennedy Institute, Frei Universität, Berlin; a key note address to the Third Roland seminar at the University of Tampere, Finland; a lecture to the graduate program in the Law Faculty at the University of Connecticut; and a presentation to the Canadian Social Science and Humanities MCRI project: "The Culture of Cities."

Finally, I wish to acknowledge the grants from the Faculty of Arts and Sciences at Concordia University, Montreal, and from the Social Science and Humanities Research Council of Canada over the course of writing the book.

INTRODUCTION

Theory on the Borders of Sociology

The work of Mikhail Bakhtin has been received and made known across the Western world largely through literary studies and the humanities. This book seeks to introduce the young Bakhtin's ideas on an ethics and aesthetics of action into a dialogue with classical and contemporary social theory. Although several theorists are discussed across the book, Jürgen Habermas, the German critical theorist, is introduced as the primary contemporary interlocutor with whom to compare Bakhtin. I am not looking for a sustained synthesis of their two positions but for a way to draw out Bakhtin's special way of theorizing creativity and the norms of answerability—a phrase I propose to describe his early philosophy of action—through a dialogue with a well-known contemporary theorist. The comparison to Habermas and others is meant to provide the bookends that support my presentation of Bakhtin's early work in terms of its place within social theory and interdisciplinary studies. The final two chapters extend a social theory situated between Bakhtin and Habermas toward an analysis of contemporary discussions and controversies around citizenship, identity, and shared sovereignty in postnational times.

The book's key idea is to link Bakhtin's aesthetically informed transcultural ethics to a theory of the interpersonal or intersubjective basis of community in a way that does not require a formal separation of the cultural sources of ethics from the emerging constellation of contemporary postnational politics. This position is drawn out of

1

Bakhtin by sharply contrasting his ideas with Habermas's theory of discourse ethics and the discourse theory of democracy. Habermas, like Bakhtin, also argues for a universalist morality, but one that cannot be fully transcultural because it is only possible within postconventional modern societies whose lifeworlds and systems of integration become uncoupled in order to resolve problems created by increasing degrees of complexity. Unlike Habermas, Bakhtin works through a conventional philosophical anthropology and is engaged in the study of what constitutes human relations in equal and coeval terms across cultures and time.[1] In simpler terms, Bakhtin begins with the question: How should I act in a world of differentiated value orientations? Habermas, in contrast, asks the question: How can I achieve agreement in a world of increasingly different value orientations and complex imperatives of administrative and economic systems? Both are normative questions but as it turns out only Bakhtin's is turned toward an answer regarding the creative dimension of action; only Habermas's answers in terms of an understanding of what holds an interaction together long enough to be able to create.

I conclude that if it is possible to conceive of a social theory situated between Bakhtin and Habermas, it is best to keep their key insights somewhat autonomous, at least for analytic reasons. For Habermas, a reasoned disagreement is the basic point of departure for the modern public sphere and his discourse theory of democracy privileges a strong procedural distinction between culture and the political. For Bakhtin, answerability is the cornerstone of the everyday and so an ethics of the political would not easily separate itself off from culture by invoking the primacy of juridical or legal procedures. On the other hand, it is argued that the two perspectives together can raise a broader range of research questions into the ethics of transculturalism than either can separately. The concept of dialogism, which would come to stand in for Bakhtin's earlier concept of answerability, refocuses questions onto lifeworlds and living linguistic relations: How should we act toward other cultures? How should we anticipate their action toward us through utterances? How can other cultures creatively take on elements from our utternaces and in part, become us while remaining themselves and vice versa? On the other hand, Habermas's discourse ethics, and many aspects of his general theory of communicative action, point to a series of normative questions: How can we get agreement through discourse? How can we introduce or change norms fairly? How do we reconcile our diverse views of the good and the just within the same social system? Can we reconcile an ethics of justice with an ethics of care? Taken together these are the intensely demanding, some say impossible questions of our time; and this is an intensity that can only increase as emerging versions of modernity become more aware of the conditions of diversity and ambivalence that have been fostered all along.

A key mediating point for a social theory situated between Bakhtin and Habermas is this need to strengthen the emphasis on the creative dimension in social action without reducing explanation to the emotional and volitional impulse of the individual or collective actor. The attempt to develop a social theory that would respect this constant requires a comparative discussion of each position and yet is not confined to their work alone. These are not theorists who are normally studied within the same discipline and so some preparation for each potential audience is necessary before a full discussion can unfold. After outlining the book, and introducing Bakhtin studies to social theorists, I introduce Bakhtin readers to a definition of social theory via a discussion of two recent books by contemporary sociologists, Jefferey Alexander and Hans Joas. The brief but instructive encounter with their work reveals some of the broader issues at stake in social theory and the importance of interdisciplinary studies for balancing a concept of creativity with the normative approach. The comparison to Habermas is suspended in chapters 4 through 6 in order to deepen Bakhtin's position through a review of acknowledged philosophical sources for his ethics, and to introduce him into a direct dialogue with Kant's moral philosophy, including the revisions to it proposed by Georg Simmel and others. The creative dimension in Bakhtin's theory of action is then brought to light by contrasting his approach with two different classical sociologies of action developed by Max Weber and George Herbert Mead. These thinkers are selected, not because they best represent social theory between Bakhtin and Habermas, but because they best articulate issues that must be considered in developing such a theory. Finally, Habermas's approach to the separation of *ethnos* and *demos* is taken up and challenged in chapters 7 and 8 via a dialogic reading of issues that he and other contemporary political theorists problematize regarding the fate of national identities in the emerging context of globalization and a "postnational constellation" (Habermas 2001).[2]

The young Bakhtin wrote extensively on the norms of answerability—the idea that ethical actions should be both individuated, or singular, aesthetic events and universal, or general, moral responses—but as he shifted the focus of his interests he never followed through with his earlier plan to write on the politics that might derive from such a theory.[3] Part of my objective, especially in chapters 2 and 3, is to reconstruct how his early interests shifted from ethics and aesthetics into a metalinguistic theory of dialogue. I return again in the final chapters to examine what his "intended" theory of an ethics of politics might look like in today's context by focusing on a case study of neonationalist intellectuals in the Quebec and North American context. This latter part of the book is based in the classical assumption, which Bakhtin presumably would have shared, that politics must be separated from ethics and aesthetics for analytic reasons and that in practice their unity is derived from the dialogue with difference that each sphere embraces or rejects.

The first chapters of the book construct general postulates for a transcultural ethics while the middle chapters on Kant et al. look to draw out some of the undertheorized sources of Bakhtin's approach to self-other relations. If the assumption about politics holds, then the thematic link to the final chapters is this attempt to think through the political from the point of view of ethics and aesthetics. This, in turn, implies that the political question has to be about more than the sheer exercise, performance, or distribution of power. Politics has to answer the question of the collective and individual relation and not just at the macro level of justice and the symbolic representation of social division but also at the micro level of lived relations. As Bakhtin might put it; "How do we consummate self-other relations without the different sides ceasing to be themeselves?" By placing Bakhtin's special theorization of the norms of answerability into a dialogue with social theory I seek to shift his philosophy of dialogue to a political level in a way that helps elucidate his original texts and points to strategies for expanding the theoretical paths laid down by those to whom he is compared. Placing his work in such a dialogue carries the risk of distorting his original project in order to serve interests he was unaware of. This begs the question, is there a Bakhtinian way of working on Bakhtin?

Syncrisis and Anacrisis: The State of Bakhtin Studies

Questions about citizenship, global migration, multiculturalism, postnationalism, and deliberative democracy were not Bakhtin's questions. Yet, his early work is filled with a variety of innovative concepts that address the philosophical and anthropological paradox of unity and difference at the core of many cultural and political issues in today's world. Should concepts conceived in another context be applied to our own worlds without a thorough understanding of their original usage and reception? If reading texts should be an immanent task of interpretation then one should try and interpret the text from its own context and point of view, as much as possible. But does this mean the reader has to give up all external positions? For Bakhtin there is an "outsidedness" or transgredience to all perspectives and so a respectful reading presumably means one should return to one's own external viewpoint only after having had a chance to understand the inherent qualities of the text's internal position. This is the boundary around which immanent understanding and external explanation typically meet in the exercise of comparison and critique.

The problem concerning the limits of internal understanding and external explanation of concepts enters any theoretical industry and certainly has frequently been raised in debates occuring within Bakhtin studies over the years. Two lines of research are easily identifiable, and I want to introduce them here and comment on them further below. One research path is to immanently reconstruct the main steps Bakhtin takes in building the ideas within his texts and situate these within his local context. This approach leads mainly to a philological or text-centered form of research that has not proven to be especially interested in speculating on how Bakhtin's ideas might be used to inform theories or research questions from other contexts. A second path compares and contrasts aspects of his approach with other theorists whom more often than not he did not know. Here, there is a danger of straying too far outside an internal reading of his corpus and imposing external ideas where they do not belong. In the latter 1963 version of his study of Dostoevsky, Bakhtin adopts the terms *syncrisis* and *anacrisis* from Socrates as a way of describing the problem of internal and external readings.[4] Following this distinction, I argue that the risk of external comparison is worthwhile if it allows us to show sharp contrasts and striking convergencies between his concepts and those developed by different thinkers, in different circumstances, at different times and for different purposes. Such juxtapositions or *syncrisis* need to be aimed at jarring loose the deeper intuitions embedded within Bakhtin's approach that are otherwise not easily articulated. The new articulation, the *anacrisis*, or the "provocation of the word by the word" provides a platform that facilitates a potential extention of theory without negating or distorting its original source. On the other hand, the comparative strategy takes us very far away from an understanding of Bakhtin's concepts as they developed within their own context. If the internal and external readings are to be reconciled, as I hope to do, some introductory remarks are necessary to briefly explain the outline of his biography and how his work developed and to outline some of the main issues at stake for those involved in the more philological reconstruction of his corpus.

The widely recognized contemporary importance of addressing the modern tension between the enrichment and anxiety of cultural and ethnic pluralism in the *polis*—of the clash between *ethnos* and *demos*—was not unfamiliar to Bakhtin's world. In the years following the 1917 October Revolution, and before he turned thirty, Bakhtin completed four works whose conceptual centers move from an ethics of two-sided answerability, or how to act in morally universal and uniquely individuated ways, first announced in *Toward a Philosophy of the Act;* to an aesthetic theory of authorship in the book-length essay "The Author and Hero in Aesthetic Activity"; to a critical response to Russian formalism and an early theorization of the utterance in "Content, Material and Form in Verbal Art"; and finally to a theorization of the transgradiant, and eventually dialogic work inherent to the whole sphere of culture in the proto-text of *Dostoevsky's Poetics* (Nicoleav 2000). Each of these works shifts the way Bakhtin addresses the norms of answerability. He begins by asking the rather simple, if not classic, ethical question: How should I act? Not because of duty, or out of my own interest, but how should I act in a specific situation knowing that each act or deed is an instance of my whole life history acted out with others who can answer back? How can we find a way to grow in our self-knowledge? He then shifts the question of two-sided answerability to the problem of aesthetically consummating the act, and then shifts again toward an investigation into the dialogic character of the verbal utterance.

Morson and Emerson (1990) argue that Bakhtin's work can be understood as having developed in four distinct but overlapping periods. To greatly simplify, they argue that in the first period he lays out his general ethics and aesthetics including the texts cited above. The first and second periods of Bakhtin's production overlap. The second period includes his shift toward a philosophy of dialogue and the so-called disputed texts published between 1925 and 1930. Some argue that several of these texts may have been authored by Bakhtin but published under different names. Others claim his early work is so different from the sociological, political, and linguistic emphasis in these works that it is unlikely he was the principal author.[5] In the last two phases he engages the linguist turn much more vigorously through a philosophy of dialogue and concentrates on deepening theories of the utterance, speech genres, and cultural practices, beginning in his essays collected in *The Dialogic Imagination*, written for the most part in the 1930s, his doctoral dissertation *Rabelais and His World*, the latter revised 1963 version of the 1929 Dostoevsky book, and articles and notes presented in his posthumously published *Speech Genres and Other Late Essays*. I examine the philosophical sources that Bakhtin draws on in developing the themes of the first period in more depth in chapter 4. Key concepts from his second, third, and fourth periods (the dialogic character of the utterance, the mixture of style, genre, and the word, of the stratification of language, or heteroglossia, of double voiced discourse, polyphony, and counterpoint) are further contrasted with Habermas's approach to subjectivity and language in chapters 2 and 3.

Remarkably, after more than thirty years of study we still have only very general ideas about the main sources of many of Bakhtin's concepts, of the steps he took in building them and of the biographic details of his early activities. This is partially due to the peculiar "doublespeak" Russian intellectuals were forced to engage in under the Soviet regime, and partially attributable to Bakhtin's own philosophical style. Rather than document the shifts in his own thinking and show how he could overcome specific problems, he liked to reformulate many of the same philosphical ideas in different disciplines (Hirshkop 1999). In a period and place where being the author of the wrong book, or having the wrong idea, could get you killed, it is perhaps understandable how a certain fictional quality enters the official accounts of one's own life history. Bakhtin offered various versions of his curriculum vitae across his career, possibly to placate Soviet authorities or simply out of a sense of personal insecurity. In any case the exact details of his early studies are difficult to determine. At one point he claimed to have studied philosophy in Marburg, Germany; at another he says he graduated from St. Petersburg University.[6] It turns out that neither claim is true, although he apparently did attend the latter institution. Bakhtin was most probably self-taught (Pan'kov 1998). He went to the gymnasium in Odessa, south of Moscow, but there are no records of his studies in higher institutions after this period (Hirshkop 1998). He moved to Nevel in 1918 to take up a job teaching high school. The circle of intellectuals at Nevel included Bakhtin's most important early mentor, the neo-Kantian philosopher Matvei Isaevich Kagan (who in fact studied in Marburgh with Hermann Cohen and also with Georg Simmel in Berlin). It also includes the linguist, Valentin Nikolaevich Voloschinov who died in 1938 of tuberculosis, the literary critic and Party bureaucrat, Pavel Medvedev who disappeared in the Stalinist purges, the young philosopher Lev Pumpiansky, and many others. The group continued to meet in neighbooring Vitebsk until 1924 or 1925 and then in Leningrad until Bakhtin's arrest and exile to Kazakhstan in 1928.

In a pioneering study of the Russian reception of Bakhtin's work, Caryl Emerson points out that Bakhtin never saw himself as a literary scholar nor would he fit well with what is today in the West called cultural studies. She argues that throughout his life he saw himself as a kind of "culturologist" and philosophical anthropologist, from his early years, through his years in exile, and through the years following his return to a teaching position at the World Literature Institute in Moscow, where he lived until his death in 1975. Emerson demonstrates how his key concepts of dialogue and polyphony, introduced in the 1929 version of his Dostoevsky book, were dismissed in a series of reviews in Russia. His concepts, it was argued, could not be applied to the works of Dostoevsky on the grounds that the novelist never intended "this sort of openness for his plots and autonomy for his heroes." As a result the book was set aside and would only reemerge, to eventually gain worldwide attention, in the 1980s. Emerson also relates some of the details surrounding Bakhtin's unsuccessful 1940 doctoral dissertation defense of what would become *Rabelais and his World*. In a second defense at the Gorky Institute of World Literature in 1946, Bakhtin was criticized on the grounds that he did not sufficiently review the Renaissance literature on humanism nor the anthropological history of folk culture for his study. In the official report of his defense, scholars were discouraged from citing the dissertation because it was considered "Freudian, pseudoscientific, formalistic and disrespectful to the spirit of Gogol" and Bakhtin was again forced to make further changes to the text before a lesser degree of *kandidat*, as opposed the first class degree of *doktor nauk*, was finally granted in 1951 (Emerson 1998, 91–92).

Not only does the scholarship on Bakhtin's biography remain inconclusive, so too does work detailing the sources of his particular approach. It is well known, for example, that Bakhtin's attempt to build a "philosophy of the answerable act" follows the well-trodden paths of neo-Kantian moral philosphy, yet there is little detailed philosophical analysis of the specific steps he undertakes in building concepts within and beyond this tradition. Vitaly Makhlin insists that the absence of understanding Bakhtin's roots in the Russian reception of Western philosophy leads to a distortion of Bakhtin's work. Specifically, he argues that the lack of rigorous definition of Bakhtin's core ideas means that his work is vulnerable to the twists and turns of the most ephemeral intellectual fads of the West. A very important book such as *Rabelais and His World*, for example, has thus received very little analysis of the origins of its terminology and points of reference because commentators have almost never asked the question of what Rabelais and his world means to "Bakhtin's time and space" (Makhlin 1998).[7]

Recovering unacknowledged sources from previous epochs used in building philosophical arguments can be a painfully slow process and relies on the work of a diverse community of scholars. In many ways, the relative absence of careful analysis of the steps Bakhtin takes in developing his approach can be attributed to a late, and as yet incomplete, preparation of a standard scholarly edition of his collected work (Hitchcock and Shepard 1998). If scholars cannot rely on a standard edition, the argument goes, explanations about how and why he developed his approach simply cannot be reliably put forth. The executors of Bakhtin's estate are promising that this problem will be gradually solved as volumes are edited and proper reference notes prepared. Yet, even if the "real" Bakhtin never ultimately emerges, the problem remains one of explaining the broader scholarly context behind his existing texts. However partial, fragmented, or simply unknown his available corpus might be and however confused the state of his intellectual biography (Poole 1998; Hirschkop 1998; Pan'kov 1998; Steinglass 1998), theoretical work within Bakhtin studies has progressed and continues to develop to the two recognizable, but not always mutually complementary, directions cited above.

A whole series of ongoing philological projects continues to reconstruct the original problematic by considering intellectual and biographical contexts along with close imminant readings of materials available in various archives. This is very much the emphasis of the ongoing industry around the production of the scholarly edition. The earliest stream of these studies begins with the Moscow students Sergey Bocharov, Vadim Koschinov, and Georgii Gachev who helped elevate Bakhtin to prominence in the 1960s. Their efforts led to Bakhtin's introduction in the West by comparative literary theorists and translators such as Ann Shukman, Michael Holquist, Katerina Clark, Caryl Emerson, Gary Saul Morson, Vadim Liapunov, Julia Kristeva, Tzvetan Todorov, and others. Many of these scholars continue to debate Bakhtin's unusual position as a figure who links post-1989 Russia with its pre-1929 intellectual history. More recently debates around the archives and the preparation of the scholarly edition have intensified. Scholars such as Nikolaev, and many others, are calling for a "scrupulous analysis of Bakhtin's terminology" against the background of the original philosophical contexts in which he developed his ideas (1997, 1).

Close studies of Bakhtin's texts and contexts have long been a prerequisite for the second, more speculative, and much more common form of external comparison that falls under the many themes of what might be called "Bakhtin and Projects." Indeed, it is difficult to think of a serious thinker to whom Bakhtin has not been compared, of a philosophical, literary, or cultural term that has not been applied, or of a set of contemporary identity politics that has not recruited some concept from his arsenal. "Bakhtin and Projects" provide an important stimulus for integrating his approach into contemporary debates and on a deeper level also nurtures an environment for speculating on unacknowledged parallels with Bakhtin's writing that the first direction of mainly philological research is often unwilling to entertain. An ongoing need for discussions concerning the absorption of world philosophy and social theory into Bakhtin's writing would seem to require a reference to both types of study. The existence of a tension between philological work and the more speculative comparative ventures should not come as a surprise given that each stream is tied to quite different requirements for fundamental research. This is not the place to elaborate a discussion of the bifurcated methodological strategies that are employed, but, practically speaking, each side maintains advantages and disadvantages. Lean too far in the direction of close textual studies and one risks missing the big theoretical picture for the philo-ideographic, and sociobiographic details (or scandals!). On the other hand, lean too far in the direction of the "Bakhtin and Projects" and one risks losing touch with the depth that is immanent to the work itself.

This book seeks to contribute to both these directions by proposing a partial sketch of the philosophical sources for Bakhtin's early work and by introducing it into a dialogue with social theory and the political context of the contemporary world. However, before proceeding, a clearer understanding about what is meant by social theory needs to be introduced in order to measure what kinds of adjustments are needed to prepare for such an exercise. Again, it should be remembered that Bakhtin's ideas have mainly been introduced in the West through literary and cultural studies and he remains relatively unkown to sociologists and other social scientists.[8] Taking into consideration both the rational and the existential poles of the norms of answerabilty is not a project that begins with Bakhtin. It is an idea that social theories of action have been grappling with for generations. In fact, much of the discipline of sociology can be seen to be a debate over just this question.

Creativity and General Sociological Theory

The idea to develop an approach that could fall between these two poles and at the same time draw from each has been stimulated by invitations from two recent books that provide an excellent introduction to the wide range of issues at stake in contemporary social theory. I refer to Jeffery Alexander's collection of essays *Neofunctionalism and After* (1998) and Hans Joas's *The Creativity of Action* (1996). The underlying tension between the two books stems, in part, from a historical debate regarding the status of philosophy's relation to sociology and sociology's relation to science and, in part, from the difficulty involved in converging different levels of analysis within a single framework and across different ones.[9] It is the outline of seemingly disparate levels of analysis and the usage of different approaches within a unified framework that is most important to the goal of presenting Bakhtin's creative approach to the norms of answerability; and it is this that I want to explore. Social theorizing needs to be able to shift between clearly demarcated levels of abstraction in order to synthesize the results of analysis and provide a general theory of its research object. Social theory is interdisciplinary given its debt to philosophy and other disciplines in the humanities, but it is also part of social science inquiry proper. Both its involvement in interdisciplinarity and the internal debates over analysis and the status of concepts divides social theorists and leaves "scientific" consensus regarding any single "general theory" in doubt.

Alexander and Joas argue that recent generations of social theorists share a common interest in overcoming the classical separation of phenomenological or pragmatic microlevels of understanding interaction and systemic, structural, or poststructural macrolevels of explanation and critique. Though Alexander and Joas adopt different solutions, each shares a common commitment to addressing the micro-macro divide through diverse strategies of convergence and critical synthesis. Neither looks to situate action theory in moral philosophy, as do Bakhtin and Habermas, but each extends the range of questions that can be asked about action beyond the latter. For example, Alexander looks to situate social theory in the realm of postpositive science defined as the procedure that takes as its research object the empirical-observational rather than the nonempirical metaphysical that is the object of philosophy. He is critical of ideal forms of positivism that would eliminate theoretical speculation, and makes a compelling argument for a postpositivism that would engage in an exchange and synthesis of conflicting theoretical interpretations.[10] Ultimately, though, Alexander warns against the speculative nature of theoretical propositions that cannot be traced to empirical analysis. He argues that the risk of the current trend in synthesizing macro and micro theories is that levels of generality get muddled and that this leads to a widening of the gap between theoretical propositions and empirical applications. In a sense, then, Alexander, like Bakhtin and Habermas, is analytically sensitive to the need to make conceptual adjustments when shifting, for example, from the question of the uniqueness of an action to its general context.

Joas reviews the long history of utilitarian and normative social theory, covering some of the same ground as Alexander but from a pragmatist rather than postpositivist perspective. He concludes that while several promising attempts have been made to point general theory in the direction of the creative dimension of action, in the main, creativity is relegated to a secondary order. What Joas says about the origins of pragmatism in part echoes Alexander's definition of postpositivism in the sense that it argues for theory construction through scientific method. On the other hand, Joas insists that the first pragmatists placed enormous importance on the moral and political dimensions of their philosophy of action.[11] Whereas Joas emphasizes the need to reach for speculative moral and political philosophies, Alexander warns against converging theories that cannot be traced to empirically tested propositions. Joas stresses the need to get at the creative dimension of action and to do so through theory construction. Their differences and similarities are reminiscent of those between Bakhtin and Habermas mentioned above, but with a fairly significant exception.

Unlike Bakhtin, Habermas, or Joas, Alexander directly questions why sociologists need to look at philosophy or twentieth-century aesthetics to develop a general theory of action. It is not so easy to answer his critique. Alexander clearly demonstrates that for many sociologists ancient and modern philosophy and aesthetics need to be treated as social facts or as purely speculative forms of knowledge. The idea that social philosophy, ethics, aesthetics, or the philosophy of history might be better understood as different genres of sociology, or as proto-sociology is not usually seen as particularly fruitful except as a means of demarcating the history of the discipline. Joas is an exceptional kind of sociologist, in that he takes great care to reconstruct the diverse philosophical backgrounds that inform sociology both as a science and an art. On the other hand, both Joas and Alexander would argue that sociological theory cannot develop without some version of theory construction based in empirical research.

It should come as no surprise to suggest that many modern moral philosophers see sociology as a narrow and overly constrained empirical science that does not add much in terms of solutions to the philosophical questions about how we should act or what we should do to live a good life. But this observation could as well be reversed, given that speculative forms of philosophy are ill equipped to provide sociological studies of knowledge and social action. Models do exist in both classical and contemporary sociology that mix the disciplines in a philosophically and scientifically mutually beneficial way. Many would agree, for example, that classical thinkers such as Marx, Weber, Durkheim, and Simmel, as well as contemporary figures such as Anthony Giddens, Pierre Bourdieu, Alain Touraine, Nicolas Luhmann, and Dorothy Smith, ultimately derive their contributions from the synthesis of ideas that belong to both empirical research and philosophical speculation. Although these are commonly read authors in sociology, they are not read by all sociologists nor is any single author heralded as a model for the discipline. Indeed, for sociologists, these thinkers tend to be thought of as "theorists." Theory and methods are usually taught separately in sociology. In part this helps hold back interdisciplinary intrusions and encourages specialization and subfield autonomy. Because of its diversity and, some argue, its lack of consensus concerning general theory, sociology is well equipped to cater to specialization but in so doing has gradually become vulnerable to takeover from emerging area studies.[12]

Why then argue for a general sociology or social theory and not cultural or other area studies? Admittedly, general sociological theory needs the political and ideological tension generated by interdisciplinary studies. Only a general sociological theory claims a comprehensive analysis of both micro and macro levels. On the other hand, and this is really the heart of the matter, sociology can only claim to offer explanations and understandings for all aspects of social life when it folds itself into social theory and addresses normative questions such as: How should I act? How can I achieve agreement? What should social justice be like? What is good power and what is bad power? What should a democratic society be like? Social theories contain sociology and social philosophy and have an awareness of their own traditions as well as a response to other traditions. Such traditions carry paradoxical questions about the relations between theory and method, the universal and the particular, and democracy and difference. Contemporary social theory has much to contribute in terms of providing coherent responses to these paradoxes, which is not to say that the rejoinders they offer do not give way to new ambiguities. To demonstrate this further I return briefly to the discussion of the debate between Joas and Alexander before summing up and outlining how I proceed in the rest of the book.

The divisiveness inherent to the question of the directives of philosophy and science and of the place of social theory in interdisciplinary studies is hardly new given that it has been present since the birth of the modern university. A very clear contemporary example of this divisiveness can be seen again in Alexander's and Joas's contradictory positions. Unlike Joas, Alexander does not emphasize a need to retrace sociology to philosophical traditions other than to show its radical break from philosophy in his plea for the renewal of general sociology. Alexander argues we should be searching to synthesize the theoretical forms that are derived from subfield empirical research.[13] He warns against polarization or the formation of such single model approaches. "A younger generation of sociological theorists has set out an agenda [and] neither micro nor macro theory is satisfactory. Action and structure must now be entertained. Throughout the centres of Western sociology . . . a synthetic rather than polemical theorizing is now the order of the day"(Alexander 1998, 163–164).

It is worth recalling that Alexander's approach to general sociology offers the advantage of bypassing sterile arguments regarding the technical and procedural relations between theory and method in subfield research. The argument also helps guard against one of the special theories from the subfields (education, economy, sex and gender, media, social movements, ethnography, demography, the family, work, race and ethnic relations, etc.) pretending to be capable of producing a general theory of society. On the other hand, after arguing for synthesizing theories, Alexander ends with a plea for a single epistemology he calls "postpositivism" or what comes "after neofunctionalism." His polemic is founded in a reductionist move that levels all approaches on the so-called soft side of sociology—including critical theory, hermeneutics, and especially aesthetic approaches—with the charge of relativism. A second limitation that immediately follows from this is that for postpositivism only traditions that can apply theory to empirical analysis need be taken seriously. The argument seeks to avoid subjectivist or ideological biases from collapsing or radically subverting theoretical logic in general sociological theory, but this comes with an unacceptable cost: the broad erasure of critical, hermeneutic, and aesthetic theories leaves no chance for the interdisciplinary dialogue sociology needs to enter into if it is to avoid a disciplinary implosion. Indeed, a better explanation of the so-called excess of metatheory in sociology might be that sociologists are increasingly forced to build corridors to forgotten philosophical traditions that its mainstream postpositivist practitioners unwittingly keep closed (Ritzer 1996).

A different plea for the renewal of general sociological theory is found in Joas. As noted above, he argues for a third theoretical option that would place creativity in human action at the center and not on the periphery of theoretical understanding. In supporting his argument, Joas shows the links of philosophy to classical and contemporary currents of sociological theory. He argues that "there is a creative dimension to all human action, a dimension which is only inadequately expressed in the models of utilitarian and normative theory" (1996, 4). The magnitude of Joas's point here should not go unnoted given that positivist and functionalist theories have dominated the mezo or middle zone of social theory not only since the 1950s but for far more than two centuries. Utilitarian theory refers to all those disciplines that explain the motivations for action as rooted in the rational maximization of the interests of the actors—whether this is in economics, behaviorist psychology, or rational choice theory in sociology. Normative theories are equally varied in approach and discipline and in general seek to explain social action as formed or oriented by fixed rules of rational conduct. Joas's claim is that each of these models reduces the creative dimension in action to a secondary status and thus can only explain creativity as a determined consequence rather than as the most important basis of social action.

After reviewing the history of theory and its relationship to philosophy, Joas concludes that while several promising attempts at conceptualizing the creative dimension have been proposed, in the main this dimension is always relegated to a second order. He does nonetheless select several key metaphors from his broad survey of ideas that describe in strikingly different ways what he means by the creative dimension of human action. He reviews the concepts of the expressive moment of any utterance (Herder), production and revolution (Marx), life (Schopenhauer, Nietzsche) and intelligence and reconstruction (Dewey and Mead). He shows how each of these concepts can be thought of as a residual fragment of a general normative theory and that in some sense the way to bring the third approach into the mainstream of social theory is to follow the impulse attached to each concept rather than to propose any kind of absolute dialectical synthesis. In this sense Joas remains a consummate pragmatist. Like Alexander, he never strays too far from utilitarian and normative theory unless he wants to remind us of the dangers that lie beyond the boundaries, and how important it is to incorporate this third approach if we want the center to hold. Yet, unlike Alexander, Joas encourages us to seek out resources in the deep traditions of philosophy and aesthetics.

For both Alexander and Joas, past generations of general sociological theorists are seen to have built their systems through the synthesis of diverse theoretical tendencies that emanate from empirical subfield research. This process has led to an understanding of theory as fundamentally rooted in empirical analysis and theory construction. My argument, in part following Alexander's plea for theoretical synthesis, is that from the point of view of subfield research, a general theoretical logic is overly restricted in its capacity to absorb the results of empirical hypothesis testing. On the other hand, Alexander's argument for a general theoretical logic in sociology, arrests the study of the potentially richer philosophical and aesthetic sources available for the renewal of general theory, because they are not derived from empirical research as defined by social science. In other words, general sociological theory must be able to join emerging interdisciplinary area studies while maintaining autonomy through reflection on its own (varied) philosophical traditions. This is not an argument to eliminate empirical research and theory construction, but a plea for a more reflexive self-criticism that would broaden research in general sociological theory in order to get at Joas's third approach.[14] In short, sociologists should read philosophy and aesthetics not only because they are social facts, which they certainly are, but more generally because they can be seen as a resource for extending theoretical genres of sociology.

The assumption of this book is that Bakhtin's nonpositivist and nonempiricist philosophy can be fruitfully read alongside sociology as a source that can provide a rich opening to a dialogical research program that privileges the creative and normative dimension of action. Joas's argument for a third theoretical option that would place creativity in human action at the center of understanding is thus very close to this position. However, there is an important difference between his definition of creativity and Bakhtin's. Joas anchors his theory of creativity in "the pragmatist understanding of human action itself" (Joas 1996, 4). His criticism of Habermas's pragmatism is that he completely misses this consideration of the creative dimension in action. Aspiration toward action is itself located in the body and so, "it is the body's capabilities, habits and ways of relating to the environment which form the background to all conscious goal-setting, in other words, to intentionality." (1996, 158) Against theories of rational action, he argues that only careful investigations of the "the intentional character of human action, the specific corporeality, and primary sociality of all human capacity for action" will lead to a sustainable theory of the "creativity of action" (148).

Bakhtin, on the other hand, proposes a phenomenological theory of action in an aesthetic and ethical mode—something none of the above attempt. Like phenomenology, pragmatism does not evoke a mind-body split. It locates thought in the sensual world, but much of its emphasis is on the cognitive. An important difference with pragmatism is that Bakhtin does not emphasize cognitivist solutions to problem solving to the same extent as Mead, Joas, or Habermas. Bakhtin is much closer to Simmel's philosophical sociology, discussed further in chapter 4. For Bakhtin, the act is more than a response to a situation or circumstance that calls on intelligent solutions to solve problems that arise. The act is also a unique response in which the self-other relation is aesthetically formed from fragmentary cognitive and ethical elements into consummated wholes (with loopholes).

On the other hand, I also want to introduce Bakhtin into a dialogue with general sociological theory and not simply define his difference. I agree with Joas that we need to bring attention to the expressive or creative dimension that remains underdeveloped in Habermas's model of communicative action and also, as with both Joas and Alexander, argue that radically subjectivist theories are not especially helpful in developing a dialogic approach to the creativity of action along the lines of a general theory. Bakhtin's emphasis on the norms of answerability is not incompatible with Habermas's general approach, and thus I will argue that his aesthetic theory is potentially an excellent counterpoint to Habermas's rationalism, and by extention a dynamic opening onto theorizing the creative dimension problematized by Joas. Although I have only touched very superficially on the debate between Joas and Alexander, it nonetheless gives an idea of the broad range of issues that lie in social theory and of the need to demarcate the levels of abstraction involved.

The Bridge between Culture and the Political

The discussion of difficulties encountered in general theorizing within sociology, along with the contrast with Habermas concerning the distinction between culture and politics discussed above, suggest that Bakhtin's approach to social theory needs to broach three levels of analysis. Firstly, a transcultural level needs to be defined in a way that allows for shifts in thinking about transcendent and concrete norms within and accross cultures. The two remaining levels include the lived dialogic self-other relations that supports the moral basis of community and the specificity of culture (ethnos) and the general level of political community (demos) and of the universal entitlements for citizens in the nation-state. I focus on the question of a transcultural ethics and the level of self-other relations in chapters 1 through 6, and in the final two chapters apply the two-sided answerability approach to the third level of demos, citizenship and national identity in postnational times. My strategy here is to work through a back and forth interplay between the levels of *ethnos* and *demos* via a transcultural ethics rather than propose an either/or judgment between them or between specific cultural notions of the good life and the application of universal rights and procedures. My argument is that Bakhtin's position lends a greater openness in relation to political issues without giving up a universal definition of the ethical as a two-sided approach to answerabilty. On the other hand, I will also argue that Habermas helps indicate why (though not necessarily where or in which cases) a procedural or deliberative form is necessary.

The comparison of Habermas and Bakhtin in the first three chapters is discussed in terms of the difference and similarity between their disciplinary orientations toward normativity. These chapters deepen the definitions of the first two levels of abstraction concerning transcultural ethics and the self-other dialogic relations. Chapter 1 develops a definition of the ideal of transcultural ethics by referring to both Habermas's and Bakhtin's perspectives. Habermas's theory of discourse ethics, or the idea that ethical action should be preceded by the open possibility of deliberation by any agent that might be effected by proposed norms of action, is given three general criticisms. These criticisms put into question the dangers of ethnocentric theorizing of universals, of the potential gender bias entailed, and of the overdetermination of juridical reason and of the definition that priveleges the supremacy of the "right" over the "good." Bakhtin's concept of the transgrediant, or aesthetically informed crossover relation and exchange between actors, is posited as an alternative way of theorizing transcendence, while the concepts of exotopy or outsidedness and of rhythm, spirit, and soul are reviewed as a way of introducing his theory of intersubjectivity. Chapter 2 continues this comparison but focuses more on similarities and differences between their postmetaphysical approaches to language with a particular emphasis on Habermas's sociological theory of the relation between systems and lifeworld and Bakhtin's shift from ethics and aesthetics to a metalinguistic theory of discourse.

Their positions on language, literature, and philosophy are discussed further in chapter 3 where Bakhtin's early definition of dialogue is traced back to the concepts he first tried out in the early essay on ethics but then left undeveloped. His attempt to create a new ethical theory through a "philosophy of the answerable act" is left incomplete, as is his attempt to shift the ethical questions toward a more aesthetic understanding of the self-other relation. Dialogue and dialogism become the key concepts that continue to be developed in his mature works, and to date, there are only partial explanations as to why he abandoned or modified the earlier concepts. In order to draw out the theoretical logic inherent to his approach I demonstrate how he might use the early definition of the concepts of dialogue and polyphony to interpret a well-known postmodern novel by Italo Calvino, *If on a Winter's Night a Traveller*. The novel is selected because it offers a counterfactual position on authorship, the genres of discourse, and their respective boundaries that helps reveal some of the hidden assumptions in both Habermas's and Bakhtin's philosophies. In the process, I try and show the steps that Bakhtin develops in his linguistic turn and how he develops the concept of dialogue out of his earlier incomplete attempt to construct a "philosophy of the answerable act." The chapter finishes with an explanation of Habermas's argument on the necessary boundaries between theory and literature and asks whether or not dialogue or communicative action can be the same with respect to the novel as to other forms of communication. Shifting Bakhtin's concern for the dialogic anticipation of response to Habermas's concern for communicative action—or the practical discourses that seek out mutual understandings at higher levels of abstraction— takes the discussion out of the history of the novel and returns it to the relation between society and culture.

In chapters 4, 5, and 6, I bracket the comparison with Habermas in order to discuss the main philosophical sources that Bakhtin draws on in his earlier works. The first works are discussed in relation to some of his most important influences including: 1) Kant's moral philosophy and some of the attempts to reform its major tenets by the Russian neo-Kantian, Alexander Vvedenskij; 2) Georg Simmel's critique of Kant's Categorical Imperative; and 3) the neo-Kantian philosopher and founder of the Marburg School Hermann Cohen's concept of fellowship. Bakhtin adds to Kant's original ethics by postulating a faith in the possible existence of an autonomous other "I" and the necessity of (intersubjective) "co-experience." Vvedenskij called this faith in the possible existence of another I the fourth postulate, and it is explained further in chapter 4. Simmel's argument for the substitution of Kant's general law with an absolute individual law is then defined as the most important assumption Bakhtin absorbs in thinking through his "philosophy of the answerable act" and eventually his concept of dialogue. The act is like a "two-faced Janus," says Bakhtin, in which the subject of action, the "I" is axiological, unique, and unrepeatable in life (being) but its action takes place in a predictable and objective culture (1993, 2). He claims that the responsibility of the "I" in the always answerable act is nontransferable and that this answerable "I" has no alibi in being: "Being that is detached from the unique emotional-volitional centre of answerability is a rough draft, an unacknowledged possible variant of once-occurrent being" (Bakhtin 1993, 42).

In chapter 5, I continue presenting the antinomies in Kant and Bakhtin while also comparing and contrasting Bakhtin's philosophy of the act with Weber's sociology of action. I highlight their differences with Kant by considering how each theorist thinks through a specific area of action. I sketch a synthesis of the contrasting ethical, sociological, and aesthetic viewpoints by comparing how each approach theorizes the example of Eros as one of a wide variety of possible action zones in human culture.

I do not propose a history of theory or a new general sociological theory as Joas, Alexander, and Habermas do. As the book progresses I introduce Bakhtin further into a dialogue with social theory in order to measure the depth of his position and to provide conceptual tools that allow a response to the challenge of joining the self-other level of action and general political levels into a unified approach. Again, Bakhtin is not a sociologist and some argue he came to disdain sociological explanation all together. It is therefore not immediately clear how his approach can contribute to a resolution of the general sociological theory puzzle.

In chapter 6 I show that Bakhtin's theory of the norms of answerability provides a rich source that symbolic interactionists who follow the tradition begun in part by Simmel and Weber and then developed much more fully by George Herbert Mead could draw on with great benefit. Following Joas, I show that both Mead and Bakhtin develop a definition of the creative event of action and that both understand the self-conscious subject as something that can only be looked back upon from a second position. I argue that Mead's and Bakhtin's projects can thus be seen as making unique contributions to the reflexive theory of the subject as an actor in a political community that remains useful to theorists of contemporary general sociology. The complementary and contradictory elements between the two thinkers are situated philosophically and each of their theoretical logics is drawn out through the application of each approach to a Dostoevsky story from *The Brothers Karamozov*—a story about murder, guilt, confession, and community.

In the last two chapters I leave the problem of defining the philosophical sources for Bakhtin's approach and his dialogue with social theory in order to solve the problem of the shift from the microlevel toward an analysis of the political community. Although the reconstruction of Bakhtin's approach is no longer part of the narrative in these chapters, my approach to the theories in question remains Bakhtinian in spirit if not in practice. As we saw with Joas and Alexander, the shift between micro and macro levels of analysis is a key problem in social theory. Sociologies of action are often limited to micro forms of description, whereas structuralist and poststructuralist explanations of social forces tend to reduce the subject of action to a function of power or discourse. Given that the aim of this book is fundamental rather than applied, I can only outline the kinds of approaches that need to be converged in order to bridge the bifurcated strategies. The interactionist, transcultural, and political levels need to be posited in terms of their proximity and distance to one another. In other words, they need to be thought through in terms of potential theoretical convergence and synthesis while at the same time allowing each an autonomy that does not collapse one into another or allow one transcendent reign over the others.

In chapters 7 and 8, I examine the conceptual shift from the level of self-other relations to a set of general political questions about citizenship, national identities, and the defense of contemporary culture in a postnational world. In chapter 7 I try to show that the reflexive approach to the individual-community relation privileged by Weber, Simmel, Mead, and Bakhtin can be used fruitfully to theorize societal dialogue that impacts on actors within political communities who seek greater self-autonomy through the state. I emphasize that although neither Mead nor Bakhtin developed distinctive political philosophies, this does not mean that their approaches are of little use for thinking through general political questions. Once the theory of the shift in levels has been explained, chapter 7 goes on to apply the two-sided approach to answerability to definitions of citizenship and national identities. The chapter concludes with a general survey and critique of various sociological and political theories of the origins of nations and nationalism as put forward by Tom Narin, Anthony Smith, Benedict Anderson, George Gellner, Eric Hobsbaum, Rogers Brubaker, David McCrone, Montserrat Guibernau, David Miller, and others.

Chapter 8 takes off from the conclusion to the previous chapter and presents a dialogue on the nation in postnational times through a comparison of both pro- and antinationalist theorists. I discuss a brief case study that examines the way in which two pronationalist sociologists from Quebec, Marcel Rioux and Fernand Dumont, have tried to theorize the question of shared sovereignty in the contexts of a Québécois ethnos within the North American continent. Their positions are contrasted with the well-known antinationalist theories of contemporary democracy as developed in the works of Habermas, Charles Taylor, and Will Kymlicka. Habermas's two-level definition of society as system and lifeworld is reviewed and his discourse theory of democracy is introduced through his debate with Taylor over the politics of recognition and Taylor's plea for a two-leveled liberalism that would address both individual and collective rights. Kymlicka's important distinction between ethnocultural and national minorities is introduced in order to help clarify the synthesis of liberal and republican theories of democracy that Habermas offers and to link us back to the dialogic approach discussed in chapter 7. I argue in the conclusion to chapter 8 that it is important to continue to bracket the problem of the unity of social relations *(bildungseffekt)* within Habermas's concept of communicative action, and the "decentred society." I also argue that his notion of "subjectless communication," derived from legal procedure, needs to be nuanced and that while his plea for "constitutional patriotism" deepens the paradox it does not offer much in terms of a dialogic solution to the national question given that *demos* and *ethnos* need to be understood in a dialogical tension rather than as monologized opposites.

1

DIVERSITY AND TRANSCULTURAL ETHICS

No matter how widely Bakhtin and Habermas might be recognized as key figures of twentieth-century social philosophy, they are rarely considered together.[1] Obviously Bakhtin was not aware of Habermas's work. Although Habermas does cite *Rabelais and his World* as an important source for his own thinking on how to revise his study on the public sphere, it is clear that he has not made any systematic inquiry into Bakhtin's approach (Habermas 1992). In a 1989 interview in the Russian philosophy journal *Vorposy filosofii,* Habermas was asked his opinion of Russian philosophy and responded by saying that while it is not well known in the West, the work of Vygotsky and new studies in language can be most favorably compared to the work of Western theorists such as Mead and Piaget. About Bakhtin in particular he says: "Bakhtin's cultural theory has had great influence in the West, this comes from his book on Rabelais and from his theory of language which I consider to be more or less a Marxist interpretation of Humboldt."[2]

The separation of Bakhtin and Habermas is not only a geographical and philosophical one but is also prepared in advance by their respective disciplinary boundaries and generational differences. Bakhtin's major works were produced at the origins of the linguistic turn in philosophy and language studies during the first half of the century but only widely received in the second half. Despite the fact that he himself did not see it this way, today his work is usually considered to speak most pertinently to audiences in literary theory or cultural studies. Coming of age in Nazi Germany Habermas had to reconcile a different kind of authoritarian context than the one Bakhtin experienced under Soviet rule. Some argue that Habermas's thought, and especially his frequent interventions into public debate should be seen as dedicated to providing the philosophical arguments that might protect democratic societies from his own nation's past (Horster and Willem van Reijen 1992; Habermas 1994b, 2001). Habermas's work has enjoyed a wide reception almost since the middle of the century as the leader of the Frankfurt tradition's second generation. In part because of this legacy, Habermas, unlike Bakhtin, has written extensively about the philosophical influences on his own work. In fact the conceptual transitions in his work are carefully documented and theorized. This is not the case for Bakhtin who remained relatively silent on the evolution of his own ideas and the conditions of the internal exile with which he struggled. Habermas speaks to audiences mainly located in, but not restricted to, various branches of philosophy, political science, sociology, and legal studies, and does so well after the linguistic turn Bakhtin and his colleagues helped instigate.

A close comparative reading of each thinker's work is thus a formidable task given not only their voluminous production and vast range of interests but also the differentiated audiences their work addresses. In this chapter and the next I limit the scope of the comparison in order to avoid overwhelming the uninitiated on one side or another while maintaining the interest of those who are familiar with each. Members of both Bakhtin's and Habermas's audiences are invited to consider the broad similarities and differences between elements of their work that address one of the most perplexing problems to face contemporary theories of creativity and action—diversity and the dilemma of reconstructing a transcultural (universal) ethics.

Transculturalism is introduced as a third term that refers to the mixing or exchange of values implied in both Bakhtin's concept of dialogism (his mature term for answerability) and Habermas's concept of communicative action. Ethnographers have used the term *transculturation* to indicate how particular dominated groups choose elements from the cultural products that are produced and distributed by a dominant culture (Ortiz 1978). In a transcultural exchange one does not become the other but one does become other than what one was before the encounter. The issue of self-other relations in transculturalism is described by one scholar this way: "[A]s a phenomenon of becoming, I cannot become the other, I can only become other than myself, and other than the other and it is this new reality that means that identity can no longer be what it was" (Bertrand 1989, 8).

An emphasis on the capacity of subjugated peoples to actively select out elements from colonizing representations is often lost in totalizing critiques of domination, while at the same time, identity theory risks erring on the side of psychologism. Both Bakhtin and Habermas provide us with different openings into the normative dimension of transcultural practice as described here without reducing norms to functions of domination or psychological elements of identity. For Bakhtin, the living utterance contains an element of "answerability," no matter how seemingly monologic the utterance, for as long as the listener is alive there is the possibility of response. In Habermas's bi-level concept of society as system and lifeworld, the internal rationalization of the lifeworld can be seen as an ongoing response to colonization by systemic imperatives. Here speakers separate the fields of culture and personality from society into abstract categories and in so doing provide a particularized response to oppressive conditions. As Habermas claims, "[C]ommunicative actors are always moving within the horizon of their lifeworld, *they cannot step outside it*" (1984, 126, my emphasis).

On the other hand, for Bakhtin a key initial concern is the aesthetic or "*eventness*" aspect of action that occurs inside cultural, political, and ethical acts whenever actors anticipate a rejoinder to their utterance, gesture, or choice. Action is not only rational, claims Bakhtin, it is also answerable. Within Bakhtin's theory of answerabilty the anticipation of response in dialogic forms of action is not reduced to a rational act in the strictest sociological sense (Alexander 1982). An action is an answerable and potentially creative deed. Thus, for Bakhtin, dialogical means something different than seeking agreement from an exchange of opposite positions that have been unified by shifting at a higher level of generality, such as it does in Habermas's theory of discourse ethics defined below. Rather, Bakhtin looks to those emotional-volitional axiological orientations that seek a response from other positions that can consummate a shared, but not necessarily conflict-free exchange. First and foremost, dialogism is understood as a creative process that actively anticipates responses from other axiological positions. On the other hand, with Habermas, it too is argued that actions are not purely autonomous creative rejoinders but are themselves implicated in normative claims.

The concept of transculturalism helps describe what happens when dominant cultures come into contact with subaltern ones and how the latter continue becoming themselves. It provides a way of thinking about shifts between levels of identity and transcendental referents without reducing one to the other. Although the question of identity is widely discussed in poststructuralist theory in terms of a critique of subject positions, performativity, and power relations, or in multiculturalism as a politics of recognition, identity has typically been posited in socialization theory as an element determined within the matrix of structure and agency, on the one hand, and as a product of socialized norms, roles, and values, on the other. Whereas the latter set of relations are thought to explain the social solidarity that holds a community together, the former provide the dynamic that explains its transformation. Norms are usually defined by sociologists as guides to conduct or as rules or standards that are expected to be followed by acting within specific roles organized and prescribed within the structure of group life. Norms vary in how closely they are connected to values. Many are technical guidelines for day to day activities that hold little symbolic importance whereas others are more culturally salient and provide the general boundaries for moral intuitions and values. Values or desires are not the same as norms or roles but the two phenomena are interrelated. Values and desires refer to particular differences and choices while norms and roles refer to limited kinds of universal expectations about how to act.

Transculturalism is an always complicated process because of the contradiction it entails between the ideal ways of doing (normative) and wanting (values), and other ways of doing and wanting. The ethnographic meaning of the term focuses attention on the way in which norms and values are created from a clash of difference. This difference is derived from a definition of the intersubjective exchange in the process of identity formation wherein questions of *who I am* and *what I am for* are grounded in the question of *how should I act* (Habermas 1996). In this way the concept of transculturalism allows a theoretical flexibility that can shift between the normative and creative levels of exchange that neither duty bound (deontological) nor utilitarian ethics contain.

The two questions that Bakhtin and Habermas ask—"What should I do when faced with someone who can answer back?" and "How can I reach understanding with another?"—take us in two different theoretical directions. The first question leads to developing a transcultural ethics that accommodates both the aesthetic creation or *eventness* that occurs when self and other meet, but also when lifeworlds cross over. The second question leads to a theoretical definition of metanorms, or the most general normative agreements within and between lifeworlds that are practically necessary. My purpose in this chapter is not to apply either Bakhtin's or Habermas's ethics or to focus on the varied cultural, political, or juridical contours of their practices but to compare the two lines of questioning, identify points of criticism, and look for the common ground between them. This comparison is developed in several stages.

First, I want to further situate Habermas's and Bakhtin's different disciplinary orientations. Next, I outline Habermas's theory of discourse ethics and identify three criticisms that suggest alternative strategies for an anthropological rather than a juridical, interpretation. These criticisms are taken as cautions that might be absorbed within Bakhtin's general approach without rejecting Habermas's model outright. Next, I leave aside the comparison with Habermas and concentrate on reconstructing the creative aspects of normative action inherent in Bakhtin's general aesthetics of subjectivity, which he introduces in his earliest essays, *Toward a Philosophy of the Act* and "The Author and the Hero In Aesthetic Activity." Bakhtin's philosophical anthropology is introduced by focusing on his concepts of "exotopy" or outsidedness and the "excess of seeing," of "sympathetic co-experiencing," and of the crossover or transgredient processes inherent in self-other relations. Finally, I reverse the field of discussion by returning to discuss the normative dimension in the creative act in order to propose a model for social theorizing that would be situated between Bakhtin and Habermas.

Disciplinary Orientations

Even though important conceptual shifts occur in the evolution of their respective writings, both Bakhtin's and Habermas's corpora maintain a remarkably unified philosophical response to the question of transculturalism. Neither thinker gives in to pluralism or a detached intellectual relativism yet each, in different ways, recognizes that modern societies develop "polyphonically" (in multiple voices, perspectives, and simultaneous points of view) and that modern jurisprudence is founded on the attempt to take into consideration the care of unique individuals and their actions in the context of increasingly disparate communal definitions of the "good life" (Regh 1994; Rzhevsky 1994). Elements of this complex neo-Kantian theme appear in Habermas's early works on political sociology, critical theory, and philosophy and return in more mature forms across his recent writings on communicative action, discourse ethics, law, and the discourse theory of democracy. Bakhtin's lifelong preoccupation with the themes of dissimilarity, answerability, and consummation can be discerned from his earliest essays to notes on metalinguistics written shortly before his death in 1975. (Clark and Holquist 1984a).

As the introductory chapter points out, the young Bakhtin's theory of creativity makes a special distinction between the aesthetic as the shaping of meaning in action and the ethical as a cognitive feature of the act itself. Unlike Habermas's discourse ethics, defined in more detail below, Bakhtin sees the aesthetic as distinct but not severed from ethics. He looks at the aesthetic as the form in which the ethical relation between subjects is consummated, and examines how a part is meaningfully shaped into a whole. This does not mean he "levels" art and literature to the same status as science or politics (a danger Habermas strongly warns against). Artistic expression is a unique aesthetic genre. The discourse of politics, science, religion, or day to day life are not artistic genres, but each has an aesthetic dimension, a special way of shaping meaning, deriving completeness, or maintaining incompleteness.

Habermas is much easier to situate in the context of general sociological theory than Bakhtin. He is considered by some to be among the most important theorists since Talcott Parsons to outline a dual concept of society as system and lifeworld that serves to provide the necessary scaffolding for moving between micro and macro levels of analysis (Layder 1994). Yet the fact that new contradictory pleas for general theory (as can be seen in the work of Alexander and Joas, for example), continue to be expressed suggests the partial nature of his success. Habermas theorizes the normative claims of social actors by connecting the seemingly opposite conceptual strategies of systems and lifeworlds through the generic pragmatic process of communicative action. Communicative actions are rationally motivated attempts to move toward shared understandings concerning metanorms within the limited horizons of the lifeworld. They are distinct from strategic forms of communication that seek to influence decisions of opponents rather than achieve mutual understanding. Communicative action is not derived from compromise. Rather, writes Habermas, "in communicative action one actor seeks rationally to motivate another by relying on the illocutionary binding effect *(Bindungseffekt)* of the offer contained in his speech act" (Habermas 1990, 58). The binding effect of communicative actions are not achieved through political compromise, but rather through the creation of unconstrained, unforced, mutual understanding.

While these two theoretical approaches differ, they each provide important arguments against contemporary varieties of relativism—

Bakhtin by returning the author/I to theories of cultural production and Habermas by shifting moral universals to discursive categories. Our question then becomes, how can we couple Bakhtin's understanding of the aesthetic shaping of meaning between individuals with Habermas's concept of the binding effects generated by communicative actions in culturally diverse societies? Bakhtinians who see only an imperious rationalism in Habermas's work are encouraged to reconsider the neohumanist impulse that returns whenever he seeks an alternative to antimetaphysical thinking. True, Bakhtin and Habermas do not share a common approach to language and intersubjectivity (Gardiner 1992; Nielsen 1994). Yet their key concepts, Bakhtin's dialogism and Habermas's communicative action, argue implicitly that the expansion of modern lifeworld solidarities can only occur through the mixing of cultures and a tolerance for differing moral intuitions.

For both Bakhtin and Habermas communicative or dialogic actions rely on interpersonal relations that have a normative dimension. When speakers from different lifeworlds are oriented toward the same symbolic referents within a single social system, they also intersect, that is, take on elements of identity from one another while becoming themselves. Bakhtin's mature concept of dialogism helps explain the creative dimension in transcultural exchange on the lived discursive plane: "Two discourses equally and directly orientated toward a referential object within the limits of a single context cannot exist side by side without intersecting dialogically." Regardless of whether they support or contradict one another, Bakhtin argues that "two embodied meanings cannot lie side by side like two objects—they must come into inner contact; that is, they must enter into a semantic bond" (Bakhtin 1984a, 188–189). In this contact zone agents meet, take on, and project elements of identity to and from one another. In this sense, identity is thought of as a creative answerable event.[3] This idea from Bakhtin's early ethics is consistent with his later theory of speech genres where he argues that in entering live speech acts, the speaker becomes, subtly or dramatically, other than what he has been while remaining himself. According to Bakhtin, "[T]o live means to participate in dialogue. In this dialogue a person participates wholly and throughout life." He or she invests his or her "entire self in discourse and this discourse enters into the dialogic fabric of human life, into the world symposium" (1984a, 293).[4]

While Bakhtin's concept of dialogism can be expanded to explain the creative dimension of transculturalism, it does not lead to an explication of normative claims that might be or should be common to all such exchanges. The difficulty of positing dialogism as a general theory is an important point to remember because as Bakhtin's ideas developed in the final stages of his work, his position only goes as far as to theorize a struggle over values that are invented in and across utterances. He does not define, at least in the materials available to us at this time, the normative conditions of transculturation outside of conventional "heteroglot" or historically stratified normative contexts. In reconstructing concepts that might explain the preconditions of both the normative and creative forces of transcultural ethics I endeavor to balance the positions of Bakhtin and Habermas. Whereas Bakhtin is inclined to overemphasize the actor's subjective anticipation of response, Habermas tends to overdetermine the question of communicative reason.[5] Lean too far in Habermas's direction and one risks erring on the side of universal pragmatics. Here, the emphasis on the aesthetically creative "acting into the utterance" is replaced with a linguistic problematic that defines language in terms of assertoric or constative sentences and speech acts. Lean too far in Bakhtin's direction and one risks erring on the side of a philosophy of consciousness that loses the capacity to reconstruct explanations of normative forces.[6]

Even the most cursory reading of his monographs on Dostoevsky and Rabelais reveals that Bakhtin privileges mythos over logos or narrative over reason as the object of study that best allows access to what he calls "the great dialogue." For Bakhtin the distinct and yet simultaneous "participation with equal rights" of all voices in a given society is only possible in modernist ("polyphonic") narrative.[7] On the other hand, this does not preclude his interest in defining ethical dilemmas across epochs and various cultural forms. Some of Bakhtin's most important commentators speculate that his theories of polyphony and carnival developed as a subversive response to totalitarian conditions in the former Soviet Union. Mikhaïl Ryklin argues that Bakhtin sought to canonize the Russian people as a "flesh bound, low-down folk" capable of overcoming the most oppressive measures. He suggests that Bakhtin's ideas are the reactions of "a representative of the Russian intelligentsia, who found himself in the 'unthinkable' situation of terror and the ever-growing and increasing dominance of a collective corporeality *(telesnost)*" (Ryklin 1993, 51). It is perhaps not surprising that in the context of a barely existing civil society, Bakhtin would claim that the "great artist," not the statesman, revolutionary, philosopher, or sociologist, possesses the gift "for hearing his epoch as a great dialogue, for detecting in it not only individual voices, but precisely and predominantly the dialogic relationship among voices" (Bakhtin 1984a, 90). The artist best hears the voices of the past, the reigning voices of the era as well as the emerging, not yet completely formed, voices of the weak, the disenfranchised, and the wretched.

Decentered Subjects and Critiques of Discourse Ethics

I will set the question aside for the moment as to whether or not Bakhtin's privileging of aesthetics and a coeval theory of ethics can be translated into a general social theory of democracy. Habermas would conclude that it cannot. Aesthetic works are expressive, dramaturgical forms of action that "embody a knowledge of the agent's own subjectivity." Compared to communicative actions, dramaturgical actions "can be criticized as untruthful, that is, rejected as deceptions or self-deceptions." Habermas explains such actions in terms of "value standards that are dependant in turn on innovations in the domain of evaluative expressions reflected in an exemplary manner" but not as ways of shaping meaning in Bakhtin's sense (Habermas 1984, 335).

Habermas rarely treats the question of the status of art and literature except through his commentary on the earlier members of the Frankfurt tradition, or in his reference to the separate status of aesthetic and philosophical texts. This makes a direct comparison with Bakhtin difficult. At the same time Habermas's controversial plea for a new critical theory based in a philosophy of language and a sociology of communication bears important consequences for the theory of aesthetics if it were to be accepted without criticism. For one thing, following Habermas's lead means that aesthetic theory is not applicable to most object domains outside of the expressive domain of culture. Like Parsons, Weber, and Kant before him, Habermas argues that modern societies are in part founded on the separation of aesthetic, practical, and scientific spheres of action and knowledge.

For Habermas, then, logos (reason, speech, action), and especially communicative reason, remains the privileged object of study from which he promises to reveal the normative foundations for his critical theory of contemporary society and politics. Society is defined as a dual concept composed of systems of administrative, economic, and political power, on the one hand, and civil society and its various lifeworlds, on the other. The relative separation of each sector accounts for societal decentering that in turn adds complex pressures on both sides to draw different kinds of resources from the public sphere. Speaking subjects get decentered in their communicative actions due to the increased need to differentiate and overlap norms, roles, and values that are situationally specific. Habermas argues that "the background of a communicative action is formed by situation definitions that have to overlap to a sufficient extent. If not actors draw on strategic action. Thus every new utterance is a test: the situation implicitly proposed by the speaker is either confirmed, modified, partly suspended, or generally placed in question" (1987, 121). Within their interpretive processes, actors discern a unique objective world and distinguish it from those of other collectivities. The cultural baggage inscribed in these decentered world views can be rationalized or separated from institutions to greater or lesser degrees. Again, as Habermas puts this, the more the world view is decentered "the less the need for understanding is covered in advance by an interpreted lifeworld immune from critique, and the more this need has to be met by way of risky agreement [then] the more frequently we can expect rational action orientations" (1984, 70).[8]

Habermas's writings on communicative action and discourse ethics contain the promise of determining—regardless of context—the justification for norms of action in decentered complex societies that entertain conflicting views of "the good." Discourse ethics provide the formal principle that replaces Kant's categorical imperative for determining the legitimacy of norms. It relies on the much-contested maxim of universalizability that states: for a norm of action to be valid, all those who could be effected by it or by its side effects must have the opportunity to enter into practical arguments about it and, from this association, form a rationally motivated agreement that such a norm should indeed come into force (Habermas 1990, 120). Despite his effort to arrive at a "context free" discourse ethics, several criticisms have been leveled at his position, each of which hints at a different aspect of the question of transculturalism.

For Habermas, communicative actions are a particularly modern discursive genre. They are not just another narrative nor are they features of every society. At the same time, all forms of communication, whatever their finality, are considered to be in some way derivative of the idealized model. Societies whose knowledge structures are rooted in "mythicomagical" or "religious-metaphysical" modes of thought are not taken to aspire to the same model (Habermas 1984). Thomas McCarthy argues that Habermas's universal maxim aims to shift the Kantian question of "How is experience possible" to "How is mutual understanding possible?" This approach to the universal concerns only the discursive interactions that actors enter into with the intention of achieving agreements. McCarthy explains the main problem this position implies for transcultural ethics: "[I]f the structures of communicative action and discourse . . . are to be found with significant frequency only in certain cultures at certain times, how then is it possible to defend the view that these structures are universal-pragmatic features of communication as such." For a transcultural ethics the argument for universal structures must be able to establish itself without chauvinism or ethnocentrism and demonstrate that "the ability to act communicatively" is a "species wide competence" whose potential is available to humankind (McCarthy 1991, 134–135).

Seyla Benhabib offers a sympathetic understanding of Habermas's discourse ethics but argues that it should be more context sensitive. She agrees that discourse ethics are based on the distinction between determining the conditions of reason for validity claims and the organizing of perceptions for the subject. In other words, she agrees that there is a shift from Kant's transcendental reason toward reason that speakers carry out in practical contexts or situations. Keeping in mind that practical reason belongs to the in-itself or noumenal subject and thus cannot be legislated, the "first step in [Habermas's] formulation," she argues, "is to shift from a substantialist to a discursive, communicative concept of rationality," while the second step comes with the idea that subjects are fragile and in need of moral protection (1992, 5). Hence, Benhabib argues that the innovation of the Kantian universal is a redundant compendium to discourse ethics. Habermas uses the universal category to explain consensus or the process of achieving understanding. Yet Benhabib points out that consensus alone is not a criterion for discourse ethics that is situationally bound and not universally grounded (Benhabib 1990). Rather, for her, universal interests are not the same as general interests, which are regulative rather than substantive. Her universalism would be "interactive not legislative, cognizant of gender difference not gender blind and contextually sensitive not situation indifferent" (Benhabib 1992, 3).[9]

In his book *The Genesis of Values*, Hans Joas puts forward an index of criticisms that chart the evolution of Habermas's ethics from its earliest formulation to his more recent work on law and the democratic constitutional state. Although several of his points do not address my topic directly, many parallel the two basic criticisms raised so far. I do not propose to address each step of his analysis but only to highlight his most general thesis that when the theoretical definition of the relation between norms and values privileges the former, and when "the broader philosophical question consistently favours the right over the good and the universally moral over the ethically specific, the net effect is that the basic idea of the actor as a reflexive agent disappears from the theoretical horizon." For Habermas, the universal "standard of justice" takes its place given that only the formula that priveleges the right over the good is able to provide a universal judgment for each agent. But there remains doubt as to whether or not the question of justice as a formal procedure actually detaches itself from "value-related propositions." If norms trump values then where do norms come from in the first place? Joas argues that if a theory of agency and a theory of value are to be retained then "the standard of justice can only ever represent itself as one point of view amongst others from the perspective of the actors" (Joas 2000, 183). If there is doubt about this relation then the predominance of the right over the good does not hold either.

Keeping in mind the strong cautions placed on the principle of universalizability, and the separation of the ethical from the moral and legal, Habermas's discourse principle could be still defined as a normative version of Bakhtin's creative theorization of the "great dialogue." Universalizability assumes an ideal speech community wherein each potential speaker might have an equal opportunity to be heard. There must be mutual recognition by the speakers of their right to speak even if their claims contradict their adversaries' traditions. Their speech claims must be acknowledged if supported by rational argument (Habermas 1990). In this "ideal speech situation" there would be no distorted communication, only attempts to achieve understanding. This is a point that is often misunderstood by Habermas's unsympathetic critics. It is argued that "the ideal speech situation" is an artificial construct in that interlocutors or speakers never act in a purely rational way and that speech is often politically or ideologically motivated. In response to this critique Habermas explains he is not arguing that speakers want to act communicatively but that they must: "The Hobbesian state of nature, in which each isolated bourgeois subject is alienated from all others, and each is a wolf to the other (although real wolves live in packs)—that's the truly artificial construction" (Habermas 1994a, 111).[10]

Communicative actions, then, are by definition situationally bound, rationally motivated attempts to move toward shared agreements concerning metanorms. In the case of contact between lifeworlds, discourse ethics argues that the only acceptable way of resolving conflict is discursive. Expanding "the great dialogue" is not done by prescribing a transcendental moral. Such a procedure might cause harm to other lifeworlds. Rather, the expansion must be done by encouraging transcultural solidarities without erasing the plurality of traditions and identities. Jean Cohen and Andrew Arato point out that Habermas's position argues that in order to achieve solidarity with other lifeworlds we must have access to "a non-violent form of conflict resolution when we encounter one another," have access to each other's cultural traditions, and retain a capacity for self-criticism of our own traditions (1992, 386).

As we have seen, it is difficult to know what response Habermas would give to the question of aesthetic invention in actual dialogue. Even though Habermas only rarely uses the term *dialogue* to describe what he means by practical discourse, the two terms are used interchangeably by his most innovative interpreters.[11] It is easy to confuse the immanent meaning of intersubjectivity with its ideal telos or outcome. For Habermas, solidarity is thought of as the local embodiment of intersubjectivity whereas justice is its universal expression. This is a logical extension of the definition of solidarity as a cohesive force that binds actors together within a lifeworld but it does not mean that a consideration of its existential meaning could not be considered. Habermas argues that while "ethical-existential" questions are more immediately pressing at the level of the lifeworld, in order to overcome insidious forms of relativism we must take up the position that the "right" prevails over the "good." Intersubjectivity in the form of moral intuition is thought to be contained in the procedures themselves by which justice is developed. For Habermas, only questions of justice "are so structured that they can be resolved equitably in the equal interest of all" (1993, 151).

On the other hand, if the reference to practical discourse hinges on the outcome of the exchange of a rational demonstration of arguments, the achievement of unforced agreements, and the binding effects they have through recourse to the justice system—what then is intersubjectivity itself?[12] This is the point where Bakhtin's approach both contradicts but also possibly helps to strengthen Habermas's discourse ethics. Given Habermas's definition of the modern decentered subject, it remains unclear how he might respond to two main problems that are fundamental to reconstructing a transcultural ethics. First, there is this question of the subjectivity of intersubjectivity, and second, the related aesthetic question of what invention or creation occurs between subjects in actual dialogue. The first question asks that we understand the "binding effects" not only as a product of mutual understanding, but also as an achievement of social communion. This completion of the social, the shaping of its meaning, is what Bakhtin means by aesthetic consummation, though with a definition that is broader than the narrowly defined expressive moment Habermas theorizes, as we will show in the section below.

The Creative Side of the Normative

In *Toward a Philosophy of the Act* and "The Author and the Hero in Aesthetic Activity" Bakhtin presents his unique philosophical elaboration of the need to reunite the aesthetic (the shaping of meaning in action) and the ethical (a cognitive element of the act itself) in explanations of the act as a unified event. The act includes any thought, deed, or sign that is both once-occurrent and open-ended. The act is composed of a two-sided form of answerability that includes both a special reference to the uniqueness of the action and a more general moral reference that situates the act as an emotional-volitional orientation in the actors' entire life history (as a non-alibi in being). The uniqueness of once-occurrent-being is axiological. Bakhtin writes: "I can love another, but cannot love myself; the other loves me, but does not love himself. Each one is right in his own place, and he is right answerably, not subjectively. From my own unique place only I-for-myself constitute an I, whereas all others are others for me (in the emotional-volitional sense)" (1993, 46).

The accumulation of each individual act makes up my life history, my once-occurrent-life. "To be in life, to be actually, is to act, is to be unindifferent toward the once-occurrent whole" (1993, 43). If I am indifferent toward the once-occurrent-whole, or if I am pretending to be someone I am not, then the fact of my uniqueness and answerability are severely jeopardized. In fact, if I ignore my active self and simply live the passive self (the self who receives), I am by definition pretending. "I can try and prove my alibi in Being. I can pretend to be someone I am not. I can abdicate from my obligative (ought-to-be) uniqueness" (1993, 42). But pretending means to risk being chosen by someone else. Even a little pretending, we might say, influences the possibilities of action across one's life. It is this collection of acts that become the content of one's life history. In the sense of unity, my life history is a single complex act. Every time I perform a particular act I perform my life history "and every particular act and lived-experience is a constituent moment of my life—of the continuous performing of acts [*postuplenie*]" (1993, 3).

The tension in the self-other relation is resolved but never finalized. Resolution comes through creative events but the once-occurrent nature of such acts cannot be grasped from aesthetic contemplation alone. Bakhtin is critical of what he calls aesthetic seeing or the abstracted effect derived from representation as if it were the already instituted act. In such approaches the content of what is seen aesthetically is not grasped as part of the two-sided reflection of answerability. The singular act "that illuminates and assigns to a single answerability both the content and the being-as performance of the act is lost in aesthetic seeing" (1993, 14). The creative dimension of the normative—finding out what I should do—has an aesthetic moment but cannot be grasped through aesthetic seeing.

Bakhtin's ethic is based on the singularity of the self-other relation and a rejection of the formal notion of an "ought" outside an emotional-volitional center that would transcend interpersonal relations. Such formal ethics "conceives the category of the ought as a category of theoretical consciousness, and, as a result loses the individual act or deed" (1993, 25). He also opposes content ethics that look to ground moral norms that "are sometimes universally valid and sometimes primordially relative" (1993, 22). For Bakhtin there can be no ethical norms in this sense. Norms are contextually constructed and can be studied by different disciplines but no norm can transcend the active will that brings it into being through an act. As Bakhtin puts it, "[T]he will is really active, creatively active, in the performed act, but it does not posit a norm or universal proposition at all" (1993, 26).

In *Toward a Philosophy of the Act*, Bakhtin develops concepts aimed at providing a personalist ethics that focuses on the self taking responsibility for action that unfolds as an event of being. The book-length essay "The Author and Hero Relation in Aesthetic Activity" is an expansive theoretical outline of the manifold problems of how the artist might represent or create the animate I of the other as a hero, and how the relation between these cognitive and ethical I's are consummated aesthetically. In Bakhtin's I-for-the self, action takes place as the I "acts through the deed, word thought or action. I come to be through my acts" (Bakhtin 1990, 138). What is added to his philosophy of the act is the I's self-reflection on its act and the way in which the I is consummated aesthetically through the transgredient relation with another.[13]

Each section of the "The Author-Hero" essay examines the perspectival uniqueness of seeing, knowing, and experiencing. The first section deals mainly with the problem of the excess of seeing or exotopy, the way in which we perceive more of the other's body than he or she might be able to see of himself or herself, as well as the way we perceive our own bodies. He emphasizes that we come to be ourselves through gifts bestowed on us by others: gifts of language and more importantly, of positive emotional-volitional tones that anchor the temporal and spatial order of our souls. In the second section he introduces us further to his usage of the concept of transgredience and of the difference between empathetic co-experiencing and sympathetic co-experiencing, or how we cross over into each other's experience without giving up who we are in order to consummate relations aesthetically. The third and fourth sections of the essay ask the question of how to represent the other as an animate other with a soul and not "just as the next man," to use Hermann Cohen's expression. Bakhtin moves us from the problem of reconstructing the transgredient I-other relation in terms of sympathetic co-experiencing to the aesthetic consummation of the other's outer body, and to the I's attempt to represent the other's inner soul. Both the inner and outer body relation and the inner-soul and outer-spirit relation are transgredient; that is, each is situated in emotional-volitional axiological orientations and each crosses over to other normative positions as it becomes itself.

Like Habermas, the young Bakhtin argues against Kantian "epistemologism" for an ethics linked to a theory of action. Unlike Habermas, he avoids the charge of ethnocentrism by maintaining a conventional ethics and concentrates on addressing his theory to the problem of how the subject should act responsibly toward the "other," and how such choices are to be seen as creative acts in the "event of Being." There is no sense in which the subject is originary or transcendental but this does not mean that the subject is not autonomous. The subject of action enters intersubjectivity through a transgredient relation with the other. In interpersonal relations the subject steps over to the other but then returns back into the self. This move toward the transgredient permits Bakhtin to posit a triadic theory of the *subiectum* and a way of theorizing the bodily and linguistic representational effect that the other has upon the subject of action. Bakhtin's theory of the self and its relation to ethics is thus revealed in his definition of the *I-for-myself, I-for-the other,* and *an other-for me* motifs for action.[14] Below I present his definition of the self very briefly in order to point out how Bakhtin addresses an aspect of intersubjectivity that complements Habermas's discourse ethics. As seen in the next chapter, Habermas draws on Mead's theory of the I, me, and generalized other in a way that is very close to Bakhtin's approach.

For Bakhtin, as an *I-for-myself,* "I calculate and evaluate all my movements internally. I see an object from the standpoint of a future inner experience." At the same time, I can never see myself except through mediations. The self in this deepest sense cannot be represented: it seeks only to be "an other for others . . . and to cast from itself the burden of being the only I *(I-for-myself)* in the world." Anything I might know about the other's subjectivity I put into his or her outward image "as into a vessel which contains his I." At the same time, I can experience the outward image of the other as consummating and exhausting the other, "but I do not experience my own outward image as consummating or exhausting myself." For me the other is gathered and fitted as a whole into his outer image, as a natural given. My *I-for-myself* is not co-natural with the world. "There is always my subjectivity which cannot be seen by me as part of the outside world, I always have a loophole to save myself from being a natural given." Before intersubjective solidarity can be stabilized by reason it must first be an "aesthetically convincing" lived experience. Only then can "I separate rational actions from aesthetic values in my *I-for-another*" (1990, 39–42). Here I have no interest in the relation between meaning and purpose as in rational action. The *I-for-another* is a moment pointing to a universal ethics of how to act toward the other. On one level, it is not simply how I want the other to see me or how I want to see the other. On the level of action it reverses the Golden Rule back onto the self. Bakhtin's ethics argue, as Morson and Emerson point out, that "we must not love others as ourselves; rather we must love others as *others,* without ceasing to be ourselves" (Morson and Emerson 1989, 21).

Bakhtin's concepts of the triadic definition of the self and the aesthetic consummation between the self-other relation can be seen as addressing the question of intersubjectivity and identity. He directly addresses the problem of transcultural ethics by posing the basic question of the problem of consciousness: "[H]ow is the action of the other experienced by me and on what plane of consciousness is its aesthetic value located?" (Bakhtin 1990, 42). This question is asked from both directions, that is, from the point of view of the effect that the other has upon me and from the point of view of my effect on the other. We can best pick up this double direction through his long discussion of sympathetic co-understanding.

In Bakhtin's early works, the category of "outsidedness" informs his aesthetics of subjectivity. He recognizes the existential interior subject and argues that the only way one can have knowledge of subjectivity other than one's own is through sympathetic co-experiencing. Any attempt to understand another's subjectivity through pure empathy or "indwelling" is not only a communicative distortion but is also unethical. He reflects on the purely expressive or empathetic contact we might have with a suffering person, suggesting that this type of contact would result in becoming infected with the other's pathology. Rather, "[m]y projection of myself into him must be followed by a return into myself, . . . only from this place can the material derived from my projecting myself into the other be rendered meaningful ethically, cognitively or aesthetically" (Bakhtin 1990, 26). Again, this is not a retreat into pure subjectivity but rather part of the transgredient process of intersubjectivity. Life history is not determined by isolated subjectivity. An ultimate issue, as Bakhtin puts it, "descends upon a life-lived-from-within as a gift from the self-activity of another—from a self activity that comes to meet my life from outside its bounds" (1990, 79). This does not contradict Habermas's understanding of intersubjectivity but it provides the reverse view of his theorization that Benhabib asks for. For Bakhtin, it is not a binding communicative reason but a gesture of care and affection that lays the basis for intersubjectivity.

Our sympathetic co-experiencing of the other does not mean we fuse the *I-for-myself* with its viewpoint or experience. Indeed, we can never be outside of our own experience (or as Habermas would say, outside the horizon of a lifeworld); we can only be outside the experience of the other. Boundaries or zones are fundamental to both the self and its discourse but they are also passable both in the imaginary and the real. For Bakhtin, "there are events which are in principle incapable of unfolding on the plane of one and the same consciousness and which presuppose two consciousness that never merge." Sympathetic co-experiencing introduces values into the co-experienced life itself whereas "pure co-experiencing of a life lacks all viewpoints except for those which are possible from within that coexperienced life itself" (Bakhtin 1990, 86). The actual aesthetic activity comes "into effect with the moment of creative love [sympathy] for the content [the life] which has been co-experiencing" (1990, 83).

Bakhtin's construction of the problem of boundaries is seen most clearly in his theory of the soul-spirit relation: "*The soul is spirit the way it looks from outside, in the other*" (1990, 100, my emphasis). It is important to recall that his discussion of this relation is not theological but aesthetic. It is derived from his study of the history of writing and artistic creations in different societies at different times. To dismiss his theory of the artist's representation of the soul as adoration of Christology is to miss the point. His main argument is that the hero's exterior is a gift from the author—much in the same way a human being receives a personality from the recognition he or she gains from others. The outer body of the hero is transgredient with the inner self's "potential and actual self-consciousness." The normative principle of "the other's inward outsidedeness and over-againstness" (1990, 101) comes about in the same way as in the inner-body aesthetic—the inner organic sensations gathered around an "inner centre" that makes my body an inner body and the body of the other an outer body (1990, 48). Ordering, organizing, and forming the soul is not a process that is fundamentally different from repre-senting the relation of the soul to the outer body. The soul is trans-gredient to the self-consciousness of the hero.

The author can order the soul in the hero because the author is ca-pable of both transposing his own soul onto another and of experienc-ing through imagination what the other might experience. This sympathetic co-experiencing gives order to the spatial aspect of the soul. It is the process by which a transposition of the experience of one's own soul outside of oneself in another is rendered possible. Such a transposition, or sympathetic co-experience, Bakhtin notes, is not a copy of one to another but "a fundamentally and essentially new valu-ation, a utilization of my own architectonic exposition in being outside another's inner life" (1990, 103). The soul in the other as well as my own soul is itself an image of the totality of everything that has been experienced in the dimension of time by me or by the other. The spirit "is the totality of everything that has the validity of meaning—a total-ity of all the forms of my life's directedness from within myself (with-out detachment from the I)" (1990, 110). Spirit is set "at every moment as a task." Like the problem of meaning in general, spirit has no exis-tence in time but is contextually situated.

Spirit cannot support rhythm or an aesthetic order on its own because it does not exist in time. Spirit does not order the future and its relation to the past or the present. Rhythm is the emotional-volitional "reaction to a reaction" and not itself an axiological point of view (1990, 117). Thus, it is rhythm that sheds light on the event by changing the future into the present or the past into the future. The temporal ordering of rhythm does not determine the normative "ought-to-be" but it can distort it by making it conditional: the "what-is, the what-ought-to be, what-is-given and what is imposed-as-a-task are in-capable of being rhythmically bound within me myself from within my-self" (1990, 118). The normative grounds of answerability "confront me from within myself as in another world—it is precisely this moment that constitutes the highest point of my creative seriousness, of my pure productiveness." Creative acts, acts that represent the animateness of the I-in-the-other, are "extrarhythmic" and once the acts are performed they fall away into "what was" (1990, 119).

In summary, then, out of his theory of the self-other relation, Bakhtin develops the observation that each subject occupies a unique space and that each is physically irreplaceable. The self approaches the other with a surplus of vision. This excess of vision allows the self to perform three interrelated tasks. First, it allows the self to center the other and to collect the image of the other who is himself or herself struggling with the ethical dilemma of what to do. The self-other relation provides the transgredient stability necessary for ethical choices but leaves the space open for each to determine those choices. Second, this centering is done by giving the boundary and providing the background ("the behind, the beside, the in front") of the other's external whole. Finally, in giving the whole, which contains as yet unknown loopholes, the author consummates the other's relation to the whole independently of the actor's own forward-looking life (Bakhtin 1990, 14).

The Normative Side of Creativity

The contradictory relation between a claim about what is universally good and the particular value context for which it is made is not easily solved and is at the heart of the theoretical paradox of transcultural ethics. Bakhtin and Habermas get at this paradox by posing different questions. In each case, though, the paradox emerges because the more we think of what might be particular or essential about a given human culture the more we wonder what is universal about it—and vice versa. For the Ancient Greek philosophers, the normative is about appearance but a norm is also seen to mediate the social. It is about appearance in the sense that it is about the way actors should appear and it is about mediation in the sense that it also determines, though never completely, just how an actor should act in order to gain understanding. Bakhtin defines a norm as "a special form of free volition of one person in relation to others" (1993, 24).[15] The norm is not imposed in this sense but is supported and sustained by actors who freely enter its realm in a kind of tacit agreement. As a voluntary agreement, a norm allows us to interact meaningfully and as a mediation it allows us to come together without crashing. Free volition does not apply to the legal metanorms Habermas wants to theorize but it does apply to everyday speech acts.

Neither Bakhtin nor Habermas hold strong versions of either a will to power, nor of a utilitarian deduction in which norms are strictly derived through a calculation of consequences. For the young Bakhtin, the social is given form through something like a will to responsibility that actors undertake in interpersonal relations in both existential and logocentric terms. He might well agree with both the classical and the contemporary idea that the social is constituted by a plurality of norms that allow a certain degree of paradox given that inside societies there are disparate views of the good. However, it is not so clear that he would agree with the classical liberal notion from Kant through to Rawls and Habermas that the right must prevail over the good. The paradox wherein norms apparently contradict one another is the trans-cultural source of Bakhtin's philosophy of answerability. The paradox allows differing degrees in which speakers from a given culture do the work of reminding each other about what they already know. In a sense enculturation means reminding each other about the norm that is aspired to in an emotional-volitional orientation. Hence, the norm is both transcendental or overarching and actual; that is, something that is practised in a transgredient way in the life of speech and action.

It is useful to recall that for Socrates one norm for knowledge was that the more you know, the more you know there is to know or be re-minded of. In other words, knowing you don't know allows one to begin to remember. We can easily extend this norm to the ethno-graphic idea of: the more we know other cultures, the more there is to know. Socrates often insisted he knew nothing. He did not want to in-struct people, he simply wanted them to learn what they already knew. Instead of lecturing, he discussed. Bakhtin reminds us that anacrisis and syncrisis were his favorite techniques (Bakhtin 1984a, 110). By confessing ignorance (Socratic irony), he showed that knowledge came from what we already know. Through anacrisis he could provoke words with words and through syncrisis he could juxtapose ideas and gener-ate new ones. In Plato's Meno dialogue, Socrates uses both techniques to draw out the answers to questions about the area of a square from someone who has no formal education. Plato takes the fact that he could get the answer as a proof of the immortality of the soul. Though he claimed he himself knew nothing he also argued that everyone al-ready knows everything before they are born. It is the shock of birth that leads us to forget (Plato 1963, 370–371). The rest of our lives are spent remembering or being reminded of what we already know. The art of this remembering is imbued with a deeper responsibility, that of knowing yourself .

In *Toward a Philosophy of the Act,* Bakhtin argues for the personal responsibility to be oneself and to resist pretending to be someone else. Another way of understanding Bakhtin's appropriation of Socrates original maxim "know thyself," is to think that humans (wherever they are) must overcome all kinds of diversity and relativity in order to become themselves. He defines Being as singular and once-occurrent, and so the event-of-Being is also seen to precede and preclude any kind of essence or identity thinking. Here, Bakhtin makes an important point in critiquing those positions that would mistake discourse on identity as somehow representing being in-itself. Shifting the in-itself existence of identity to the *vita contemplativa* (cognitive and even political thinking on identity) is the most general level of the error Bakhtin calls theoreticism. Yet, it is paradoxical in this text that Bakhtin might also be convinced by Aristotle, and later Hegel and Habermas, that recognition of the many—of diversity, and by way of extension, the struggles for this recognition—also precedes the recognition of the singular unity of the world.

The unity of Being-as-event cannot be grasped theoretically but can only be described. A reflection on the representation or the sign of Being can only ever be a reflection on "once-occurrent-being." Something that represents something to someone is also something that means something to someone. Bakhtin's doubling of the symbolic means that I find myself passively in being but I also actively participate in it. My uniqueness is given and I participate in its consummation or what it has not yet achieved. I am both what is and what ought to be. This moral presence in the act is one side of its answerability whereas the specific content of the act is its other. Two-sided answerability is required to join the individual and the collective or life and culture (28). "In all being I experience only myself—my unique self-as an I. All other I's (theoretical ones) are not I's-for-me" (1993, 46). These are the I's for-the-other or the other's-for-me. My non-alibi in Being means to struggle with the seduction of pretending to be who I am not through an imagining of how the other might see me or how I would like the other to see me.

One side of philosophy, so it seems, has always theorized that reminding each other about the transcendence of the norm is the best way to live ethically while the other has taught that the only way to live ethically is to first be true to oneself. If we somehow confuse our value relation to the norm as being independent of any transcendence (solipsism); or if we pretend that the transcendence of the norm is extra-historical (i.e., does not pass through a transgredient relation and therefore is not bound to a value relation—Stoicism, Platonic forms), then we risk giving up on the theory of the good as being plural and multiple as well as unique and universal. In the case of a strongly stated nonseparation between norm and value we end up in a dogmatism that insists no unity or foundation for truth is possible except of course the proposal of the one who posits such a statement ("The end of history," "The last man," "The death of philosophy"). In the case of too strong a separation between the norm and the value, we give up the spontaneity and source of diversity that makes the stability of the norm possible.

If, with Bakhtin, we adopt the neoclassicist position that the ability to choose between right and wrong lies in the transgredient relations of speech and action *(vita activa)* and not in transcendental categories then we also maintain Socrates' position that suggests people who have good insight will choose the right way. There is not enough space here to go into all the sociological differences between us and the Ancients, or the history of ideas that distances us from that civilization. Hannah Arendt explains, for example, that our sense of the concept of excellence is measured in terms of productivity and not by the achievement of great deeds achieved through speech and action. Our sense of reason is that it is instrumental and administrative whereas for the Ancients it was the highest virtue. Our sense of equality is about justice and even the guaranteed equality of outcomes, whereas for the Greeks it meant being among peers. One of the most profound differences Arendt speaks of is the precedent we afford to the private over the public sphere, and how the private was seen as the space of unfreedom for the Ancients whereas for us it is privileged as a precious escape from the administrative rationalization of our public lives (Arendt 1958, 22–78). Still, for both civilizations, it is the question of values about right and wrong and good and evil that gives rise to the problem of orienting morality and justice to the status of norms.

Between the Creativity and Normativity of the Act

If we hope to understand the difference between Bakhtin and Habermas a clear distinction of the concept of dialogue must be better developed. For Bakhtin, intersubjectivity or co-being is predicated on what he calls the "transgredient outsidedness" that allows for taking on aspects of the other while remaining oneself. This is the primary criterion we saw above for expanding the solidarity necessary for a transcultural ethics. In other words, what can be considered to be an ethical occurrence—a *live entering* into the "ongoing event of Being" with another subject—is very much what an ethical occurrence between lifeworlds should be like. Still, it is difficult to see how we might move from specific kinds of intersubjective ethics to Habermas's universal category. Bakhtin's understanding of transgredient value-orientations is inspiring not so much as a site for working out resistance or coping with the trauma brought on by the context of terror, as Ryklyn would have it, but rather as a site from which one might discern how the clash between lifeworlds necessarily brings on hybrid identity formations that challenge "once-occurrent being."

More readily than Habermas, Bakhtin would answer the question of what creative invention actually occurs in discursive acts as the aesthetic mixing of style and word in actions. Utterances or speech acts are not vacuous communication vessels that facilitate mutual understanding. They are not necessarily fully understood by the participants in dialogue even when unforced agreements are achieved. Utterances carry traces of intersubjectivity because every speaker is influenced by the potentially active response and possible misunderstanding of the listener, much as the writer might guess at a response from an imaginary reader or a lover from a beloved. Bakhtin's position differs from Habermas in that he sees that the creative content of actual dialogues has to do with the extra, unfinished residue that actors produce in their discursive associations, despite the rational motivations that might be deduced from their actions. "The actually performed act in its undivided wholeness is more than rational—it is answerable" (Bakhtin 1993, 29).

Still, Bakhtin's concept of answerability and the consummation of the whole of intersubjectivity in the "act" or "deed" closely resembles Habermas's pragmatism and the postulate concerning the three forms of validity claims in every communicative utterance. For Habermas, communicative practices, wherein actors seek out a "rationally motivated consensus," share a common structure. Here the speaker makes a universal validity claim concerning the truth, justice, and sincerity of the proposition.[16] "Pragmatic questions" are drawn from the perspective of the actor's "goals and preferences" whereas "ethical-political questions" address individual or group interests, and "moral questions" refer to the "normative point of view from which we examine how we can regulate our common life in the equal interest of all" (Habermas 1996a, 159–161). The triple validity claim refers itself to something in either personal experience, objective knowledge, or the social world of a community. Obligations linked to the binding effect among participants arise "only insofar as the speaker and the hearer agree to base their actions on situational definitions that do not contradict the propositions they accept as true at any given point. As soon as the hearer accepts the guarantee offered by the speaker, obligations are assumed that have consequences for the interaction, obligations that are contained in the meaning of what was said" (Habermas 1990, 59).

Bakhtin defines the ethical as a non-alibi in being and does not differentiate it from the morally universal but rather posits it as one side of the same question. Nor does Bakhtin venture beyond the practical level of discourse when he argues, "[T]he answerability of the actually performed act knows a unitary plane . . . in which its theoretical validity, its historical factuality, and its emotional-volitional tone figure as moments in a single decision or resolution" (Bakhtin 1993, 28). The unity of the answerable act is derived from its combined claim of objectivity, normativity, and sincerity. When we act we take into account the consequences of our action. This taking-into-account (objectivity) means imagining or reasoning the valid effects of our action as well as our response to a possible response. Every act is answerable. Emotional-volitional tone (sincerity or conversely the lack of sincerity) is where we find the force of active answerability. Being-as-event is measurable by the degree of sincerity indicated in the emotional-volitional signature. When one is describing once-occurrent being, Bakhtin employs the term *faithfulness* (being-true-to). "The emotional-volitional tone, encompassing and permeating once-occurrent, being-as-event . . . is a certain ought-to-be attitude of consciousness, an attitude that is morally valid and answerably active" (1993, 36).

Given that Bakhtin's and Habermas's disciplinary orientations are both complimentary and contradictory, it follows that their definitions of the universal aspect of intersubjectivity are also somewhat distinct. For Habermas, the moral universal is grounded in situations of practical discourse. In Bakhtin's philosophical anthropology, holism and the universal remain unfinished. Transcendence is achieved through transgredience rather than abstraction through experience as implied in Habermas's communicative reason. For Bakhtin, consumation implies a certain objectivity and the loophole implies a certain opacity within intersubjectivity. The three moments in the constitution of intersubjectivity (I-for-myself, I-for-the other, the other-for-me) are set against each other in Bakhtin's approach and so there can never be any final consensus. This is where the most fruitful difference lies with Habermas. The unfinalized openess of the self-other relation is at the core root of answerability and the creative, aesthetic turn Bakhtin proposes. For both, the metaphysical explanation of a common origin or foundation for all subjects must be challenged so that a more open sense of the diversity of subjects might be defined. Inside of this diversity, intersubjectivity works itself out. To better understand the concept and its importance for developing a transcultural ethics, it is necessary to compare their respective definitions of subjectivity and to expand on their approaches to language and culture. This is the theme of the next chapter.

2

COMMUNICATIVE ACTION OR DIALOGUE?

This chapter continues to compare Bakhtin's and Habermas's approaches in terms of their core concepts of dialogism and communicative action. Habermas's argument that the philosophy of the subject develops through Fichte, Humbolt, and Kierkegaard to Mead's theory of symbolically mediated communication is reviewed in the first section. I discuss his defense of universal categories and the theory of postconventional socialization he adopts from Lawrence Kohlberg. Four pressure points are identified concerning the problem his theory raises for a transcultural ethics. Specifically, I argue that 1) the universal category that supports discourse ethics also directs his theory of moral development and thus should be nuanced in order to avoid charges of elitism and chauvinism; 2) his bi-level systems/lifeworld concept creates a paradox that makes it difficult to account for transcultural hybrids at the level of lived language; 3) the bi-level concept does not clearly distinguish language as a potential colonizing medium; and 4) risky (transcultural) agreements need to be seen as aesthetically, as well as practically, convincing. In the final section of the chapter I discuss the adjustments that are required when shifting from the concept of communicative action to dialogue and once again compare the two positions.

Habermas develops his approach to the subject of action out of a paradigm change from the philosophy of consciousness to a philosophy of language and a theory of communication. Bakhtin does not enter the "linguistic turn" without a strong critical response to formalism and a plea for locating a creative dimension inside the lifeworld. He proposes a theory of language and subjectivity that takes into account the intersubjective basis of the utterance, stylistics, and relations between consciousness and discourse. Habermas, on the other hand, bases his claim in the break that Wilhelm von Humboldt and George Herbert Mead make from the philosophy of consciousness toward a postmetaphysical approach to language. He argues his concept of communicative action is an extension of Mead's theory of symbolically mediated communication and is better suited for an explanation of the processes of individuation that is at the core of the modern project. In the final section of the chapter, I compare Bakhtin's reception of philosophies of language, discourse, and subjectivity with Habermas's position.

Habermas explains that metaphysics is the ancient branch of philosophy that looks to explain parts of things as having issued from an original or unique source. Postmetaphysical thinking contests the idea that one origin or tradition can explain all parts of a phenomenon. Cultural universals, for example, have their sources in definitions derived from some local consensus about them. Postmetaphysical thinking understands unity as being constructed from diversity rather than the reverse (Habermas 1992b). Bakhtin's concept of holism is a good example of postmetaphysical thinking. He defines the whole as containing a "loophole" that allows a way out of any finalization. In postmetaphysical terms, unity should not be understood as a closed off or finished exercise but rather as the unique consummation of the ensemble; "the uniqueness of a whole that does not repeat itself anywhere and the actuality of that whole and hence, for the one who wishes to think that whole, it excludes the category of unity" (1993, 37). Unity exists in the answerable act; that is, in the moment of decision and of resolution. Unity is unique and unrepeatable. It is not being in any originary sense, it is the event of being for which I take responsibility. "It is only my non alibi in being that transforms an empty possibility into an actual answerable act (through an emotional-volitional referral to myself as the one who is active)" (1993, 42).

Communicative Action and Moral Development

Habermas's critique of the philosophy of consciousness is perhaps one of his best known and provocative philosophical arguments. His argument for a postmetaphysical (pragmatic) definition of intersubjectivity is clearly distinguished from deconstruction and systems theory even as it shares a common critique of metaphysical definitions of the subject. On the one hand, he maintains that antimetaphysical thought goes too far in completely abandoning the moment of inter-subjectivity in language and hence he charges that it directs critique toward a totalizing negation of reason. On the other hand, traditional metaphysics remains trapped in foundational or originary logic, the notion of the first One or founding subject. Neither tradition, he argues, permits a theory that would explain the way the object works back on the subject, or how subjects work on each other through the mediation of language.

For Habermas, among the first thinkers to move toward a post-metaphysical definition of the subject was Fichte. He was the first to problematize Kant's definition of the transcendental subject, the subject defined by its capacity to reason outside experience. Fichte moves away from the latter definition when he argues that subjects become subjects by an original act of self-positing and that they negotiate objects on the basis of this self-initiative. "The I comes into being only by means of a *self-referring* activity. By observing oneself while engaged in this activity, one becomes immediately conscious of it; i.e., *one posits oneself as self-positing*" (Fichte 1992, 65). Yet, the relation of the subject to others is still determined by the original or transcendental ego and so Fichte's argument is often described as a solipsism.

In entering the arena of intersubjectivity subjects risk their freedom by becoming objects to other subjects. Habermas argues that Fichte's theory of the knowing subject as self-positing is a step toward a contingent theory of intersubjectivity. However, he also argues that Fichte's subject ultimately turns itself into an object and then returns back to its originary and hence transcendental status because the subject can posit itself only as an individual. "Fichte's original ego comes on the scene in the singular, as one over and against everything, thus freely active subjectivity . . . unveils itself in every individual consciousness as something universal" (Habermas 1992b, 161). And so the argument collapses back into a metaphysics of origins.

For Habermas, Fichte's return to metaphysics is the result of the blind spot brought on by the philosophy of consciousness that does not permit a theory which would explain the way the object works back on the subject through the mediation of language. He claims that Humboldt was the first to argue against the theory of the transcendental subject by suggesting that it could not maintain itself outside of language. In postmetaphysical fashion, Humboldt rejects the originary and foundational subject. According to Habermas, he conceives a theory of dialogue defined as an unforced agreement from which subjects create a unity out of the plurality of differences. This said, there is nothing subjective in language itself. Language is, rather, that which makes a linguistic community possible (Humboldt 1988). Habermas summarizes the definition of Humboldt's theory of language as "the whole comprising the system of grammatical rules and speech." He attributes to Humboldt the important contribution of having advanced a theory that could explain the "unforced synthesis of linguistically reached understanding" (1992b, 160). On the other hand, he objects to Humboldt's tendency to limit analysis to the examination of pronouns and various minimal elements of speech.

Whereas Humboldt proposes a positive theory of the relation between the subject and the linguistic system, for Søren Kierkegaard, subjectivity is inconceivable without individuation. Habermas argues that Kierkegaard's contribution to the theory of identity and intersubjectivity is that he was the first to criticize the reifying effects of reason on the subject. Kierkegaard showed that individuation requires that the subject must choose to become himself or herself. In so doing one is revolting against the overwhelming force of reason in modern society. The choice to become a subject replaces Fichte's concept of the original act of self-positing. For Kierkegaard, choosing to become a subject among subjects becomes part of every moment of existence. If I don't choose to become myself, someone else or something else will choose for me. If I don't make the right choice I will suffer. Once one chooses or is chosen by someone else to become a subject then that choice encompasses a package of possibilities that in turn suggest other choices that will have to be made and that are always contingent on the positions of other subjects. It is this package of choices that becomes the content of one's life history (Heller, 1990). As Kierkegaard puts it: "In choosing itself the personality chooses itself ethically, and exludes absolutely the aesthetical, but since he chooses himself and since he does not become another being by choosing himself but becomes himself, the whole of the asthetical comes back again" (1972, 182).

In the two volumes of *Either/Or,* Kierkegaard defines the three main stages of human existence as the aesthetic, ethical, and religious (1959, 1972). The aesthetic phase is characterized by the absolute pursuit of the satisfaction of desires. "The aesthetical in a man is that by which he is immediately what he is." It begins with unhappy consciousness and ends in despair. The ethical stage resolves the despair through a commitment to universal societal values but at the same time takes away from individuality. "The ethical is that whereby he becomes what he becomes" (1972, 182). The ethical subject is the one who acts on the choices that have been made and in so doing becomes that person. The ethical subject is identical to the totality of choices he or she has made. As Kierkegaard puts it: "[T]he person who lives ethically cancels the distinction between the accidental and the essential, for he takes responsibility of all himself" (Kierkegaard 1970, 250). The religious stage is a paradoxical one in that the actor is seen to transcend the universal through a "leap of faith" that once again can become a unique individual choice. The traces of an authentic life can only be read across the history of this interior life. This is the point on which Habermas finds Kierkegaard's position most problematic.

> Since Kierkegaard we have been in a position to know that individuality can only be read from the traces of an authentic life that has been existentially drawn together into some sort of an appropriated totality. The significance of individuality discloses itself from the autobiographical perspective, as it were, of the first-person—I alone can performatively lay claim to being recognized as an individual in my uniqueness. If we liberate this idea from the capsule of absolute inwardness and follow Humboldt and George Herbert Mead in grafting it onto the medium of language that crosses processes of socialization and individuation with each other, then we will find the key to the solution of this final and most difficult of the problems left behind by metaphysics. The performative attitude we have to take up if we want to reach an understanding with one another about something gives every speaker the possibility of employing the "I" of the illocutionary act in such a way that it becomes linked to the comprehensible claim that I should be recognized as an individual person who cannot be replaced in taking responsibility for my own life history" (Habermas 1992b, 144)

Habermas turns away from existential approaches to theorizing language, identity, and intersubjectivity and looks to the tradition of American pragmatism instead. He looks to Mead's theory of intersubjectivity as a point of departure for establishing his theory of communicative action and discourse ethics. For Mead, identity is formed in the search by the self to achieve understanding from the process of interpersonal communication. Individuation occurs within both socialization and intersubjective comprehension. Mead distinguishes between the *I* and the *me* and between what Habermas refers to as the theoretical or *epistemic I* and the *practical me*. The *I* is a part of the self that becomes a *me*. The *I* in Mead's sense has no knowledge of itself and "is never entirely calculable." The *epistemic I* knows herself as subject from the memory she has of herself and from what she sees in the other's gaze. In remembering the *I* we are no longer in the experience of the *I* but the *me*.

Mead says that "the me is the organized set of attitudes of others which one assumes" (1934, 175), that "represents a definite organization of the community there in our own attitudes, and calling for a response, but the response that takes place is something that just happens" (178). The *theoretical I* is the detached self-conscience whereas the *practical me* is the me that acts. The *theoretical me* develops its self-comprehension by recognizing itself in the image that it discerns from seeing itself in the other. For Mead, the self only knows itself through this mediation of the other to whom he addresses himself. In Mead's terms, the self is the object of the *generalized other,* or to put it more directly, the *theoretical me* is conscious of the rules of its own culture whereas the *epistemic I* can create a unique response to those rules "the attitude of the *generalized other* is the attitude of the whole community." It is "the organized community or social group which gives to the individual his unity of self" and carries the knowledge of a general consensus of norms that lead to action (Mead 1934, 156).

Habermas looks to Mead's pragmatism in order to reconstruct a theory of action that might take into consideration the processes of socialization and individuation that operate simultaneously in communication practices. Like Mead, and Peirce before him, Habermas withdraws from theorization of the interior world of the "epistemic" subject *(I)* in favor of a theory of intersubjective *(me)* comprehension through language. The autonomous and individuated *I* remains key to his communication theory, but the *I* is redefined in terms of its performative function. Habermas argues that for the modern individual "both autonomy and a certain behaviour are institutionally demanded from individuals" (Habermas 1992b, 183). This double demand in turn serves to differentiate the freedom of actors and their knowledge of themselves *(me)* or their self-determination and their self-realization. As social division becomes more complex, conflicting and even multiple "role taking" becomes more commonplace. Mead's theory of symbolically mediated communication that organizes the I, me, and generalized other does not account for the development of intersubjectivity within the context of a decentered society and the increase in social complexity that Habermas is looking to explain. Space allowed for disagreement between lifeworlds is vastly broadened in this context. Habermas attempts to overcome dilemmas accompanying the theorization of this widening gap by demonstrating his concepts of discourse ethics and communicative action discussed previously in a theory of postconventional moral development as explained below.

While admitting that his argument does not always "sit well with the spirit of the times," Habermas states that anyone "who maintains himself in the network of reciprocal expectations and perspectives built into the pragmatics of the speech situation and communicative action, cannot fail to have acquired moral intuitions" in the sense discussed within the "egalitarian values of the radical democratic tradition" (Habermas 1993, 114). He argues that these values are not merely expressions of subjective points of view, but are derived from the interaction of individuals within their communities as they move through three phases of moral development. With Kolberg he defends the idea that the phases of socialization—from preconventional (childhood socialization) to conventional (Golden Rule ethics) and postconventional (legal universals)—are processes of learning. Both preconventional and conventional phases can be considered natural developments in human psychology whereas the postconventional phase is defined as a social construction.[1]

The solution to the problem of establishing moral universals in complex modern societies is drawn from the postconventional level of socialization. It is at this level that subjects learn a universalist moral point of view that is itself divided between the values and rights of individuals and those of the social contract. "Moral decisions are generated from rights, values or principles that are (or could be) agreeable to all individuals composing or creating a society designed to have fair and beneficial practices" (Habermas 1990, 124–125). One reason that laws must be respected is because one is committed to the social contract and that each must contribute to the well-being of all. In its most mature phase, postconventional morality teaches the principle that all humanity must be respected, not as a means toward achieving some other goal, but as an end in itself. Habermas sees international human rights—the ultimate postconventional universal principles of justice—as the result of "collective efforts and sacrifices made by sociopolitical movements over the last two centuries" (208). Put most succinctly, Habermas defines identity and intersubjectivity in terms of the simultaneous processes of socialization and individuation. Only conventional ethical subjects that have first learned to reason on the behalf of the other can hope to attain such postconventional universals.

The Limits of Universal Reason

Habermas's most controversial claim remains that postconventional morality maintains its universal status despite the often conflicting situations of different lifeworlds. This claim suggests a series of pressure points that work against a transcultural ethics as defined up to this point. I already argued the need to respond to McCarthy's charge of ethnocentrism, but a response to Behabib's charges of elitism and chauvinism is also needed. The charge of elitism has to do with the relatively few citizens who are thought to actually evolve to the postconventional "stage 6." Carol Gilligan was among the first to challenge the Kolberg theory of universal moral development on the grounds that it justifies an unequal distribution of moral responsibilities between the genders.[2] Habermas responds that empirical evidence remains inconclusive as do the number of citizens that enter the final phase.

While recognizing Habermas's response to Gilligan, Benhabib also challenges the distinction between the moral principle and personal experience that Habermas appears to be making. She again expresses her critique of the universal category: "My thesis is that Habermas as well as Kolberg conflate the standpoint of a universalist morality with a narrow definition of the moral domain as being centred around issues of justice" (1992, 185). Benhabib and Gilligan share the common concern with the separation of the moral elements of "care and responsibility" from the universal concept of justice, yet it is not entirely clear how they might account for the normative force of social norms that Habermas's analysis addresses.[3]

Habermas continues to argue that universal caring can be maintained while wrestling with culturally diverse discourse ethics. He dismisses the relativist dilemma by defining ethical differences between cultures as belonging to diverse stages of moral development. He locates the intersection of system and lifeworld as the key that defines the potential for maintaining postconventional morality. The phases of moral development are not restricted to modern societies and so it seems reasonable to assume that Habermas's point is not to exclude women or premodern cultures, rather, it is to provide the normative base for the critique of traditions that are protected by systems imperatives. If gender and premodern cultures are excluded it is done "within a selectively rationalized civil society, and it is precisely the blockages to its further modernization in the normative sense that Habermas's theory tries to articulate" (Cohen and Arato 1992, 539).

Habermas is thus concerned that the production of meaning within lifeworlds is blocked by steering mechanisms that keep the system in place.[4] Media-steered structures of administration and money block the lifeworld's potential for autonomy, equality, and the freedom to produce a universal postconventional morality. This second pressure point suggests a paradox that accompanies the bi-level social theory. While the colonization of the lifeworld by systems of power can be defined as an obstacle to achieving a postconventional discourse ethics, it is also part and parcel of the history that made the differentiation of lifeworlds possible. Hence, in modern societies, emerging gender, racial, ethnic, or national identities are defined as struggling both offensively and defensively at the same time. As Cohen and Arato argue, in "a politics of influence" they seek the defense of specific identity interests for the autonomy of their own lifeworlds, and "in a politics of inclusion" they search for universally equitable representation within the same social systems that otherwise colonize them (1992, 526).

It follows that the challenge to traditional norms on a transcultural scale would also mean a challenge to the way in which the private and public spheres are linked to the economy and the state in different societies. A transcultural critique of gender relations, for example, would have to proceed under the assumption that traditional norms are already postconventional so that social actors might have access to nonviolent forms of conflict resolution and to a critique of each other's traditions. This does not mean that critique could only come about within formations whose moral and political economies were in relatively similar stages of development. On the contrary, serious differentiations in development should be seen to influence the content but not the form of normative agreements. In other words, if postconventional norms emerge where system and lifeworld are separated, that is, where the system is not directly controlled by social integration, challenges to conventional norms could potentially abet the influence of dominant systems themselves.

A third pressure point where Habermas's definition of universal morality becomes problematic for a transcultural ethics is on the level of practical discourse itself. As soon as the speaker enters into a communicative relation, he or she shares certain responsibilities with the addressee. Speakers must have a degree of communicative competence. Utterances must be intelligible and must respond to certain criteria for establishing validity. But if communicative competence is inscribed in the social processes of transformation and differentiation and are not simply a static mechanism that allows one to master linguistic rules, then the question must be asked, how does the speaker or addressee from another lifeworld—one who does not share the communicative competence (vernacular, accent, vocabulary, syntax, etc.) of the other—hope to achieve a coherent response?

Indeed, transculturalism, defined here as the process that leads to hybrids that occur when different lifeworlds clash or come into contact, would appear to threaten the "ideal speech situation." Habermas relies on this ideal as a "bridging" mechanism for achieving universal moral justification. Interlocutors or speech actors from different lifeworlds must share a common public language. There is no recognition of public language as a colonizing system itself. In other words, whose language do we assume for a transcultural ethics? This is a universal question whereas the kinds of sanctions placed on speech inside different societies becomes a particularistic one. It is difficult to see where Habermas might conceive of public language as a colonizing system. He argues that language is part of the system and the lifeworld. Yet, in many places in the world, language is very much linked to colonization. Language, then, should be understood sociologically as a potentially colonizing steering mechanism when it represses the lifeworld from developing its own meaning. In other words, the colonization of one lifeworld by another is a violation of communicative action due to systemic power differentials. Under normative conditions, however, language is a creative resource speakers draw on to express validity claims supported by the nonproblematic background convictions of the lifeworld. This is why isolating language as a colonizing mechanism is not always appropriate.

Language potentially belongs to both system and lifeworld. It is a good example of the difficulty that is presented to us when we seek to define empirically where the lifeworld ends and the systems imperatives take hold. A way of adding to an understanding of the boundaries is to consider more carefully the aesthetics of practical discourse; that is, the foreground or "outsidedness" of the actors' intervention. Like language, the aesthetic dimension also belongs to both system and lifeworld. This is the fourth concern raised against Habermas's usage of the universal category. I argued above that he confines the aesthetic dimension to the expressive feature of speech. The main difficulty remains how to recouple the aesthetic with the practical (ethical) realm, as we have seen with Bakhtin. Habermas's pragmatic turn rejects the retreat to metaphysical categories. In this sense, he leaves the problem of recoupling open to further discussion by bracketing his own analysis at the expressive level. In other words, he leaves the question of the existentially based revelation of sincerity in speech open to further speculation.

It does not therefore negate his position to argue further that the "outsidedness" of speech, to employ Bakhtin's notion, is not only a question of taste or judgment. It refracts an intuitive content of inter-subjectivity as well as a rational force of unification or binding effect. Crossing the boundaries in transcultural communications means the expressive plays a larger role than either the objective or authoritative validity claims in communicative actions. If transcultural communicative action means taking on elements from other lifeworlds without ceasing to be oneself, then it can be argued that such an achievement requires something more than a risky agreement. As will be seen below with Bakhtin, transcultural actions require first and foremost that one act in an aesthetically convincing manner.

Habermas's problematic argues for an understanding of modern societies by examining very closely the formal and pragmatic organization of language that helps allow for the coexistence of distinct lifeworlds in the same social systems. While he succeeds in grafting on a philosophy of language and a theory of communication previously absent from the Frankfurt tradition of critical theory,[5] he so steadfastly refuses the philosophy of consciousness in his "pragmatic turn" that he appears to abandon any attempt to understand intersubjectivity as a category that persists despite and not only because of the rationalization of the lifeworld. I have suggested that Habermas's argument presents four pressure points that need to be paid attention to in further developing a transcultural ethics: 1) the exclusionary bias of the moral development theory, 2) the system-lifeworld paradox, 3) the treatment of language as an element of lifeworld rather than as a potentially colonizing medium, and 4) the separation of the creative sphere from the construction of risky agreements within and between lifeworlds. This sets the stage for an interesting reflection on how Bakhtin's theory of intersubjectivity and of the dialogic nature of the utterance might help balance an overemphasis on reason that many argue centers Habermas's approach.

Dialogism: Mixing the Word and Style

A consideration of the different receptions of Fichte, Humboldt, and Kierkegaard by Bakhtin and Habermas in terms of the relation between language and subjectivity is an important point of comparison and an excellent place to reintroduce the ensuing discussion of Bakhtin's approach. I set aside the topic of Mead's theory of symbolically mediated communication for a fuller comparative discussion in chapter 6. For Bakhtin, the possibility of response from the listener must also be theorized if one is to develop a thoroughly dialogic theory of the puzzle concerning the relation between unity and diversity in speech performance. His ideas on the subject contrast well with those of Fichte. For both Bakhtin and Habermas, the subject is always outside of other subjects but is never outside of experience. For Bakhtin, the subject enters intersubjectivity through a transgredient relation with the other. This means that the subject may take steps toward the other but should never give up the I-for-the-self in order to consummate a relation. As demonstrated in chapter 1, this move toward the transgredient permits Bakhtin to posit a triadic theory of the subject that allows a way of theorizing the bodily and linguistic representational effect that the other has back on the subject without slipping into Fichte's solipsism.

For Bakhtin, Humboldt does not explain how language both separates and unifies speaking subjects within and between groups. For Habermas, this breakdown occurs in the application of the theory whereas for Bakhtin it is already present in Humboldt's reduction of the actual communication between speakers to a secondary role. Humboldt is discussed by Bakhtin in order to situate a point in his own history of ideas and to clarify his theory of speech communion, vis à vis nineteenth-century linguistics.[6] We can note that his commentary in these instances is very much in line with the criticism against Humboldt's linguistics raised by Bakhtin's colleague Voloshinov in *Marxism and the Philosophy of Language*. Voloschinov contrasts Humboldt's "individualistic subjectivism" with Saussurian "abstract objectivism." He argues that the former approach reduces language to "an unceasing process of creation realized in individual speech acts [and that] the laws of language creativity are the laws of individual psychology" (Voloshinov 1986, 48). Bakhtin also claims that Humboldt's formulation ignores the creative role the addressee plays in forming the dialogic position of the speaker. Humboldt reduces the listener to a passive recipient and sets up the speaker-subject as the singularly active participant in the communicative process. As Bakhtin puts this:

Nineteenth-century linguistics, beginning with Wilhelm von Humboldt, while not denying the communicative function of language, tried to place it in the background as something secondary. What it foregrounded was the function of thought emerging *independently of communication*. . . . The essence of any form of language is somehow reduced to the spiritual creativity of the individuum. . . . Language is regarded from the speaker's standpoint as if it were only *one* speaker who does not have any *necessary* relation to *other* participants in speech communication. If the other is taken into account at all, it is the role of a listener, who understands the speaker only passively." (1986, 67)

Unlike Habermas, the young Bakhtin embraces to a greater extent the emphasis on interiority not only as it collects itself within the speaker but also within the listener. His ethics assumes a faith in the other's existential animateness (discussed in more depth in chapter 4) and thus can be seen to be based on themes that are consistent with Kierkegaard's concept of total responsibility—although it is not clear that this is the source of his thinking. The subject is always becoming itself by entering or choosing to enter into translinguistic communicative, or aesthetic acts of communion. Responsibility toward the other is not a formal requirement nor a simple empathy toward the other. One does not become the other through "pure-indwelling" (taking on the identity of the other). Rather, in "live-entering" the open event or act of being "one enters another's place while still maintaining one's own place, one's outsidedness with respect to the other."[7] In later works, the dialogized process of intersubjectivity is described as an unfinalized communion of the utterance based on the anticipation of response from the listener, and the shared responsibility that develops from the background of the social diversity of speech, which Bakhtin terms heteroglossia.

For Bakhtin, a dialogical approach to discourse ethics would understand language as being created in the movement that designates the relation between the responsibility of the speaker and his or her anticipation of rejoinder from the addressee in terms of a reference to an object or an event. In the most general schema, the dialogic can be discerned on both the level of language and consciousness; on the level of the signification of the word, of the discursive style, and beyond these limits across cultural contexts themselves. A sociology of communicative actions, such as the one proposed by Habermas, defines actions as communicative when they are geared uniquely toward achieving agreement and thus does not include such a wide view of the dialogic as a creative process. The theory of communicative action is not concerned with vernacular speech, intonation, or accent, or with any other stylized nuance available to living language. Is it the agreements achieved through communicative actions that generate hybrids or is it where the speakers themselves cross over opposing values in their discursive associations?

The tension between the monologic and the dialogic informs Bakhtin's general theory of culture and language. For example, he defines national languages as being unified but internally stratified and in constant opposition to heteroglossia (the stratification of language). It is only possible to conceive the unity of language in an abstract sense. The diversity of speech in language and the stratification and divisions of communicative competence are seen as centrifugal and centripetal forces. Unitary language imposes specific limits on heteroglossia "guaranteeing a certain degree of mutual understanding and crystallizing into a real, although still relative unity—the unity of the reigning conversational (everyday) and literary 'correct language' " (Bakhtin 1981, 270). The process of linguistic "unification and disunification intersects in the utterance itself" each time the subject attempts a speech act and enters into an interpersonal relation (272). "Consciousness finds itself inevitably facing the necessity of having to choose a language. With each literary-verbal performance, consciousness must actively orient itself amidst heteroglossia" (293). Thinking of the speech act as a "live-entering" problematizes the question of communicative competence for our transcultural ethics. So-called national languages are already subverted by the vernacular from within and by various "other" languages that cross over their territories. Living language is already transcultural but is always limited by centripetal forces. Expanding the already transcultural basis of language would require an enlargement of the translinguistic character of the word and mixing of styles that shape it.

Bakhtin argues that no living word relates to its object in a single way. The orientation of a word toward an object is not so much determined by the object's resistance, but more generally by the diverse orientations toward the object of other possible words and arguments. "Between word and object there is an elastic environment of other words about the same object, the same theme" (Bakhtin 1981, 276). It is in this gap that style shapes the utterance. Style shapes the word that comes from an already "dialogically agitated" space. Style is an aesthetic category that allows an analysis of hybridization otherwise not yet taken up in Habermas's problematic. Style merges the word into the speaker's lifeworld and actually confronts contradictory or colonizing values that might be attached to elements of its universe. This universe is made up of "thousands of living dialogic threads" which the utterance potentially brushes up against. And when different utterances, different speech manners orientated toward the same object, merge, they have the potential of producing hybrids. Style both conserves the unity of language and adds to it by synthesizing the diversity of speech. Stylistics is that part of communicative competence that facilitates hybrid constructs.

A dialogic definition of an ethical discourse would look to utterances that can create hybrids, that anticipate response, that can include the other within its horizon of expectation and that can keep from imposing the final word. It is inconceivable to imagine attempts at achieving shared understanding that could occur outside of a dialogic context. Bakhtin states that "any understanding of live speech, a live utterance, is inherently responsive, although the degree of this activity varies extremely. Any understanding is imbued with response and necessarily elicits it in one form or another" (1986, 68). The speaker counts on the active understanding of the listener. The orientation toward the listener is an orientation toward the imagined horizon of the listener's expectation. The speaker is looking for an interpretation of his or her word, and his or her own perspective, from "the alien conceptual system of the understanding receiver." One enters into dialogical relationships with certain aspects of this system (1981, 282). This internal *dialogism* gives the word a double voiced quality. To encounter the alien word within the object itself is to enter the arena of the "subjective belief system of the listener." For Bakhtin, style is the dispute mechanism that is determined by its relation to external discourse. "Discourse lives on the boundary between its own context and another, alien, context. The rejoinder in a dialogue also leads such a double life ... [it is] an organic part of a heteroglot unity" (1981, 284).

Disputes over truth claims are "from one side highlighted while from the other side dimmed by heteroglot social opinion, by an alien word about them" (1981, 276). From a dialogical perspective, agreement is never far from a disagreement where the word must enter the "arena of doubt and shadow." The author of an utterance is never its owner because the dialogic is never closed. Bakhtin argues, "[T]he word in language is half someone else's. It becomes 'one's own' only when the speaker populates it with his own intention, his own accent, when he appropriates the word, adapting it to his or her own semantic and expressive intention" (293). Bakhtin's dialogical theory of the speech act does not analyze the succession of constative or assertoric propositions

that would constitute an exchange or a conversation between two interlocutors orientated toward achieving understanding. The dimension of
moral argumentation could be seen, though, as a part of his larger definition. In the life of speech acts, says Bakhtin, active understanding
"assimilates the word to be understood into its own conceptual system
. . . indissolubly merged with response, with a motivated agreement or
disagreement." Dialogic relationships "permeate all human speech and
all relationships and manifestations of human life—in general everything that has meaning and significance" (1984a, 40).

A transculturalism that allows one culture to take on elements of
another while remaining itself is not a requirement of communicative
action and it is not the goal of postconventional ethics. But for
Bakhtin, it is what happens in the aesthetics of self-other relations and
in the dialogic practices of everyday language. On the other hand,
Habermas demonstrates much more directly than Bakhtin can that
transcultural relations between lifeworlds are not possible without
communicative actions and postconventional ethics. Universal moral
discourse on human rights, for example, is geared toward eliminating
often violent disagreements that in some cases have been handed down
across centuries. Transculturalism necessitates keeping the space for
nonviolent political disagreement as large as possible so as to gain access to the critique of different traditions and thus to create the possibility of their transformation.

Bakhtin's concepts of holism and the transgredient relations within
intersubjectivity shift from a philosophy of "live entering" into an act,
to a theory of authorship and to a theorization of the dialogic work of
the utterance itself. It is not difficult to imagine how close Bakhtin's approach comes to Habermas's pragmatic theory of speech in that he
would agree that a claim of sincerity coordinates the construction of
the utterance and that normative and objective validity claims are in
fact part of almost any dialogue. On the other hand, for Bakhtin, the
open ethical event where questions of "oughtness" are worked out has
no universal grounding. What is universal about the utterance is its
varying degree of answerability. Even monological or strategic forms of
utterances—those that make no space for transcultural hybrids, and
that, in extreme cases seeking no response at all from a listener of the
same lifeworld, presume the last word—are still answerable.

In this chapter I have shown that Habermas both contradicts
Bakhtin's theory of language and subjectivity and complements it
through his proposal of a normative rationale for the universal categories of intersubjectively shared identity. I have also argued that he

minimizes the aesthetic or creative moment in communicative reason. His pragmatic turn backs up an attempt to reconstruct a normative critical theory aimed at outlining the reasoned agreements that actors could work out together. At this point though, his own followers argue that he in part succeeds and in part disappoints. On the one hand, many are persuaded by his plea concerning the need to theorize how modern subjects seek out agreement together through their communicative actions. On the other hand, fewer are persuaded by the principle of universality that accompanies the pragmatic turn he takes in founding his discourse ethics. I propose that critiques posited against Habermas's theory of communicative action and discourse ethics can be responded to by enlisting several aspects of Bakhtin's approach. For example, the charge of ethnocentrism and elitism is to some extent diffused by cautioning, but not abandoning, the universal principle and by reconsidering the definition of language as a centripetal normative force as well as a potentially creative one.

On the other hand, it is easy to see why Bakhtin's early work, considered in greater detail in chapter 4, is relegated to the quirky status of philosophical and even religious metaphysics. His synthesis of theories of consciousness and language that inform his theory of dialogue are indeed developed with regular reference to Christology (Mihailovic 1997; Felch et al., 2001). Given the emphasis in his early works on the soul-spirit-body relation (discussed in chapter 1), it is difficult to see what kind of postmetaphysical ethics would be possible. Yet, like Habermas, his emphasis on the analysis of the relations between subjects ("individual, personal relations, dialogic relations among utterances" [Bakhtin 1986, 138]) does point to a postmetaphysical ethic that refuses both a formal definition of the "good," or the "just," as well as a practical mapping of what one should do or how we should act together.

The point of converging two theories should be to mutually reinforce them. The key to such an exercise is to point out the weaknesses of the one and to reinforce it with the strengths of the other. The concept of dialogism helps refocus questions onto the lived relations of transculturalism while discourse ethics points to a series of normative questions that must be considered. The question of how we should act toward others needs to be theorized from both angles.

3

THE WORLD OF OTHER'S WORDS

Both Bakhtin and Habermas search for solutions to problems posed on multiple levels: the one, the particular, the unique, the many, the general, the universal. Each thinker makes conceptual shifts that break away from their previous attempts to explain problems and yet each carries forward part of their already achieved understanding into new concepts. In order to better link his theory of communicative action to a general sociology and moral and legal philosophy, Habermas shifts his focus on discourse ethics to a study of the discourse principal of democracy. Law becomes the hinge that allows unique ethical issues to be simultaneously distinguished and yet connected to universal morality and politics. The discourse principal supports his argument regarding the normative separation of *demos* from *ethnos* and his proposition for a macro political definition of self-other relations expressed through constitutional patriotism.

In an effort to deepen his general theory of the relation between ethics and aesthetics, and to avoid sociological reductionism and legal theoreticism, Bakhtin shifts his focus from two-sided answerability to the dialogical principle. Traces of the understanding he was able to achieve through the concepts of transgredience, outsidedness, consumation, sympathetic empathy, and the loophole are carried over into his philosophy of dialogue, while the sociological and sociolinguistic concepts of heterglossia, the chronotope, and ideology critique, added in the 1930s and '40s, appear to be less emphasized in his subsequent works.[1] Bakhtin's linguistic turn, present in his earliest work, reaches one of its highest expressions in his final notes published posthumously. In these notes he jots down part of his deeper understanding of intersubjectivity in strangely unique and universal terms: "I understand the other's word to mean any word of any other person that is spoken or written in language that is not mine. In this sense all words (utterances, speech, and literary works) except my own are the other's words. I live in a world of others' words and my entire life is an orientation in this world" (1986, 143).

"The world of others' words," that is, the communities, nations, and cosmopolitan cultures in which we live together are populated , with multiple voices. The national chronotope, the specificity of timespace relations, the stratification of language and the dialogism within and between cultural communities needs to be theorized both on a micro lifeworld level of *ethnos* as well as on the macro level of the political community or *demos*. Dialogism is embedded with notions of transcultural exchange that redefine the relation between *ethnos* and *demos*. Habermas's critique of nationalism and the dilemma posed by the emerging postnational constellation of nation-states in the era of globalization calls for a separation of culture and politics, a problem that is taken up in more depth in chapter 8. In this chapter I look to deepen the comparative discussion of Bakhtin and Habermas through a closer examination of how each thinker theorizes the utterance and the boundaries of speech genres. Most importantly, I look to outline the key steps each takes in shifting their original philosophical positions to the later philosophy of language each adopts. This is the final attempt at a theoretical comparison and convergence of these two thinkers before I discuss Bakhtin's sources in the next chapter and then discuss his commonality and difference with other social theorists—in particular Weber and Mead—in chapters 5 and 6.

I start by outlining Bakhtin's and Voloshinov's definition of the utterance and by explaining how Bakhtin looked to Dostoevsky's art as a communicative utterance that could help him understand ethics and aesthetics, a goal that dominated his first intellectual phase. The shift in Bakhtin's thinking between the 1929 and 1963 versions of his book on Dostoevsky is analyzed in order to point out some of the steps he takes in developing his theory of the polyphonic novel out of his earlier interests. Voloshinov's early work on the sociology of language is compared with Habermas's pragmatism. Habermas's position is situated in terms of his break from the aesthetic theories of the early Frankfurt tradition. Finally, Bakhtin's concepts of polyphony and dialogue and Habermas's theory of the communicative utterance are reconsidered through a discussion of how each thinker might respond to Italo Calvino's contemporary novel *If on a*

Winter's Night a Traveller—a novel that challenges their respective concepts of speech genres.

Calvino's novel challenges the postmetaphysical theory of boundaries that differentiate speech genres or genres of discourse. Instead of
a story of moral paradox from the novel, to help explicate
al ethics, analysis is focused on the evolution of the novel
uous and even unstable form of utterance. Calvino's novel
nticipate the question of the relation between literature
al, and between literature and theory—questions posed by
eration of the Frankfurt School and questions Habermas
ed in several places. Habermas's pragmatic theory of lan-
esented in terms of its break with the Frankfurt tradition
at is shown to be compatible with Bakhtin's and Voloshi-
r formulations.

Bakhtin and Voloshinov on the Subject of the Utterance

Bakhtin leaves his early essay *Toward a Philosophy of the Act* with the problem of the subject's state of inner responsibility and the effect of the other's reaction upon that subjectivity—the doubling process of answerability. Here, Bakhtin's theory of two-sided answerability provides a unique position within the philosophy of the subject: The subject is ultimately the author of its actions and the subject is interpellated by the power and authority of its circumstances. In the aesthetics of the author-hero relation the sociological importance Bakhtin lends to the way in which the I is authored by significant others—"our communities, our cities, nations and Gods"—is still quite prevalent (Bakhtin 1990, 121). Both these early essays extensively theorize the transgredient relation between self and other as an aesthetic and ethical problem. The connection between the responsibility of the actor and the authoring of others is that each takes into consideration the animateness of the existence of the I in the other. In the pre-1929 draft of *Problems of Dostoevsky's Poetics*, Bakhtin announces the discovery of the new artistic genre of polyphony, a genre that expresses his ethics in terms of the distinctiveness of each unique voice emanating from an author. In other words, the autonomy of voice is a way of describing how it is that actors can come into contact with one another and not merge or stop being themselves. It is interesting to note here that as Bakhtin develops his study of polyphony and dialogue, the theorization of the social-community sphere as a normative force shifts once again. Bakhtin looks to Dostoevsky as the inventor of the polyphonic novel. In Dostoevsky's novels, Bakhtin argues, "a character's word about himself and his world is just as fully weighted as the author's word usually is. It possesses extraordinary independence in the structure of the work; it sounds, as it were, alongside the author's word and in a special way combines both with it and with the full and equally valid voices of other characters" (1984a, 7). The conceptual metaphors of polyphony and counterpoint are as concerned with the plurality of voices as with the plurality of once-occurrent-Beings. The plurality of voices imply internal conflicts between the many and the one. For Bakhtin, and even more so for Voloshinov, the struggle is over the ownership and meaning of the word or utterance.

Both Bakhtin and Voloshinov see the center of the utterance as the scene for a battle over the ownership of the word. Given the highly regarded principles of unfinalizability and the loophole of subjectivity at the heart of Bakhtin's approach one might ask: Why focus on something so closed off as an ownership claim? If it is agreed that Voloshinov is the main author of the 1929 text *Marxism and the Philosophy of Language*, then why relate a definition of the word through a theory of production to Bakhtin? The simple answer to the question is that the young Bakhtin appears to have held to a conflict sociology and not a consensus sociology of the word or discourse *(slovo)*. The later Bakhtin introduces concepts such as heteroglossia and dialogism that leave linguistic acts completely open ended but also entertain the notion of their social determination. This is not to say that for the early Bakhtin the struggle over the meanings and explanations of events, as well as the privileges and truth claims regarding their interpretations, is entirely about a struggle over power and knowledge. Although he might argue that there is no innocent reception, no passive speech genre, no neutral distribution system, no institutional receptacle empty of values that would universally sculpture an utterance, he recognizes that the word is received and it does make universalizing claims. "Bakhtin is no relativist," as Emerson claims, for he recognizes that there are judgments to be made and events to be witnessed (Emerson 2001).

The paradox between the poles of consummation and unfinalizability is embedded in Bakhtin's philosophy of the act from the outset. Let us set the paradox aside for the moment with the understanding that he would eventually come to favor a theoretical emphasis that leaned toward the unfinished and mutually reinforcing search for values rather than the already arrived at norm. The dialogical rather than the sociological definition of the utterance means that it is intersubjectively consummated but never finalized. His early dialogical theory is not looking for an agreement but for an understanding of the social struggle over the definition of the creative (eventness) aspect of interaction.

Voloshinov goes even further into a conflict sociology of the word than Bakhtin when he defines the most minimal point of the utterance, the signified concept or "word," as a semiotic purity (Voloshinov 1986, 14). It is a plane of sheer meaning. As a sovereign form of the utterance the "word" is at once an explanation and an evaluation. Among all possible signs only the word is a neutral sign. But when a speaker comes across a word, as Bakhtin notes elsewhere, "it is not as a neutral word of language, not as a word free from the aspirations and evaluations of others" (1984, 202). Thus, the word is never "just" an explanation. It is also an emotional-volitional axiological position, implicated in an event of Being. As a neutral exterior sign it always has the potential to become part of "inner speech." Here the word cannot be neutral. It carries a stock of knowledge from other users. The potential of the word to become the "semiotic material of inner life" is proof of its dialogicality; that is, of the capacity of the self to anticipate rejoinder from an exterior but not necessarily fictional other. At the center of the utterance, then, is a specific kind of ownership claim lodged in the cognitive, ethical, and aesthetic relations between self and other. These relations, and not simply the ownership claim, are constantly shifting, being challenged, and holding off finality.

Bakhtin's later version of the concept of dialogue comes to cover more than the exchange of information between speakers across various media of communications. He comes to understand the concept of dialogue as extending far beyond the relations between rejoinders in a formally produced linguistic exchange. In this sense, dialogue is more than the achievement of a shared understanding or agreement, and in the most general sense is quasi universal in that it incorporates everything that has meaning or value. Ultimately, dialogue implies the semiotic sign, given that signification, which is always contextual, stems from the interaction between voices. Bakhtin is drawn to Dostoevsky's literary art because he sees in it a dialogical object *par excellence* that can incorporate the full scale of possible dialogical characteristics such as hybridization and polyphony on the level both of language and of ideas. Hence, dialogical phenomena exist on an unlimited number of levels beginning with the signification of the word and reaching toward discourse and then beyond discourse to social context itself.

Social and Ethical Worlds of Dialogue in Dostoevsky

The most important point I want to make here is that Bakhtin's approach moves farther into the linguistic turn between the 1929 and 1963 versions of his book on the *Problems of Dostoevsky's Poetics*. The 1930 essay "Discourse in the Novel" and the posthumously edited essay "Forms of Time and Chronotope in the Novel" already foreshadow the shift that is presented in chapter V of the 1963 book on Dostoevsky but, again, in the latter the strong sociopolitical slant is reduced. Further, in the 1963 version of Dostoevsky there is much less talk of heteroglossia and ideology. Interestingly, his signature concept of dialogism has come to be the concept (along with carnivalization) that has most excited Bakhtin's Western readers despite the fact, previously noted, that Caryl Emerson reports it is also one of the concepts which came under early scrutiny from his Soviet reviewers (1997). I do not propose to address the questions of whether or not Dostoevsky's novels are truly examples of open-ended polyphonic novels, or whether or not Bakhtin was a bourgeois existentialist or an ultra-formalist; nor am I interested in defining his studies of the novel as a critique of modernity itself. Instead, the question I want to address is, if it is true that this shift in theoretical orientation is more than cosmetic, then why the shift? A satisfactory response in the secondary literature on Bakhtin to date remains only partially developed. The position I want to defend is that the linguistic turn in his existential-phenomenology, along with the reorientation of the original sociological concepts this entailed, is an attempt to advance his earlier attempt to deepen his ethics and aesthetics of "a philosophy of the answerable act" (1993, 28). I present a full discussion of this earlier phase of his work in the next chapter. For the moment, however, it is less important to understand his philosophical source than to try and address the scope of the shift in his problematic.

According to N. I. Nicolaev (2000) a prototext of the Dostoevsky book had already been sketched out as early as 1922. It coincides with the period in which Bakhtin wrote *Toward a Philosophy of the Act* and the author-hero essay—his earliest look at a new theory of authorship wherein the hero becomes self-determining. Bakhtin's inspiration, according to Nicolaev, was directly related to a book on the crisis of the author written by one of his closest collaborators, Lev Pumpiansky. The 1984 English translation, *Problems of Dostoevsky's Poetics*, is based on the expanded 1963 version that includes new chapters on the genesis of carnivalization, and on his theoretical typology of discourse. It is the only publication to place both the new version and chapters omitted from the 1929 version together in one volume. Apart from the additions of the new material, the main change from the 1929 version is the sharp shift away from sociological categories describing the determining effects of social context. An original foreword, a short section on the adventure plot, and the early summation of his 1929 survey of the types of dialogue were dropped for the 1963 edition but are included in the first appendix in the 1984 English language edition. A second appendix includes his notes for the 1963 revised edition.

Bakhtin drops the strong definitions of sociology of literature from his original 1929 foreword and deletes it from the first chapter, which presents a literature review of scholarship on Dostoevsky where he sharply rebukes various forms of sociological reductionism. The softer utopian notion of community, articulated both negatively and positively in the "Author-Hero" essay and in *Toward a Philosophy of the Act,* is further developed from Dostoevsky's own work. The creative act is seen as something that is both produced by the community and that produces the community. In the 1929 version, there is still a strong sense in which literature is considered both a social force as well as a cultural product, though he also states that a creative act is something more than a reflection of something that already exists. In the 1963 version, literature is more of an example of philosophical investigation. This does not mean that Bakhtin's new concept of the dialogic shifts exclusively toward unique individual utterances. He also adds the distinction between the great and the micro dialogue that retains something of the original tension between his libertarian and communitarian tendencies. The dialogic in the larger sense includes a more utopian definition of community, as we will see further below.

While it is true that the 1929 version is more preoccupied with the types of sociological questions one finds at the center of the books published under Voloshinov's and Medvedev's names, there is also more emphasis the "the solitary person" (rarely on "the individual") as opposed to the firm "monologic we" of a unified community. In one section dropped from the 1929 version, he reflects on the way in which "The Great Inquisitor" (the famous scene from *The Brothers Karamazov*) is described as an example of "man with man" where "an exceptionally keen sense of the other person as another and of one's I as a naked I presupposes that all those definitions which clothe the I and the other in socially concrete flesh . . . have lost their authoritativeness and their form-shaping force." Bakhtin focuses his attention on the unmediated "idea" in Dostoevsky. "A person, as it were, senses himself in the world as a whole, without intervening stages. . . . Dostoevsky's heroes are motivated by the utopian dream of creating some sort of human community that lies beyond existing social forms." His novels are not set in a complete hoplessness of the "social disintegration of the classless intelligentsia, whose members must orient themselves in the world one by one, alone and at their own risk" (1984a, 280–281).

The 1929 version of the Dostoevsky book includes part of the critical review of literature that Bakhtin uses to draw out his own definition of polyphony as an artistic genre and provides an excellent example of immanent critique. Various classic types of studies on Dostoevsky are reviewed in which Bakhtin negates the claims of each to have provided a definitive explanation of Dostoevsky's art, and at the same time draws elements from each that he sees as most significant for his own approach. Some positions are dismissed outright but one senses that even here Bakhtin is using them to orientate his own approach. For example, Vasily Rozanov and others present an explanation of Dostoevsky's art through a crude dialectics that seeks to unify the separate voices in his novels into a single unified consciousness. Bakhtin dismisses the position but at the same time presents a prime example of what he means by philosophical monologism. Several other positions are negated on the same grounds. Each contributes some angle of interest to Bakhtin's own construction. While Vladimir Ermilov and others are charged with sociological reductionism, Sergei Askol'Dov's personalism is a more typical example of the positive critique backed by a negation of the approach. Bakhtin praises the personalist understanding of the "inner man" in each of the characters but then shows how he also monologizes Dostoevsky's aesthetics by reducing each voice to a mere psychological profile.

In the 1963 version, Bakhtin argues that among the most important but incomplete descriptions of Dostoevsky's art are studies by the symbolist poet, Vyacheslav Ivanov, and an "official party critic," Valery Kirpotin. On the other hand, the best explanations of the poetic characteristics are found in the concepts of polyphony, counterpoint, and dialogue described by the Dostoevsky scholars, Leonid Grossmann and Vasily Kormarovich. According to Bakhtin, Ivanov is the first to "grope" for an understanding of the separateness of the characters and the dilemma this relation presents for ethics. "To affirm someone else's I—not as an object but as another subject—this is the principle of Dostoevsky's art." Ivanov articulates Bakhtin's earlier plea for an ethics of answerability as the principle of Dostoevsky's art, but according to Bakhtin he reduces the ethical to the author's vision of the relation and does not proceed with an analysis of the dialogue between the characters. Kirpotin also grasped the ethical terms of answerability in arguing that "Dostoevsky had the seeming capacity to visualize directly someone else's psyche. He looked into someone else's soul as if equipped with a magnifying glass that permitted him to detect the subtlest nuances, to follow the most inconspicuous modulations and transitions in the inner life" (Bakhtin 1984a, 36–37). However, like many other official Soviet critiques, Kirpotin also emphasizes historical and sociological context over analysis of the poetic or formal characteristics of the art. For Bakhtin, paying attention to someone else's consciousness in itself is not what makes a new artistic vision. Grossmann, on the other hand, focuses analysis precisely on the question of multivoicedness and dialogic relations. But he simply describes the separate ego-voices in terms of simple contradiction and misses the "dialogism" (transgredience) between the axiological positions. Kormarovich looks at the poetic problem of counterpoint in polyphony but, in the same sense as Grossmann, ends up defining each ego-voice as a completely separate will.

In the 1963 version, Bakhtin takes the concepts of multivoicedness from Grossmann, and polyphony and counterpoint from Kormarovich, but adds that "the artistic will of polyphony is a will to combine many wills, a will to the event" (Bakhtin 1984a, 21). An important distinction is introduced under the concept of the dialogic that helps clarify what he means by the "will to the event." The new distinction referred to here is between the great and the micro dialogue. Again, each of these concepts strongly link Bakhtin's concept of the dialogic to a communitarian philosophy ("the will to combine many wills"). Right through to his last writings in metalinguistics in *Speech Genres and Other Late Essays,* Bakhtin never gives in to a formalism wherein codes (linguistic, psychological, or political) themselves would be seen to structure normativity. While Bakhtin withdraws from the sociological determinism outlined in the version of the 1929 book he never loses sight of the community as a reference for the "normative" idea of "fellowman" (Cohen 1972).

Bakhtin's new definition of the dialogic provides a more complete response to his early ethics of answerability than any of his previous formulations. Dialogue, he says at one point, requires the condition of at least two separate noncoinciding consciousness, the condition of polyphony that allows an ongoing and unfinalizable anticipation of rejoinder in discourse. The musical metaphors of polyphony and counterpoint are directly tied to the concept of dialogue that Bakhtin links to the Socratic tradition. He contributes a mixture of linguistics and ideology critique to the concept. Bakhtin rejects Boris Englehardt's sociological reduction, which defines the work as the coming together of three action contexts (the environment as a functional system, the soil as an organic evolution of the "people's spirit," and the earth as all of nature) but retains the notion that Dostoevsky's hero was in some sense the idea itself developed dialogically. Again, this is an extension of the notion of the transgredient in that the idea can only develop through crossing over to other ideas. For Dostoevsky, according to Bakhtin, ideas have no copyright. Ideas are not individuated to the point that they might have "permanent resident rights" because they exist in "a person's head." The idea is intersubjective: "[T]he realm of its existence is not individual consciousness but dialogic communion between consciousness. The idea is a live event, played out at the point of dialogic meeting between two or several consciousnesses." The close relation between the transgredient and the dialogic is obvious here. The new emphasis is on the linguistic act. The crossover involved in the verbal act is not only cognitive but also aesthetic and ethical. An idea takes on life "only when it enters into genuine dialogic relationships with . . . the ideas of others." Thought is genuine "only under conditions of living contact with another and alien thought, a thought embodied in someone else's voice, in someone else's consciousness expressed in discourse" (1984a, 88).

Bakhtin's earlier presentation of transgredient relations presented in the author-hero essay are strengthened by adding the concept of dialogue. Monologic words anticipate no response: "A monologic artistic world does not recognize someone else's thought, someone else's ideas as an object of representation" (1984a, 79). A thought is affirmed or repudiated. In a negative reference to Plato's metaphysics, Bakhtin says that in monologism the unity of consciousness replaces the unity of existence. In dialogue, words and phrases anticipate response from the animated other. A dialogic understanding means that another is always axiologically positioned over and against an addressee. I take into account the other's animateness as I engage the utterance. In monologue, I exclude the other as the object of my consciousness. In dialogue, the other's response is anticipated and in this sense is included in the interlocutor's consciousness. Monologue assumes it has the last word. Dialogue assumes no last word, no finality.

As has been stated more fully in chapter 1, dialogism is Bakhtin's signature concept. I have tried to show how the concept evolves across his ethics and how he is increasingly drawn away from sociological reductionism into the linguistic turn. While Bakhtin's ethics and aesthetics are distinct from Georg Simmel's and Alexander Vvedenskij's positions, as will be seen in chapter 4, their influence on Bakhtin leaves him carrying the main postulates of neo-Kantian moral philosophy: the necessary existence of the idea of God, the possibility of immortality, of free volition of the normative and of faith in the animated existence of uniquely individuated subjects. As was seen in chapter 1, Habermas's discourse ethics also takes from Kant's ethics but in such a way as to keep the original distinction of practical reason separate from aesthetics, metaphysics, and theology. The next section retraces Habermas's place in the Frankfurt tradition and explains his sharp break from the aesthetic theories that the tradition carries.

The Frankfurt Tradition

Although Habermas is not known for his contribution to the development of the theory of the novel, his problematic is in part drawn from the Frankfurt tradition, which is very well known for its debates around the relation between art and the social. By incorporating the linguistic turn, Bakhtin and Habermas avoid reflection theories that characterize this tradition. Both argue for a separation of genres of discourse and both seek to join their theories of discourse with ethics. As was seen in chapter 1, Habermas looks to build a new social theory that can break free of the constraints of historicism and the philosophy of consciousness, on the one hand, and avoid the antimetaphysical trap of deconstruction, on the other. A review of the general outline of the original position of critical theory will help clarify Habermas's shift and better demonstrate his difference and potential compatibility with Bakhtin on the question of dialogue.

Some of the twentieth century's most experimental intellectual projects challenging a variety of disciplines, ranging from philosophical anthropology to political economy, psychoanalysis, aesthetics, and literary criticism, are found in the Frankfurt School of critical theory.[2] For almost seventy years the tradition has been both divided and held together over a debate concerning the definition of its central concept: critical theory. First announced in 1931 in Max Horkheimer's programmatic work, *Critical Theory*, the concept is offered as a rejection of the purely immanent form of interpretation in traditional hermeneutics best exemplified in the philosophy of Wilhelm Dilthey. On the other hand, it also attacks scientific approaches that make claims of pure explanation based on objective experimental techniques of analysis. All knowledge is seen as being rooted in ideological interests. This position may be seen in three dominant problem motifs that each successive generation reassesses as they enter or cross through the tradition.

The first problem motif might be called historical relativism. Horkheimer attacks the problem of historical relativism, which states that all forms of knowledge including literary and aesthetic forms are related to specific social interests. The motif is problematic because it poses a philosophical and political dilemma to those who would claim there are universal and metaphysical synonyms of truths regarding the nature of fascism, for example.[3] Historical relativism is challenged by critical theory within its other two problem motifs as well. How is literature possible? How is art possible? Posing the question of the conditions in which knowledge is possible suggests a second problem motif for critical theory. It demonstrates the Kantian side of the Frankfurt tradition's definition of critique and its shifting reliance on transcendental (negative) reason as the means to access the critical interest of emancipation. But adapting the concept of negative reason as its second problem motif means that explaining the real takes on two different definitions of reason itself: universal reason and critical reason.

Universal reason is seen as a form of instrumental reason. It is a means to an end. But universal reason can be subverted through critical reason. These two conditions in which knowledge is possible refer to two distinct processes. Instrumental reason seeks to protect its own interests. It is utilitarian in that it seeks an absolute identity with its truth referent. Critical reason seeks to dissolve the rigidity of the referent that is fixed in the immediate present or "the actual" by introducing negativity. Negation of instrumental reason opens up the potentiality of the truth referent; that is, it opens up the conditions of possibility in which literature or art might be possible.

But negation of instrumental reason is not enough for critical theory to be able to overcome instrumental reason. Critical theory must also be self-critical. In the third problem motif, critical reason requires a sustained will to self-reflection that allows it to overcome its own rigidity. Without this third problem motif critical theory could not claim an immanent critique of some other object. In order that the critical interest does not collapse into an identity with its object, critique must shift back and forth between the position of its own place in the mass of possible approaches to the object and the immanent construction of the object itself; that is the hermeneutic technique of understanding the object from its own point of view. The referent to which the object refers is negated but it is also reconstructed in the critical process through self-reflection, immanent critique of the object, and appropriation of positive elements that might be derived from other critiques of the same object.

Aesthetic and literary questions remained central to the project of critical theory in different ways for the diverse members of the inner circle during its first phase.[4] For Walter Benjamin, the evolution of art and literature is tied most importantly to the manner in which the conditions of its reproduction are handed down.[5] He argues that art is no longer defined as a reflection of the social but as a mode of production among many. Art is thoroughly mediated by the organizing and aesthetic practices that precede it. Modes of production are composed of a division of labor founded in a particular definition of the artist or writer to their means of production and, therefore, to the technical means of reproduction. In the case of the artysanal "story teller" (Benjamin 1969), for example, the oral means of reproduction depend on a social formation that has all but disappeared in the "age of mechanical reproduction." At the same time, art has its own specificity which lends it a very distinct beauty or "aura." In spite of Benjamin's theoretical break from Lukàcs and Brecht, there is still a strong sense in which a representational aesthetic theory informs his approach. This comes across most clearly in his concepts of *allegory* and *dialectical images*. All modern art and literature is seen by Benjamin as allegorical in the sense that characters, stories, and narratives are seen as the symbolic surface of some deeper social signification that takes the form of remembrance, or lamentation, of an aura lost to emergent technologies of reproduction and distribution. At the same time, these emergent technologies generate new allegories based on a sense of the present as loss or "ruin" juxtaposed with elements of memory, dream, and fantasy that coalesce in the form of *dialectical images* (Benjamin 1978).

Adorno and Horkheimer's critique of Benjamin is aimed at his belief in the inevitable revolution of the proletariat and his conviction that art must ultimately take on a political identification.[6] The contrast between great and average works is best represented in Horkheimer and Adorno's apocalyptic discussion of the culture industry in their landmark work *Dialectic of Enlightenment,* written in 1944 while in exile in Southern California. Both in this work and in Adorno's *Introduction to the Sociology of Music,* art is defined as the negative knowledge of the real world. Only "great works" have the capacity to overcome the commodification or reification process henceforth technologically inherent to the modern culture industry. For Horkheimer and Adorno, the reification process of the industry is totalizing. The culture industry has become so omnipresent that it now transforms virtually every aspect of culture into "mass mystification." In the modern cultural apparatus all cultural products are submitted to crushing rational models of repro-duction that require increasing standardization of reproduction tech-niques, a repetition of forms and contents that leave no creative chance, and a requirement of a uniformity of signs and images. As they put it, the culture industry creates a constant conformity even regulating rela-tions with the past: "That which is new is the exclusion of everything that could be new" (Horkheimer and Adorno 1972).

Habermas's Break

Almost forty years after *Dialectic of Enlightment,* Habermas launched a blunt attack on some of the ideas put forth by Horkheimer and Adorno in his essay "The Entwinement of Myth and Enlightenment: Re-reading the Dialectic of Enlightenment." Habermas argues that the work of his predecessors suggests such a nihilist critique of moder-nity that it eliminates the possibility of any kind of reasoned emanci-pation. He argues that their negation of rationalism, or the idea that knowledge is inherently emancipatory, demonstrates the limits of a theoretical logic founded in historicism and a philosophy of con-sciousness, an approach that posits the will of the social actor as the determining force in the historical process. The elaboration of a new critical theory that would need to go beyond these limits and recover the critical reason of the Enlightenment project, he argues, must shift to a philosophy of language and a sociology of communication.

Although Habermas has never specialized in the analysis of art and literature, his controversial plea for a new critical theory based in a philosophy of language represents an important departure from the theory of aesthetics that the Frankfurt tradition has been famous for. From his earliest work on the public sphere, to his essays on technol-ogy, and to his recent and ongoing critical encounters with poststruc-turalism, Habermas warns against the collapse of theory into literature and vice versa in order to protect a place for positive reconstruc-tive criticism. In one of his early essays he cites the traditional neo-Kantian distinction between the natural and cultural sciences as the best place to situate the demarcation of the scientific and literary gen-res of discourse: "Science has meant the strictly empirical sciences, while literature has been taken more broadly to include methods of interpretation in cultural sciences." His essay on "Technical Progress and the Social Lifeworld" presents an early illustration of his original reference. He distances himself from Aldous Huxley's plea for an unmediated interface between the two genres. Huxley argues that these genres are only distinguished in so far as they are derived from different experiences—literature belonging more to the lifeworld, science to the world of technology and administration—and so the "law-like" generalizations of science need to be better integrated into literature as a means of introducing science into the lifeworld. Habermas argues that this postulate is unfounded given that science only enters the lifeworld through the application of technology. He argues that the relation between the genres needs to be situated in the larger question of "how is it possible to translate technically exploitable knowledge into the practical consciousness of a social lifeworld" and not how to collapse one discourse into another (Habermas 1970, 51).

Habermas argues in a similar way against contemporary poststructuralist positions that would level the genre distinction between theory and literature. As seen in chapter 2, he advocates a postmetaphysics that would not erase subject positions that have the capacity to respond to critical problem solving. "Whoever transposes the radical critique of reason into the domain of rhetoric in order to blunt the paradox of self-referentiality," he says, "also dulls the sword of the critique of reason itself. The false pretense of eliminating the genre distinction between philosophy and literature cannot lead us out of the aporia" (Habermas 1997, xx). His attempt to overturn the philosophy of negation with a positive pragmatic form of criticism requires that various spheres of discourse, knowledge, and power be clearly demarcated from one another. Let us now return to comparing his position with that of Bakhtin.

Genres of Discourse in Literature and in Theory

Given that for both Habermas and Bakhtin discursive genres are, to a certain extent interchangeable but are not reducible to one another, the problem becomes: how does one distinguish the specificity of a given utterance within a genre? Bakhtin argues that utterances have a specific dialogical form that is intimately implicated in the vast variety of intricate and complex threads that provide unity and diversity within lifeworlds. Recall that for Habermas, communicative actions are forms of speech acts in everyday lifeworlds where interlocutors seek out a common understanding. The interlocutor makes a universal claim regarding the validity, justice, and sincerity of his utterance that corresponds to the objective, social, and personal worlds.

Everyday discourse genres are seen by Voloshinov (1976) and Bakhtin (1993) as carrying all three levels of Habermas's pragmatics. They need a common spatial purview, a degree of common knowledge and a minimally shared set of values and norms. Voloshinov presents the example of two interlocutors in a room where one says the word, "Well," and the other gives no response. Without understanding the extraverbal pragmatic situation we can have no idea what the adverb "Well" could possibly mean. If we know that the two speakers are in Russia and are looking out the window at a late spring snowfall, we can assume the utterance is a bit ironic, and perhaps even comic. They are tired of the winter. Communicative utterances are not reflections of the pragmatic extraverbal purview but rather emergent elements of the interlocutor's shared, but unexpressed assumptions, which permit evaluative conclusions. As Voloshinov puts it: "[T]he concrete utterance is born, lives and dies in the process of social interaction between the participants of the utterance" (1976, 105).

This way of arguing assumes, as Habermas points out, that the utterance is inserted into a communicative rather than a strategic form of the act of utterance. Would a tourist from Southern California visiting Russia grasp the ironic complexity of the shared common understanding of a northern chronotope? Communicative action is not looking to transfer knowledge or to manipulate the listener with humor or threats. Transgredient to the illocutionary act, the speaker is motivated by the other to act conjointly. The question in part, though, is what exactly is in the illocutionary act that brings speakers into the conjoined solidarity of communicative action?

For Habermas, the speech act supports expressive as well as regulative and constative structures. The listener accepts the argument that the winter has gone on far too long not only because it is a spatially and temporally true observation, but because the intonation expresses sincerity and gives it a social meaning. For Bakhtin and Voloshinov, sincerity is almost completely expressed through intonation. "Tone," says Voloshinov, "lies on the border of the said and the unsaid. It is where discourse comes into contact with life" (1976, 102). The listener can accept the claims about the winter because the sincerity is guaranteed by the emotional-volitional tones in the utterance and in each other's life.

Emotional-volitional guarantees enter into the coordination of the relation between the speaker and the addressee. This relation is grounded in regulative and constative speech acts. In the case of a disagreement about truth or rightness, according to Habermas, a regulative speech act would allow the guarantor to redeem himself discursively; that is, "by adducing reasons; in the case of claims to truthfulness, he does so through consistent behavior." On the other hand, constative speech acts are uniquely addressed to situations about which the speech participants are in agreement. Obligations linked to the binding effect among participants arise "only insofar as the speaker and the hearer agree to base their actions on situational definitions that do not contradict the propositions they accept as true at any given point." For Habermas, a guarantee is at the center of the communicative utterance. "As soon as the hearer accepts the guarantee offered by the speaker, obligations are assumed that have consequences for the interaction, obligations that are contained in the meaning of what was said" (Habermas 1990, 59).

Bakhtin and Voloshinov share Habermas's pragmatic distinction between the genres of discourse and their dialogic theory, as opposed to the monologic theory of the utterance, comes very close to Habermas's distinction between communicative and strategic forms of action. On the other hand, as was argued in chapter 1, Bakhtin highlights the aesthetic dimension in all genres of discourse. The theory of dialogism Bakhtin sketches is not simply a semiotic relation between the author and the reader. It is a theory of the contextual and cultural particularity of the speaker's anticipation of response from the active listener. For Voloshinov, the key difference between discourse in life and discourse in art is that the latter "is wholly absorbed in the creation of a work of art, and its continuous re-creations in the co-creation of contemplators, and does not require any other kind of objectification" (1976, 98). As soon as it steps out of this objective, it gives itself up as a literary or artistic practice. I am not saying that Habermas, Bakhtin, and Voloschinov would define Italo Calvino's book as a work of nonfiction, because it breaks out of any kind of primary aesthetic function. This is not the point of raising the example. The point is to probe some of the questions that the novel raises regarding the ways in which communicative utterances work in both theory and literature.

From Dostoevsky to Calvino

Keep in mind that Bakhtin was not aware of Calvino's novel and although he was interested in the evolution of discourse in the modern novel, his most systematic analyses are best seen in his books on

Dostoevsky and Rabelais and in his essays in *The Dialogic Imagination*. Habermas briefly discusses the importance of literary genres in his early study of the emergence of the modern bourgeois public sphere, but one of the only literary works he discusses in any detail is Calvino's novel. His discussion of Calvino's novel is mainly focused on a critique of how the poststructuralist aesthetic conceives the communicative utterance. As a postmodern aesthetic form of literature, Calvino's novel significantly departs from both Bakhtin's and Habermas's theories of the relation between the genres of discourse in literature and in social life.

For Bakhtin, Dostoevsky's polyphonic novels are an art form in which speakers express ideological interest that in turn allows the reader to apprehend the world. The principle of polyphony includes "the great dialogue," as well as micro compositional and interior discourse in the novel. The author's task is to perceive the "great ideas" of the epoch and to provoke dialogue by giving voice and representation to all possible points of view. The interaction of the separate voices (polyphony) that clash and form new hybrid forms is made possible through the dialogic narrative. In Dostoevsky's novels, hybridization is derived from characters who express distinct points of view. The characters interact among themselves not only at the level of speech, but also at a much deeper discursive level where the slightest or most nuanced utterance can be identified as belonging to a character or the author. This is an important creative aspect in the dialogized dimension of polyphony that clearly and mutually demarcates the distinction between world views. If the author's work consists of positively developing this polyphonic condition for the novel, then analysis should look to elaborate as precisely as possible the mutual, though not necessarily reciprocal, relations between the voices. Herein lies the problem from a Bakhtinian perspective. This type of analytic objective is achievable in Dostoevsky's novels given that its major elements conform to a more or less conventional modern novel genre that meets the reader's expectation. It includes the conventional elements of description and representation among its formal structure, interior monologues and syncopated syntax normally associated with the insertion of a speaking subject in the text. These conventional elements are clearly discernable in Dostoevsky's novels. However, if the dialogical principle is an immanent process that unfolds and becomes something that it has not been before, then addressing the evolution of the novel more than one hundred years after the early modern genre Bakhtin theorized, one should expect to find important formal differences (Sabo and Nielsen, 1984).

The formal differences between Dostoevsky's *Brothers Karamazov* and Calvino's *If on A Winter's Night a Traveller* are immediately apparent. Calvino's novel is composed of a series of independent unfinished stories grafted onto a background narrative that holds to the novel form. The background narrative concerns the search of a male and a female reader for misplaced, lost, or as yet unfinished chapters from different books. Chapters in the novel tell some of the different stories that belong to different novels. Through these incomplete narratives the author (Calvino), according to Habermas, seeks to establish the intertextual truth about literature and theory. The novel's structure is subverted by cutting off the stories as well as by parodies of the subgenres, especially the popular adventure and suspense novel. The narrative dissolves into an event of searching for texts. Habermas argues that "Calvino turns the search for the books that have apparently disappeared into an exercise that is supposed to bring light to the truth about literature: there are no originals, only traces, no texts, only readings, no fictional worlds in contrast to reality." For Calvino to demonstrate this new form he "must carry through with a novel that is consistently written in the second person before he can show that the relation of the novel to the reader need not remain external to the text" (Habermas 1992b, 218). If the experiment succeeds then literature and literary theory are assimilated.

How then can we discuss the dialogic form of such a novel when its structure bears so little resemblance to the novelistic utterance? The voices in the text and their interrelations are problematic, especially the author-reader relation, but also the relation between the author and the characters. In the first lines of the novel, the voice of the author directly addresses the reader in a discourse that is in the form of a preface: "You are about to begin reading Italo Calvino's new novel. Relax. Concentrate. Dispel every other thought. Let the world around you fade. Best to close the door; the TV is always on in the next room" (Calvino 1981, 3). But the novel does not begin as we are told in the opening lines. Although the title on the next page is "Chapter One," the direct address to the reader is continued. It quickly becomes apparent that the reader the author addresses is not a reader outside the narrative of the novel. It is rather the author's imaginary reader who is attributed certain characteristics: "It is not that you expect anything in particular from this book. You're the sort of person who, on principle, no longer expects anything of anything" (Calvino 1981, 4). The "you" in this direct address, could also be a noun created by the author. As the text unfolds, this imaginary reader takes on an identity that is increasingly based on the assumption of the real reader, who in turn is progressively drawn into a series of events along with other imaginary characters. The author also inserts his own voice into the text through an imaginary author, Silas Flannery. The view of the concrete reader is presented through Flannery's diary, which would normally only be read by its author. In the text, though, the author imagines how his neighbor might read the diary and in the process he observes the way she reacts and goes on to structure his writing in a way that corresponds to her reaction. On the other hand, Flannery is not especially conscious of his relation with the reader. It becomes apparent that his words simply become attached to the reader.

Convergence and Difference

Several points of convergence and difference between Habermas's and Bakhtin's approaches can now be better identified. Calvino's novel can be seen to work in three areas of operation for which both Habermas and Bakhtin (for different reasons) seek autonomy. First, Calvino eliminates the aesthetic productivity that distinguishes the author from the hero. He actively seeks to eliminate the author by assimilating theory and literature into the same discourse. Second, this results in an erasure of the boundary between fiction and reality. Third, as a result of the latter operation, the reader is placed in what Habermas calls "a fourth world position," meaning that the text does not recognize the reality of the reader, only some aspect or level of reality. From each of these operations, Calvino's novel dissolves into an event of searching for narratives.

It would appear then that if Calvino is to Habermas what Tolstoy was to Bakhtin then for Habermas, Calvino is still very much the author gazing down from above. But this conclusion is completely beside the point of Habermas's discussion and an unnecessarily harsh deduction from Bakhtin's approach. Calvino's novel is an excellent counterfactual example of a poststructuralist aesthetic. It is antimetaphysical and yet it manages to articulate multiple voices both within and across their divergent speech genres.

On the other hand, there is a very important difference between Bakhtin and Habermas on the point of the relation between genres of discourse. Unlike Bakhtin, Habermas argues that everyday utterances of speech lose their force when they enter a literary universe. Bakhtin argues the contrary position. He claims that the transposition of everyday speech utterances into the literary genre is a deep dimension of heteroglossia or the stratification of language. This is the main aesthetic device for creating character zones. For Habermas, the reader of literature does not have the burden of finding a solution to the dilemma. In everyday speech genres, the addressee and her partner in dialogue must find their way to solve the problem at hand, and achieve understanding together. In the novel, sincerity, validity, and objectivity are derived through the presentation of heroes or characters. But validity in this instance, as Habermas points out, is "illocutionarily disempowered." This is because a validity claim between author and hero is already interpreted by the text and so "it does not get all the way through to the reader" (Habermas 1992b, 223). Finally, in contrast with Bakhtin, only the author determines what is or is not valid according to Habermas. For Bakhtin, the polyphonic novel is about the separation of each voice from the author, which does not mean the elimination of the author, but does, to a certain extent, suggest that validity claims are made by characters.

The point of this chapter has not been to categorize Calvino's novel as a monologic, strategic, or dramaturgical utterance but to draw out differences and points of convergence between Habermas's pragmatist theory of the utterance and Bakhtin's dialogic theory. For Bakhtin and Voloshinov, a creative anticipation of response is what characterizes dialogized utterances. Words carry traces of different voices and only express their "own words" once they are internalized by the speaker. On the other hand, in "the world of other's words" the struggle between voices argued by Bakhtin and Voloshinov—and, we could add, over Habermas's guarantees about validity—is what is at the center of the communicative utterance. Habermas shares Bakhtin's and Voloshinov's definition of the distinction between the genres of discourse and the pragmatic terms of the struggle over the event of ownership at the center of the communicative utterance. The political ramifications of this theoretical convergence at the level of community, nation, and global geopolitics needs to be further explored in the final chapters by looking more carefully at Habermas's discourse theory of democracy and contrasting it with Bakhtin's dialogic approach. At this point, though, we need to turn our attention to an explanation of the deeper philosophical sources that Bakhtin draws on in his earliest attempts to construct a "philosophy of the answerable act."

4

ON THE SOURCES OF YOUNG BAKHTIN'S ETHICS

(Kant, Vvedenskij, Simmel, Cohen)

A series of questions guide the following discussion of some of the
sources of Bakhtins' earliest work. What are the origins of his
concepts? What is his unique contribution? What did he mean by mixing this or that concept? How did he get to this or that proposition
from the place he began? Why and what conceptual shifts does he engage in from one text to the other? How can the core philosophical idea
that is directing his program be explained and expanded toward an
ethics of the political? These questions cannot be fully answered by any
one researcher and so, once again, inquiry is limited to revisiting a background that is already partially covered in the literature with the hope
that further nuance and possibly some further explanation can be
added. The place to begin is a reconstruction of the most relevant
arguments from Kant's moral philosophy against which Bakhtin proposes his "philosophy of the answerable act or deed" (1993, 28). A re-
examination of selective theoretical arguments from three other
thinkers that are known to have had an important influence on the
young Bakhtin is the next crucial step. The analysis here is necessarily
incomplete as I am looking to deepen the understanding of the creative
dimension of social action and transcultural ethics that can be derived
from his early work, and not to provide a definitive study of his texts.

After reviewing the main postulates of Kant's ethics in the first
section below, I introduce two other less acknowledged arguments that
have an important influence on Bakhtin's *Toward a Philosophy of the*

Act. These include the argument for the fourth postulate in Kantian ethics proposed by the turn of the century Russian philosopher, Alexander Vvedenskij, and Georg Simmel's lesser known discussion on individualism and moral philosophy in *Das Individuelle Gesetz*, or "The Individual Law."[1] Mihailovic's well-documented study of the theological and religious ideas that underlie much of Bakhtin's early ethics does not pretend to have provided an explanation of the most important philosophical sources. On the other hand, he does suggest that Bakhtin's positive reading of aspects of Kant's Categorical Imperative need to be read through the interpretation given by the orthodox religious philosopher, Vladimir Solovyov. I do not contest that Solovyov's religious ideas influenced Bakhtin but I do contest the implication that Bakhtin borrowed mainly from his reading of Kant's Categorical Imperative. Instead, I argue below that Simmel's text needs to be recognized as the key influence on Bakhtin's interpretation of Kant. Brian Poole also makes a case for considering the philosophical influence of Max Scheler and Nicolas Hartmann—most notably on Bakhtin's use of the concepts of "empathy"and of the "I-for-the-self" and the "I-for-the-Other" (Poole, 1997). Although there is good reason for considering the influence of these thinkers on later works, it is more difficult to demonstrate their impact on the development of Bakhtin's early ethics. It is true that these concepts first appear in the early essay and that on many points Bakhtin's philosophy of the subject and participative thinking approximates Max Scheler's distinct brand of personalism and especially his sociology (1970). On the other hand, Bakhtin's core argument for the primacy of practical reason is expressed in an ethics of answerability and *not* an ethics of intentionality, as is the case with Scheler. Bakhtin's ethics asks the question: How ought I to act?—not exclusively because of my axiological position of intentionality, but how I ought to act toward another so we can both grow in self-knowledge. Scheler's (1973) ethics, on the other hand, ask the question: How ought I to act, given my axiological position of intentionality and the values that correspond to my idea of the good? Although there is much overlap between the two positions, they are, in fact, posing two very different questions.

The young Bakhtin's works in ethics and aesthetics are thus the subject of a certain degree of controversy regarding the interpretation of his earliest influences. Bakhtin's ethics derive from, at best, a very general critique of Kant and of Hermann Cohen's attempt to reform Kant via an ethics of pure will and the transcendence of the juridical subject.[2] Cohen is a third major influence that has been cited since the earliest studies on Bakhtin but again has received little systematic attention outside Clark and Holquist's original article (1984b). His interpretation and critique of Hermann Cohen and his later reception and appropriation of other members of the Marburg School is thought to be filtered through his closest mentor and friend, M. I. Kagan, who studied with Cohen and attended various German universities at the time.[3] Again, this influence is difficult to demonstrate because Bakhtin's ethical theory also contradicts Cohen's. In *Toward a Philosophy of the Act,* Bakhtin rejects Cohen's attempt to reform Kant via an ethics of pure will and the transcendence of the juridical subject when he argues that "the concept of legality [law] is incomparably wider [than Kant's Categorical Imperative] and contains moments that are completely incompatible with the [ethical] ought" (1993, 25–26). On the other hand, a strong sense of Cohen's influence can be read analogously by comparing the concept of fellowship and community he presents in his book *The Religion of Reason* to Bakhtin's complex understanding of the individual-community relation. I take this question up in the third section of this chapter before concluding.

Keeping in mind the difficulty of pinning down Bakhtin's precise argumentation,[4] this chapter focuses on the influences of Kant, Vvedenskij, Simmel, and Cohen on the young Bakhtin's attempt to construct what he calls a "philosophy of the answerable act." My main argument is that his conceptual shifts do not simply spill over from one part of an essay to the next nor from one text to the next, but can be seen as a concentrated effort to move beyond the fourth postulate of neo-Kantian philosophy. As will be seen below, Vvedenskij defines the fourth postulate—the fourth necessary precondition for an ethical action to be possible—as a faith in the existential animateness of other egos. The implications that such a postulate holds for normative actions make Bakhtin's ethics quite different from those of Kant and the neo-Kantians. The question remains, though, is his position original or is it derived from some other source?

Bakhtin's concepts can be presented in a unified and original theme I have been calling the norms of answerability. In other words, the question of how I ought to act is not resolved by following the rules or the expectation of my duty (Kant), nor by rigorously applying juridical reason (Cohen, Habermas). The question of how I ought to act needs to be resolved through the imaginary, but not fictional, subjectivity of another who can answer me back (Vvedenskij)—however different that subjectivity might be from my own. Bakhtin's notorious reverence for the most shady characters in Dostoevsky's novels and the most fantastic and twisted bits in Rabelais's version of grotesque realism attest to his sustained interest in this moral faith in the other as both a unique individual and a potential collective friend (Simmel). As was seen in chapter 1, well before the monographs on the latter artists Bakhtin defines normative action as the emotionally and volitionally orientated act toward another axiological position that can answer back. Kant's question of how I ought to act becomes for him how I ought to act toward this other "I," this other emotional-volitional orientation and in what aesthetic form can we consummate this action?

It seems clear that this philosophical understanding the young Bakhtin reaches for can only be achieved by balancing the needs of normative authority (consummation of an intersubjective act between two or more individuals) with the principle of infinite openness (the unfinalizability of self-other relations). To achieve this he develops a series of doubling concepts that are designed to uncover different layers of crossover or transgredient relations. Bakhtin doubles the concept of responsibility into the individual responsibility of being oneself and being in relation with another. The highest expression of the self-other architectonic is the "contraposition of *I* and the *other*. Life knows two value-centers that are fundamentally and essentially different, yet are correlated with each other: myself and the other; and it is around these centers that all of the concrete moments of Being are distributed and arranged" (Bakhtin 1993, 74). Bakhtin achieves the first level of this understanding of intersubjectivity by doubling the relation between consummation or completion and open-endedness in self-other relations. He claims that the whole world is unitary in content when it is correlated with me or with another. This transgredient meaning of the world is both particular and universal and raises the question of its unity to the level of a unique event.

The question I have is what are the fundamental ideas that brought Bakhtin to these doubling propositions? Simmel's *Das Individuelle Gesetz* provides several clues as to the source of Bakhtin's interest in individuality and the "philosophy of answerability." On the other hand, Cohen's work may have had a potentially stronger influence on Bakhtin's idea of community. Vvedenskij, Simmel, Cohen, and Bakhtin share a common interest in overcoming the wedge Kant's transcendental critical philosophy drives between experience and knowledge. There is not enough space to provide a detailed description of their approaches nor to present a full critique of their reception. Instead, I concentrate on how each looks for a way to join experience with knowledge and account for the unity of the world.

Kant's Three Postulates

To begin with it is helpful to remember that Kant remodels both the Ancient Greek and the Enlightenment way of thinking for modern society with his three critiques, which are couched in the form of three fundamental questions: What can I know? What should I do? and What may I hope? Kant no longer holds to the eternal forms as put forward by Plato nor the priority of practical experience as developed by Aristotle. He synthesizes aspects of Descartes's rationalism and Hume's empiricism into a new model that is critical of both pure reason and pure experience. Kant's questions belong to the autonomous object domains of theory, ethics, and aesthetics.

Theoretical knowledge begins with experience but it is not reducible to experience. This nonreducibility applies to the other spheres as well. Ethical or practical reason is contextual but not reducible to context, and aesthetic judgment comes from the experience of beauty in the world but is not reducible to this experience. For something to be judged beautiful, or sublime, the beholder needs to be able to claim that everyone must see it so. The source of pleasure is in its common sense and communication. A subject might know his or her own experience but he or she can only know what another's experience might be like from outside. Practical ethical knowledge is not simply a feeling based in experience. A subject might have a feeling about right and wrong but the knowledge of right and wrong is not reducible to the feeling. An action should unfold in reference to a formal duty that is tied to the "ought" and not to an impulse. In the same way, a valid judgment about good or bad taste needs to be couched in a universal form of beauty. Thus, a person who decides something is beautiful, or sublime, implies that everyone ought to give the object his or her approval.

Kant maintains that our experience of the world can only be made sense of through a priori conditions such as space and time that in turn allow understanding in terms of the categories of quantity and quality and through modalities such as unity, plurality, substance, necessity, existence, possibility, and so on. In each sphere, knowledge is derived from experience but is not reducible to it. Transcendental knowledge lies beyond the realm of immanent experience because it is derived from the dialectical synthesis of formal categories. Transcendental practical knowledge is possible through the synthesis of the formal categories of duty and transcendental aesthetic judgment is achieved through the synthesis of formal claims about the beautiful and the sublime.

In the practical, rather than the theoretical and aesthetic spheres, Kant argues that actors must embrace three postulates if they are going to be able to know what it means to act ethically. He argues that for any action to be a good action we must be able to make some sort of measure of what the ultimate form of the good might be. His first postulate is that for an ultimate norm of the good to exist there must also be some infinite time span in which the norm might occur; hence, there must also be the possibility of immortality. Secondly, a concept of the ultimate good (such as God) must exist in order for such a measure of the good to be possible. Without the analytic concept (of God), we could have no mechanism for agreeing on what the good might be like. Finally, Kant's third postulate is that human subjects must be free to choose between good and evil for there to be such a thing as the good in the first place (Kant 1990, 18).

Kant's ethics contain three levels that can be considered deontological and universalist: 1) the level of autonomy; 2) the level of respect for the dignity of persons; and 3) the level of the law of the moral community. These levels are distinguished in terms of maxims or formulas that are derived from the general Categorical Imperative; a kind of obligatory ultimate rule for moral conduct. Each maxim of the categorical imperative contains traces of each other maxim and all are, in general, applicable to any social action situation. The first two maxims are only slight variations on the Golden Rule whereas the third is more a justification for a moral community that establishes the right over the good through the rule of law. On the first level of the categorical imperative, Kant says we should only ever act on a maxim that could be willed by everyone (1990, 18). On the second level, he argues that we should never act in a way that another person would be treated as a means and not as an end (1990, 46). On the third level, he declares that "all maxims that proceed from our making of law ought to harmonize with a possible kingdom of ends as a kingdom of nature" (Kant 1990, 53). In other words, find a way to reach agreement through legal procedure, do not treat anyone as a mere object and base your actions on the universalizable question: What would happen if everyone were to act this way?

Vvedenskij's Fourth Postulate

The return to Kant in German philosophy began after the 1848 revolutions in France and elsewhere in Europe, which occurred in the context of a collapse of political, ethical, and epistemological systems. In philosophy the movement is understood as a return to the starting point of critical idealism and not a plea to defend Kant's overall system. Some, such as Kuno Fischer and Eduard Zeller, returned to Kant from Hegelian perspectives while others, such as Rudolf Lotze and Albert Lange, were looking for a way out of mechanical materialism and the rising dominance of positivism. In Marburg, Cohen and his students, Paul Natorp and Ernst Cassirer, developed neo-Kantianism toward logic and epistemology as well as social democratic or liberal-socialist political models. In Baden, Wilhelm Windelband and Heinrich Rickert, and later in Berlin, Georg Simmel and Max Weber, were more concerned with defining the fundamental tasks of the cultural sciences and were less concerned with political theory. For all, the crises of the epoch set the backdrop for a revival of moral philosophy that developed around highly tentative and experimental interpretations of Kant's critiques (Willey 1978).

The main figure who led the neo-Kantian revival in Russia was the well-known professor Alexander Vvedenskij who had attended various German universities in the 1880s before graduating from St. Petersburg and receiving the chair in philosophy. Vvedenskij's work has not been translated, he has written no book-length manuscript on ethics, and very little secondary commentary has been written about him outside of encyclopedic entries in various histories of Russian philosophy. A recent study by Thomas Nemeth (1996) of Vvedenskij's dissertation and of the importance of his contribution to neo-Kantian philosophy in Russia is thus a very timely contribution. Unfortunately for our purposes, Nemeth does not discuss Vvedenskij's most important definition of the fourth postulate proposed in his essay "On the Limits and Symptoms of Psychic Life," which was written in 1882 and will be discussed below. However, Nemeth does explain the philosophical argument Vvedenskij uses to posit the question of faith in the "in- itself." To begin with, Nemeth explains that Vvedenskij thought he was simply improving on Kant's already acceptable critical philosophy. He thought that "he held to the spirit rather than the letter, to the chief principals rather than all the specifics, and therefore that made him in his own mind a Neo-Kantian rather than a Kantian" (Nemeth 1996, 121).

Vvedenskij proposed the fourth postulate as an addition to Kant's ethics. He claimed that "the three postulates of practical reason established by Kant are not sufficient for the full understanding of moral behavior." He formulated the fourth postulate as "a belief in the existence of other egos, as a morally established faith" (cited in Lossky 1952, 161). Like Kant, Vvedenskij maintains that the other's inner life is unknowable and that one can only ever know oneself. For Vveden-skij, however, this defied the common sense notion that the represen-tation of the self in time has to be about an actual, or in itself, time. He assumed his concept of "a time in itself" would help correct Kant's oversight. Nemeth shows that Vvedenskij understood that "by provid-ing for freedom of the will, Kant was forced to postulate an immortal soul. Yet such a metaphysical soul is plausible only if we locate it in a metaphysical time, time in itself, certainly not that mere representation of time of which we are conscious." This is the deeper theoretical ar-gument that supports the fourth postulate. For Vvedenskij, "the basis of our acknowledgment of the existence of things in themselves, then, is a peculiar, conscious faith, a faith resting on moral, not cognitive, demands" (Nemeth 1996, 140).

Bakhtin hesitates when confronted with the question of whether we can actually know the other's I-for-the-self. Partially at least, he al-lows the more neo-Kantian assumption that breaks from Kant by as-suming we might completely experience the other's being through empathy. But he immediately counters that pure empathy is impossible because it would mean completely giving up on the empathizing indi-vidual's once-occurrent Being (1990;1993). It would not be correct to argue that Bakhtin's approach is simply the extension and working through of the fourth postulate even though he eventually sees in Dostoevsky's novels an example of an artistic vision that is capable of completely imagining the other as an unmerged voice. Hence, an-other influence on the development of his problematic needs to be accounted for.

Simmel's Shadow

Bakhtin's ethics can also be seen to lie in the long shadow cast by Georg Simmel's radical replacement of Kant's universal absolute (Cat-egorical Imperative) with an absolute individual law. Simmel's essay *Das Individuelle Gesetz* can be seen to have held a fundamental impor-tance for the development of Bakhtin's philosophy of answerability. Bakhtin's standpoint on ought *(Sollen)*, on answerability *(Verantwor-tung)*, on formal ethics, and on the whole of a life history cannot be understood without reading him in direct relation to Simmel's argu-ment. Concepts of individuality and the uniqueness of the act also need to be understood in Simmel's special sense as a repetition of uniqueness *(Einzigkeit)* and not as a singleness *(Einzelheit)*, as is usually meant in the German philosophical tradition. Other concepts have Simmelian overtones but may well be borrowed from other common sources of nineteenth-century German philosophy. One interesting example of this is how the expression *emotional-volitional* gets translated from Bakhtin's Russian, where it originally reads "emotional and volitional." Simmel also uses the phrase in *Das Individuelle Gesetz*, but here it is "emotional or volitional."

It is important to recall from the onset that Bakhtin tries to unify his ethics by drawing together two branches of traditional philosophy into one model. He puts first philosophy *(prima philosophia)* together with the Kantian argument on the "primacy of practical reason." This combination is not a common maneuver. By opposing "theoretism" or "fatal theoretism," Bakhtin ends up pleading for what appears to be a completely new moral philosophy, that would stand virtually alone in its contradiction to the dominance of the "epistemological turn" at the end of the nineteenth century. One of Bakhtin's main points, then, is a very rigorous standpoint against modern moral philosophy, which he claims "cannot pretend to being a first philosophy, that is, a teaching *not* about unitary cultural creation, but about unitary and once-occurrent Being-as-event. Such a first philosophy does not exist, and even the paths leading to its creation seem to be forgotten" (1993, 19). Here, Bakhtin is speaking as if he is about to create a completely new path. However, other research has made it sufficiently clear that he often falls into the habit of not citing his sources (Hirschkop 1998; 1999; Poole 1997), making it difficult to determine what is actually original in his argumentation and what is borrowed. Bakhtin's unacknowledged debt to Simmel seems to be one of those sources that is fairly easy to see.

Simmel reverses Kant's general rule with an ethics of individual law. For Kant, an ethical action cannot be derived from acting out of an impulse but only by acting from duty. As was seen above, the orientation toward duty is rooted in the universal law that I ought only ever act in a way I could will everyone else to act. According to Kant, the universally objective law cannot be individual, whereas for Simmel, the law is both individual and objective. In other words, while the sources of moral obligation are found in a reality that transcends the individual's life for Kant, for Simmel the ought emanates from the individual's life as a whole and so individuals are understood as mutually complementary with respect to the uniqueness of each.

Simmel begins his analysis of the conception of the moral ought with a critique of the classical ideal that a law must be universal for it to be valid; an ideal that achieves its highest expression in Kant's ethics. Simmel reverses the position by arguing that if the general law means the agent can give a universal value to action and yet the action can only be carried out by the agent's own definition, then law is no longer general but only particular to that agent's case. Thus, each specific case would have to include the formulation of a new law that would only ever be valid for a singular case (Leger 1989, 131). The relation between generalizability and the law does not actually "require any . . . mutual necessity" and if the relation between these two categories is not one of mutual dependency, then neither should be the relation between subjectivity and individuality, as is also presupposed in rational Kantian ethics (Simmel 1968, 217). In opposition to general law, Simmel sees individuality as resting in an objective realm: "This in turn necessitates a new differentiation and a new synthesis of terms: the individual does not need to be subjective, and the objective is not supra-individual. Rather the crucial term is the objectivity of individuality"; that is, objectivity of unique individuality—what Bakhtin would come to call once-occurrent-Being. Simmel goes on to argue that "the decisive point is that individual life is nothing subjective but—without somehow losing its restriction to this individual—it is as an ethical ought that is absolutely objective. The malformed connection or combination between individuality and subjectivity has to be dissolved like the one that requires the generalizability of law. Thereby the terms become free to build the new synthesis between individuality and legality."[5]

Simmel argues that the general law does not always suit an individual, but the individual law always does. The ideal ought changes constantly through actions and in this sense the individual ought is also objective (1968, 230). For Simmel, the act defines one's entire life history if one accepts that life is not the sum of several actions but one continuous act (1968, 235). Every deed is responsible for the entire life history of the agent and vice versa. "For this reason the responsibility for one's life history lies in the ought of every single doing."[6] The individual law does not come from the contents of life but rather from the process of life. The ought is based on all we have ever done, been, and ought to have done or been (1968, 238).

To summarize, Simmel situates the ought in individual law. At the same time, he insists on the importance of carefully distinguishing between the "individual" and the subjective. Unlike juridical law, Simmel's moral law is simultaneously individual and objective. Individual law is not at all a convenient refuge for the individual's subjectivity but rather the most rigorous of imperatives as it challenges the individual to come to terms with the whole of his or her life history in each and every act (Leger 1989). Simmel's reversal of the categorical imperative thus prepares a new orientation for moral philosophy and a new general sociology. It is especially Simmel's moral philosophy that is at the heart of Bakhtin's philosophy of the answerable deed. The most important place to begin to examine his attempt at positing a moral philosophy is in his critique of formal ethics. His critique of content ethics is really only important for understanding the disciplinary approach to norms and thus is fairly secondary to our topic here, as are his preliminary attempts at sketching out a critique of aesthetic seeing and the problem of pure empathy, which are taken up in more detail and possibly under different influences in his subsequent works.

Bakhtin appears to follow Simmel's reversal of Kant's imperative and his argument that the ethical ought does not come from a universal subject but from the individual I in a reciprocal relation of exchange with others. Simmel argues that subjectivity is as unique for each individual as is the content of happiness or sadness that might be felt. He also argues that the terms *individuality* and *subjectivity* need to be separated because as an ethical ought the individual is also objective. It would be a mistake to accuse Simmel of championing an atomistic concept of individuality; that is, one that ideologically opposes the individual to the community. On the contrary, anyone familiar with Simmel's sociology knows the importance he places on reciprocity between social actors.[7] Moreover, Simmel uses the word *individuality,* not to express uniqueness but to express the origin of the ought in the individual.

Bakhtin and the Formal Ought

Bakhtin intuitively understood the complex meaning of Simmel's individual law. The first proof of this intuitive understanding is seen in the fact that he does not give us an immanent reconstruction of Kant's arguments on formal ethics, yet he adopts them as a kind of foil to develop Simmel's argument regarding the individual nature of the ought within the act. Using the same inner logic Simmel uses in his reversal of the general law into an individual law, Bakhtin argues that, "the ought is really absolutely compellent or categorical—for the individual" (Bakhtin 1993). Bakhtin builds his criticism on the concept of individuality, and especially, on unique individuality: "The ought," he says, "is precisely a category of the individual act; even more than that—it is a category of individuality, of the uniqueness of a performed act, of its once-occurrent compellentness, of its historicity, of the impossibility to replace it with anything else or to provide a substitute for it" (Bakhtin 1993, 25). This is Simmel's original idea.

Bakhtin gives very little explanation as to why the individual act is lost in formal ethics except to repeat that "formal ethics . . . conceives the category of the ought as a category of theoretical consciousness, i.e., it theorizes the ought, and, as a result, loses the individual act or deed" (1993, 25). The question should be asked here, What theoretical consciousness is he referring to? It turns out that he is no longer talking about moral consciousness but something much wider, which he calls legality. And so the second point that demonstrates Bakhtin's usage of the individual law is seen in the direct way he follows Simmel's critique of Kant's understanding of the law as a general law of nature, or as juridical law. In other words, Bakhtin is repeating Simmel's contention that "the categorical imperative has the logical structure of a law of nature, on the one hand (Kant himself hints at this), and on the other, that of juridical universality" (Simmel 1968, 183).

Bakhtin argues against juridical universality as not being a valid principle for the moral ought. We just saw how Simmel dismisses Kant's concept of the law but the question now is: What proposition does Bakhtin formulate against Kant's Categorical Imperative? His sole argument here is that the principle of formal ethics is not the principle of actually performed acts at all "but is rather the principle of the possible generalization of already performed acts in a theoretical transcription of them" (Bakhtin 1993, 27). But this is not an original argument. Indeed, we see again that it is, in fact, Simmel's thesis. The Kantian formula, Simmel says, is seen to "determine the morality of an action and even to establish a possible generalization. However, if our action is understood as it *really* stands in life—with its seamless, interwoven wholeness—then it cannot be generalized, because this would mean nothing else than to think the whole life of this individual as a general law" (1968, 189–190).[8]

Bakhtin makes three points regarding formal ethics that appear to be directly drawn from Simmel's individual law: those of individuality, law, and possible generalizations from already performed acts. The final point in Bakhtin's argument concerns the unique aspect of moral subjectivity. This point requires a closer examination of the concept of individuality. The question of moral subjectivity is perhaps the most complicated of Bakhtin's points because it is also at the same time the basis for his architectonics of the self-other relation. Again, though, Bakhtin's discussion of moral subjectivity is directly outlined by Simmel, whose own thinking on this point is inspired by Schleiermacher and the German Romantic tradition. Simmel writes that "the moral task is that each person should represent mankind in a particular manner . . . that is the moral duty of the individual. Each person is called to realize his own, his very own prototype" (Simmel 1971, 224). Kant's moral imperative calls for an abstract equality between agents, whereas for Simmel, and by implication Bakhtin, the imperative is rather about the differentiation of individuals. Rationalism assumes homogeneity of individuals whereas for the German philosophical tradition, "each person is called to realize his own, his very own prototype." Architectonic relations thus assume qualitative differences between unique individuals.

Thus, a key unacknowledged source of Bakhtin's philosophy of answerability can be seen in Simmel's essay *Das Individuelle Gesetz*. Bakhtin's approach to answerability *(Verantwortung)* and the critique of formal ethics cannot be properly understood without reading him in direct relation to Simmel's argument. To repeat Nicolaev's plea cited in the introductory chapter, closer examinations of Bakhtin's thought are needed to "explain the novelty of his approach." This needs to be done "by placing a scrupulous analysis" of his terminology against the background of the original philosophical contexts in which he developed his ideas (1997, 1).

With Simmel, Bakhtin is very critical of Kant's ethical formalism. Keep in mind, however, that he does not dismiss the content of the latter's three postulates even though he does not develop his approach in terms of postulates or necessarily undemonstrable principles. As his biographers are continually stressing, and as is evident in his own texts, Bakhtin never left the soul-immortality-individual freedom assumptions behind. On the contrary, he retains and develops the premise of the existence of God (the soul-spirit-body relation), the possibility of immortality (e.g., Dostoevski's capacity to divine aspects of the future from the present and the past) and of free volition (of the normative). In *Toward a Philosophy of the Act* and "The Author and the Hero in Aesthetic Activity," Bakhtin presents the most significant philosophical elaboration of the need for a special effort to reunite the aesthetic (the shaping of meaning in action) and the ethical (a cognitive element of the act itself) into one unified event. Kant, on the other hand, insists that while knowledge is derived from experience it cannot be reduced to experience. Knowledge needs to be supported by the further division of spheres of possible knowledge (theory, ethics, and aesthetics) in order to provide the condition for its transcendental synthesis—a condition Bakhtin describes as "fatal theoreticism."

One of Bakhtin's points in criticizing Kant's formalism is that as we reflect on the aesthetic representation of another's life through empathizing, or construct a philosophical ethics about how someone should act, we have already left the domain of once-occurrent-Being. This does not signal a postmoralist nor a relativist dilemma. The rules of conduct and the translation of desire into virtuous acts are not separated. On the contrary, once-occurrent-Being is never outside a normative deed. Bakhtin's insistence on the immediacy of once-occurrent-Being is an implicit component of the fourth postulate. Bakhtin argues that any position that does not take the understanding of the other's coeval and equal existence as in itself can only be a formalist understanding of how it should be or what it should be like.

By positing the animated existence of another I, Bakhtin addresses the larger question of the "consummation" between parts and the whole in the experience of the action itself. Kant's ethics are seen as flawed in that the norm is not defined inside the act but from an appropriate belief system or discipline outside the act that places it into context. "What is needed is something issuing from within myself, namely the morally ought-to-be attitude of my consciousness toward the theoretically valid in-itself proposition." Deontological ethics correctly assumes that the ought is a category of consciousness, "a form that cannot be derived from some particular material." But such duty-bound ethics further "conceives the category of the ought as a category of theoretical consciousness, and, as a result loses the individual act or deed" (1993, 23). For Bakhtin, the ought is not only an element of the act, it is a category of individuality itself. Neither the unique aspect of the individual act nor its universally valid claim can be repeated or performed by someone else. The uniqueness lies in the I's affirmation of its non-alibi in being.

Cohen's "Discovery of Man as Fellowman"

As we saw in the section on "Vvedenskij's Fourth Postulate," a common theme of the return to Kant at the end of the nineteenth century was the attempt to find a way to bring the spheres of human activity back into one unified philosophy. Hermann Cohen became a leading figure in neo-Kantianism and one of the most important influences on Bakhtin and his friends. Cohen's first works were close commentaries on Kant's three critiques. The essence of Cohen's new form of Kantianism "resides in the conception that all three directions of reason that Kant had educed and explored, are exhaustively conditioned by rational constructions that themeselves are not derived from but transcendentally prerequisite for and of their respective realities" (Scharzschild 1981, VII). In each work, *The Logic of Pure Reason* (1902), *The Ethics of Pure Will* (1904), and *The Aesthetics of Pure Feeling* (1912), Cohen looked for ways to narrow the gap between experience and knowledge and thereby to create a position that would greatly concretize the categorical imperative.(Zac,1984). Cohen establishes a philosophical system for a theory of law and of binding social relations in practice and not only in transcendental synthesis. As Wiley points out, Cohen "developed the main thesis of Marburg socialism by broadening the Categorical Imperative into the fundamental rule of society directed by moral reason and constituted under law" (1978, 124).

While the first two critiques in Cohen's philosophical system are connected through his earlier work on mathematics as a form of scientific reason (Cohen 1999), the "ethics of pure will" is more attached to the philosophy of natural law. His project to develop a fourth critique of psychology that would follow the "aesthetics of pure feeling" was finally dropped in order to give way to a major shift in his program toward the philosophy of religion (Launay 1999, 9). His theorizations of the will of the subject turned themeselves into an ambitious and broadly historical attempt to reduce the gap in Kant's philosophy between the theological understanding of God as a postulate of transcendental reason and the direct experience of God. As Clark and Holquist put it: "He seeks to reduce the gap between the God of the philosopher and the God of Abraham" (1984b, 304). Cohen's philosophy of religion is itself derived from readings of the *Ancient Testament* and Jewish theology. For Cohen, the problem of the norm originates in the correlation between God and man. This relation itself is defined as the holy spirit. The reintroduction of experience into the relation between "God" and "man" leads to the theoretical problem of man as plurality and man as individual. Out of plurality comes the problem of unity. The unity of man means the extension of the power of the One "over every individual member of the plurality." This is a founding question of monotheism: what to do with the foreigners who do not believe in the one God? In fact the problem of the foreigner is a key political problem for all societies.

For Cohen, an individual man is but a unit in a series; he is only "one man next to another" or just the next man *(Nebenmensch)*. The concept of "the next man" is taken from historical experience and "poses for ethics and also for religion . . . the problem of the fellowman *(Mitmensch)*" (Cohen 1972, 114). The next man is not a fellowman. The fellowman is not just there innocently or unobtrusively. The correlation of man and God cannot be maintained if man and fellowman are not corelated. The problem of fellowman becomes the highest problem of morality—it is the problem of the contraposition of the I-other relation Bakhtin defines at the end of *Toward a Philosophy of the Act* (1993, 74). Ethics are not possible unless they are attached to the question of the fellowman. If the fellowman is leveled down to the concept of the next man, sociability could not arise and normative orientations (mediations and breaks) would be impossible.

Cohen's definition of the fellowman is based in a theological orientation but it is also situated genealogically. He argues that monotheism, specifically Judaism, gave rise to both the humanist concepts of man-as-all-mankind and man-as-an-individual. But monotheism had to solve the problem of how to deal with the other who would not share the beliefs and customs of the one religion. It solved the problem through the concept of the stranger. The concept of the fellowman has its origins in the older concept of the foreigner, a concept that predates Ancient Greece. The state creates the distinction between the foreigner and the native. Cohen adds that as sociability increases and locals come to know the stranger he may be elevated to the status of the guest-friend, the immigrant, the one who is invited to eat and to stay and participate. "The stranger is not thought of as a slave, but as a guest-friend, who requires the piety of guest-friendship. Humanity is already so rooted in the stranger that the slave, as stranger, can be admonished to the bond of gratitude" (Cohen 1972, 120). The guest-friend may be excused from strict observance of the laws and is not required to believe in the one God. The guest-friend evolves into a more legal status and is called the guest-sojourner. Here, a foreigner-stranger may enter into another's territory and be recognized as having the same legal rights without being expected to observe the same cultural laws or even believe in the one God. Eventually, as enough guest-sojourners begin to immigrate they eventually take on the status of "brother" and the unity of brotherhood leads to the solution of the problem of the fellowman (Cohen 1972, 127).

It is not difficult to see how the ethical and the political implies the capacity to shift around the categories of "just the next man" and "the fellowman." But moving from "just the next man" to "the fellow-man" requires some form of community backed by the rule of law (1972, 137). The foreigner, the guest-friend or immigrant, the stranger, and the sojourner-stranger are the release valves and side entrances to the absolute law of community. The political, as well as the ethical, evolve out of the movement between these categories and the interests they get attached to in the social division. As Cohen argues, whereas one cannot be indifferent to the tragedy of the good fellow-man it is easier to be indifferent to "just the next man"; or to the fellowman who does bad; but not to the fellowman who does good.

In one sense, for Cohen, social division is rooted in the inability to maintain the integrity of the fellowman (1972, 130). Cohen refers to the biblical example where Cain kills Abel because he possessed more than he did. A flash of fratricide became possible at the point where Abel could be leveled down to the status of just the next man. But the question becomes how is social division possible given the necessity of the common good of the community (man) and God? Does not social division create opposition to the fellowman? The next man becomes the opposing man *(Gegenmensch)*. "Even more than the question of the stranger, the question of rich and poor is asked in one's native land and among one's own people; this human question is asked with regard to every man, with regard to every fellowman" (1972, 128). Out of the question of poverty and suffering comes the primary emotion of pity, a kind of glue for the sociability of fellowship.

Cohen succeeds in concretizing the Categorical Imperative by introducing the dynamic between the opposing man, the next-man, and fellowman. His sideways shift from a transcendental metaphysics that separates knowledge from experience to a religious metaphysics (from "the God of philosophers to the God of Abraham"), leads him to theorize an "ethics of pure will" in itself. However, the shift to religious metaphysics only brings the individual-community problem into sharper focus. It remains a question whether his shift can offer a solution to the normative puzzle that is generated with the fourth postulate. The larger anthropological question of how to approach others as coeval partners whoever and wherever they might be is still not fully answered. The category of the stranger-immigrant solves some of the political dilemmas of the one society and the one religion, but does not begin to theorize the phenomenological effect the stranger has on the community, nor does it answer the question of what effect the community has on the stranger. In a way, Bakhtin's starting point from the fourth postulate and the individual law is not how to solve the problem of the stranger but is the more difficult question of understanding the effect of the animated I ("the man in the man") as a more permanent condition of the stranger category. We will explore this argument in the next section before coming to a conclusion.

Influences and Steps

I have argued that to understand what Bakhtin calls the highest level of architectonic relations, the self-other relation, it is necessary to have a clear idea of the steps he takes to build his "philosophy of answerability." These steps are: 1) the retention of Kant's postulates of the existence of God, immortality, and freedom; 2) the absorpsion of Vvedenskij's fourth postulate; 3) the rejection of Kant's theory of action through an appropriation of Simmel's argument concerning the Individual Law; and 4) a qualified appropriation of Cohen's notion of fellowship. In some ways, the author-hero essay drops the overriding concern with ethics in order to deal more explicitly with aesthetics. But I read his essay on aesthetics and his monograph on Dostoyevsky as an attempt to try and deepen the "philosophy of the answerable act." I say this because each essay adds an expansive theoretical outline of the manifold problems of how the artist might represent or create the animate I of the other as a hero and how the relation between these ethical I's are consummated in unique aesthetic acts. In the process other theoretical influences are absorbed but the starting point of his "philosophy of the answerable act" is not disturbed. In Bakhtin's I-for-the-self, action takes place as the I "acts through the deed, word, thought, or action. I come to be through my acts" (Bakhtin 1990, 138). What is emphasized much more in these essays is the I's self-reflection on its act and the way in which the I is consummated aesthetically through the crossover or transgredient relation with another—a point covered in previous chapters.

Like Cohen, and even Simmel, Bakhtin attributes the origin of the "I" to the community's production of fellowman. But here Bakhtin goes further by reintroducing his theory of the non-alibi in being under the guise of a theory of "alienation." Here, the I lives "in the other and for the other. In my lived life, I participate in a communal mode of existence, in an established social order, in a nation, in a state, in mankind, in God's world." In each of these "worlds of the other's words," Bakhtin argues, "I experience, strive, and speak here in the *chorus* of others. But *in a chorus* I do not sing for myself; I am active only in relation to the other and I am passive in the other's relation to me." Acts are performed in a context that is relative to day to day life, to a universe of social and political values, and of aesthetic and ethical values. In communitarian ("fellowman") action, "I exchange gifts, but I do so disinterestedly; I feel in myself the body and the soul of another.... Not my own nature but the human nature in me can be beautiful, and not my own soul but the human soul can be harmonious" (1990, 121).

More so than Vvedenskij, and especially more so than Simmel, who would continue to develop his sociology of objective and subjective cultures through a priori categories, Bakhtin shares the more common neo-Kantian critique of Kant's a priori doctrines. Bakhtin also distances himself from Bergson's and Simmel's later *lebensphilosophie*. On the other hand, he is clearly influenced by several neo-Kantian criticisms of Kant and not only Vvedenskij's, Simmel's, and Cohen's. He shares the more common suspicion of Kant's doctrine of the inability to ever know the thing-in-itself. In his first essays, in particular, and as we saw in earlier chapters, he relies heavily on Jonas Cohen's and Wilhelm Windelband's concept of the transgredient.[9] On the other hand, he retains Kant's postulates, embraces his architectonics as a means of constructing the whole from the parts, and he privileges moral and practical responsibility over utilitarian theories of ethics. Bakhtin never wrote on the fourth postulate, never acknowledged Simmel's "Individual Law," and gave no credit to Cohen for any of his philosophy of dialogue. Yet his moral privileging of the other and his notions of once-occurrent Being, sympathetic-empathy, and the uniqueness of the act remain outstanding features that lurk behind concepts he would develop in his linguistic turn. The fourth postulate, the absolute individual law, and Cohen's social philosophy of emotion should be understood as a starting point for thinking through the background motives for Bakhtin's early conceptual shifts rather than as a set of converged axioms that explain his program. A point to keep in mind is that Bakhtin was not alone in his search to shift emphasis away from an a priori synthesis of knowledge toward an interest in the ethical and aesthetic problems raised by our more direct experience with each other.

Finally, we saw that for Bakhtin the open ethical event, where questions of "oughtness" are worked out, has no transcendental category. This does not mean that he has no normative theory. Each of Bakhtin's first essays shows him coming to terms with limitations based on a series of conceptual doubling: 1) of the ethics of being yourself through others; 2) of the inner and outer body-soul-spirit aesthetic; and 3) of the individual and community character of culture. The key definition of varying norms of answerability and the argument concerning the responsibility to be oneself are two core principles that are absorbed in the shift to define the transgredient or crossover relations between self and other as an aesthetic activity. This principle is brought out further in the comparison with Kant's and Max Weber's theories of action in the next chapter.

5

ACTION AND EROS

(Kant-Weber-Bakhtin)

This chapter continues to explain Bakhtin's deep affiliation and difference with Kant's ethics and introduces a comparison with Max Weber's sociology of action. The similarities and differences among the three approaches are reviewed by contrasting separate discussions of their general approaches. In order to economize on the presentation, discussion is directed to a more limited focus on how each might theorize the example of Eros as one of a large number of possible action zones in human culture. I comment on the relevance and irrelevance of Kant's ethics for contemporary actors and argue that although Weber and Bakhtin work through different streams of neo-Kantian epistemology, neither retains a strictly Kantian orientation. Weber learned enough Russian over a period of three months in 1905 to be able to report to his German readership on the complexity of Russian political culture and the geopolitics of the time (Weber 1995b). However, he had no knowledge of Bakhtin's group nor is there any evidence that Bakhtin read Weber's writings. It should be kept in mind that this is not a study of contrasting local influences and contacts but an attempt to continue to outline a broad general theory of the normative and creative dimension in action. In the final section I link the erotic zone of action to a sociological definition of intimacy and contrast the ways in which these three thinkers theorized intimacy with how it might be thought about today.

Kant: Duties Toward the Body Concerning the Sexual Impulse

In *The Critique of Practical Reason* Kant asks the question, How ought I act in a way that is universally good and right, that is, regardless of any given context? He initially poses the ethical question of action on an existential and pragmatic level. Action is a problem of immediate creative sensibility. Sensibility is divided into "sense" or the "faculty of intuition in the presence of an object"and "imagination" or "intuition without the presence of an object" (Kant 1978b, 15) But imagination is also an impediment to knowledge and so his treatment of it is further divided in terms of its different roles in logic and metaphysics *(The Critique of Pure Reason)* and taste and genius *(The Critique of Judgement)*. In the realm of practical reason he retreats from the specifically creative sensibility to an a priori form of explanation that downgrades the sensual impulse in favor of a universal rule for all action.

One of the most intriguing ethical problems that Kant thought through using the Categorical Imperative is to know how humans might ethically consummate a natural sexual inclination toward one another. Kant defines sexual appetite as a universal inclination we have for enjoying another human being's sex. Sexuality per se "is not an inclination which one human being has for another as such, but is an inclination for the sex of another" (1963, 164). He calls this appetite for another human being "the sixth sense." Acting on such an appetite means turning the other into an object of impulse. Polygamy, concubinage, prostitution, bestiality, and incest are some of the forms of sexual practice that Kant gives as examples that deviate from the Categorical Imperative. All violate the notion of the person by separating human and sexual love, or by exploiting the other (the object of sexual inclination or possession) as simply a means and not an end. According to Kant, the sexual inclination toward another can only be exercised by all genders ethically should the sexual act with the other be achieved under the umbrella of the monogamous marriage contract. "Sexual love makes of the loved person an Object of appetite; as soon as the appetite has been stilled, the person is cast aside as one casts away a lemon that has been sucked dry" (1963, 163). Sexual love needs to be combined with "human love" and placed under the construct of rights over the body in order to escape degrading the other person. Only when both partners have the same full rights of access to each other's bodies can one actually give oneself up or abandon oneself in order to get oneself back (1963, 167). Thus, it is only through a contract of marriage rights that we might exercise our sexual impulse without violating the Categorical Imperative.

We see in the above example that Kant grasps an important aspect of the creative dimension of Eros. One risks the most intimate and vulnerable parts of the self as one exercises the sixth sense. One abandons one's body to the other in order to get oneself back. Kant leaves an absolute freedom to the creative impulse and gives no prescription as to how sexual behavior should be practiced between consenting (married) adults. There is no code regarding how the consummation of the sexual act should be exercised. This is surprising given the conservative, not to mention the implicitly homophobic, impression we are left by his definition of the monogamous marriage contract. Still, as contemporary actors we have to come to an understanding about the values of intimacy, fidelity, friendship, and trust. The relation between these values and the uses of pleasure leave us with coeval ethical dilemmas; that is, dilemmas that occur across different societies and epochs. Kant's universalist solution is perhaps no longer our solution and yet, the dilemma of the objectification of the other would seem to remain.

One of the most obvious changes that distances us from Kant's discussion of action and Eros is that the legal consensus he had in mind is no longer held as a universal criterion for entering into sexual relations. On the other hand, in the era of safe sex, most would agree that it is at the very least mutually respectful and a sign of good will to fully disclose one's sexual life history before engaging in sexual relations. In this sense an a priori element continues to dominate the contemporary normative approach to sex albeit in a prudential rather than ethical form. A second factor that has been transformed since Kant's time is the growth of concubinage in the form of common law marriages. On the other hand, these relations are also legal contracts and therefore continue to provide something of the legal definition Kant insisted on in terms of "grounding desire" in the rule of law. Indeed, despite thirty years of so-called sexual revolution, kinship patterns in Western societies remain overwhelmingly monogamous and patrilineal. But perhaps the most important and most obvious change since Kant is the radical relativization of cultural values on a global scale. For many, this change leaves any kind of universal formal claim in doubt. Deontological or duty bound ethics are considered to be limited by an overreliance on transcendental universals that can be criticized as being anchored in either ethnocentrism or authoritarianism. Here the critiques of Kantian philosophy, along with the rejoinders to critiques, are simply far too numerous for us to go into in any depth.

Common criticisms of Kant's philosophy argue that the three postulates that underlie the general theory of practical reason cannot be empirically demonstrated and so the levels of the Categorical Imperative remain formalist abstractions with little concrete validity (Habermas 1990, 195–215; Benhabib 1991, 334–346). Consequently, deontological or duty bound ethics are considered to be limited by an overreliance on practical reason that borders on a form of (patriarchal) authoritarianism. For Kant, the postulates are deduced as necessary prerequisites for both individual and collective existence and in order to establish reverence for moral law. Yet, the existence of actors or collectivities remains distanced from Kant's theory of them. By driving a wedge between knowledge and experience he presents a philosophy that almost eliminates the possibility of a more direct understanding of the interpersonal basis of action even though he frees philosophy from metaphysics—at least enough to establish the relative autonomy of the zones of action that both positivist and critical sociologists would go on to explore to this day.

Weber: Action, Ethics, and Eros

Late nineteenth-century neo-Kantian philosophers either looked for ways to bring the theoretical, ethical, and aesthetic spheres of human activity back together again, as in the Marburg School led by Cohen, or sought to further differentiate them into what Weber, following the southwestern school led by Windelband and Rickert, would come to call "the value spheres of culture," thereby designating the new object domains of science: technology, law, the media, etc. As Wolfgang Schlucter describes the intellectual climate at the time: "The desire for a new value synthesis was everywhere. One no longer was willing to live without it. The fact that one has to live without it, if one wants to be honest with oneself, was what Weber had taught in 'Science as vocation'" (Schlucter 1996, 44). Max Weber is often charged with carrying Kantian epistemology into the discipline of sociology. This is sometimes disputed given the influence that Nietzsche is known to have had on his overall approach to the social. I continue to argue as if the original idea of the Kantian influence still dominates, not in order to dispute the edges of nihilism that can be read in Weber's work, but to situate him within the more general neo-Kantian context that even Nietzsche reacted to. In the posthumously published First Volume of *Economy and Society,* appropriately subtitled, *An Outline of Interpretive*

Sociology, Weber defines the question of social action as all those acts that take into account the behavior of other actors given their specific orientations to social relations. His sociology of social action is backed by a double ethics of responsibility and conviction that holds that every social actor can find their daemon, or personality, if they follow the calling that emerges from their choice of values. Hence, Weber also posits action as a creative impulse but like Kant, and unlike Nietzsche, he downgrades the theoretical status of the creative impulse to its a priori form of conviction and responsibility.

Weber's well-known reservations against historicist voluntarism and positivist objectivism strengthened the original Kantian distinction between the natural and cultural sciences. His *verstehen* sociology both continues a kind of Kantian epistemology but also contradicts Kant's original understanding of the way in which practical reason requires a universalizable dimension for social life to be possible. Weber's pivotal Kantian assumption is that reality contains an infinite number of elements but that the human mind is only capable of grasping a limited number of these elements. The social actor abstracts those elements that are meaningful. Those meaningful elements, abstracted from the infinite number of elements in empirical reality, are chosen on the basis of the presuppositions of the actor. In other words, the meaningful elements are chosen because they have significance for the actor, or as Weber suggests, are "value-relevant." Hence, prostitution, concubinage, bestiality, and incest are types of social action that fit certain orientations to social norms in highly specific contexts.

Modern societies are composed of conflicting value spheres and the mark of modernity is that the juridical problem of right and wrong becomes an autonomous sphere unto itself. Though the legal and the ethical spheres are autonomous, they do overlap and influence each other. Our value judgments about actions can be made more or less objective but they are not universally objective and they cannot be applied to all situations. For Weber, universal objectivity is claimed in both the domains of the law and the ethical. At the same time, social actions are valid only given the empirical context and subjective valuation that we lend to them. "Action is instrumentally rational *(zweckrational)* [in either ethical or extraethical modes], when the end, the means, and secondary results are all rationally taken into account and weighed" (Weber 1978, 26).

While Weber's debt to Kant's invention of modern epistemology and the analytic status of concepts seems fairly direct, it does remain a matter of some debate as to whether or not Weber's sociology and ethical philosophy remains strictly Kantian. Indeed, part of Weber's genius is that he embraces Kant's original separation of experience from knowledge but his philosophy also includes a more contextual element of interpretation. Weber has it both ways, as can be seen in his classic definition of sociology as "a science concerning itself with the interpretive understanding of social action and thereby with a causal explanation of its course and consequences" (Weber 1978, 4). Similarly, in his famous essay on "Science as Vocation," he implicitly upsets Kant's universal category by posing a classic ethical duality concerning the distinction between the political and pedagogical duties of the teacher. The professor is doing a good job when political convictions are not imposed on students but also when the professor succeeds in getting students to look at "inconvenient facts" as well as convenient ones (Weber 1946).

Weber's ethics should be understood as going beyond Kant in better balancing an ethics of conviction with an ethics of responsibility. The ethics of responsibility includes a commitment to act on the basis of duty, whereas the ethics of conviction is more committed to ultimate values and to following the calling that comes from the choice of those values. Following such a path leads the individual to become a personality: finding your daemon is the final element of Weber's ethics.

Weber's ethics include the idea of the singular value-orientation but also suggest a serious consideration of alternative values and ethical possibilities that need to be chosen from amongst possible ultimate choices. Kant's Categorical Imperative is also bridged to this version of ethics inasmuch as he grounds the universal principle in the assumption that an individual can think for herself or himself, can also think from the standpoint of everyone else, and can think consistently. Neither Kant nor Weber develop their ethics on the dialogical foundation that this principle implies though both point to the need for dialogue as the main mechanism for resolving conflict between competing value orientations. Hence, Weber never develops his theory of social action in terms of answerability even though it is derived in part from an analysis of how the actor would respond given certain value orientations (Schlucter 1996, 99–101).

In Weber's defense, it is quite true that in his essay on "The Meaning of Ethical Neutrality in Sociology and Economics," he directly addresses Kant's Categorical Imperative and shows that it is not merely a formalist abstraction as critics charge. Here, Weber does not put into question the empirical or subjective validity of the Categorical Imperative; rather, he tries to flesh out even further the substantive grounds uncovered by Kant's original position. The example concerning the consummation of a sexual inclination is treated by Weber not as a way of understanding any universal norm of action but as a way of further cataloguing the spheres of possible action as an interrelated problem in the theory of value. Weber sees Kant's moral critique of objectification as a deeper theoretical revelation of other value spheres. He argues that the importance of Kant's maxim is that, at a deeper level, it also indicates that "autonomous, extra-ethical spheres" do exist and can be delineated from normative, ethical spheres and that, therefore, "different degrees of ethical status may be imputed to activity orientated towards extra ethical values" (1949, 17). That we treat each other as means is in fact a very widespread and even common type of rational-purposive social action in modern society. Weber would agree without passing judgment that such actions should be considered success-orientated rather than morally-practically-orientated. "Value-rational action may thus have various different relations to the instrumentally rational action. From the latter point of view, however, value-rationality is always irrational" (1978, 25).

Arguing this way, Weber does not exactly stand Kant on his head. Nor does he lead us to an absolute normative theory about how we might consummate sexual inclinations ethically. Instead, he points to the necessary foundations for a theory of normative action under pluralistic conditions. Meaning is not simply deduced from an ultimate belief. Rather, meaning is made meaningful against other meanings. In other words, the ethical and the extra-ethical are conditioned by contingent value orientations. Weber's special twist is that specific elements are meaningful only because of the axiological orientation of the actor. All social action is meaningful in the sense that it involves taking into consideration the purpose, motives, and values of other actors (Weber 1978, 4).

In Weber's sociology, concepts of normative social action are orientated to time in either a rational mode or in a more subjective or passionate one. All social action takes place between these extremes. A sexual inclination that is a pure stimulus response is not a foundation of social action because it is not motivated by a consideration of the behavior of other social actors. An action based in the erotic sphere, though, might become a social action. Weber addresses this distinction in a section on eroticism in his essay "Religious Rejections of the World and Their Directions" in which he distinguishes between the primitive class of sexual inclinations and the sublimated erotic interest (1946, 344). Eroticism comes from the sublimation of sexual desire.

Sublimation suggests a division between the interests of a rational calculation of sorts and a direct physiological stimulus response. The former is closer to the domain of social action, the latter is not. Social actions come from working through the instrumental or emotional interests of the actor. Eroticism as an inner expression of an emotional interest is autonomous from any institutional representation and, hence, defining the erotic as a form of objectification or power does not address its immanent meaning as a social action.

Put another way, erotic love is a category of the emotional type of social action for Weber because it can be separated from the body even though it is of the body. In a way, for Weber and even more so for Simmel, one of the purest forms of sociability is located in the erotic. Specifically, Weber sees the erotic interest in sociability as an inner-directed action that follows from the ethics of responsibility and conviction, an action that implies both the subjective anticipation of response and the construction of the other as means. Eroticism, then, as Weber links it to the inner-erotic and the inner-directed action, is much more a wish for a response to our own intimate self than the objectification of the other through power.

Once again, Weber points us to an ethics of answerability that opens onto dialogue but for Weber actions are not defined as social because they can be answered back, as is the case in dialogue. Actions are social because on some level they can be separated from the other's value sphere and behavior. We can plot either overtly or passively to settle our accounts with someone in the future, who has betrayed us in the past, perhaps because they treated us as a means and not an end. Traditional, absolutist, and emotional types of social action are less calculating than rational-purposive types but each fits within the general definition of social action. This does not mean the basis of action is purely voluntarist and yet neither is it entirely determined by social structure. The paradox is that the social actor moves toward a norm that he or she posits even as the norm has already been posited through previous practices. Choosing the value sphere of ascetic Protestantism, for example, implies a set of responsibilities, the undertaking of building a particular personality, and the assumption of a particular approach to Eros.

I have argued that while Weber leaves us with a fairly clear definition of a monologic and cognitive ethics of conviction and responsibility, the dialogic ethics of answerability is left relatively underdeveloped. Though I should note that the dialogic mode can be discerned in Weber's sociology of law where he might argue that one should only act on the conviction that their action could be made into a law that could, in turn, be legitimated by legislation following a parliamentary debate. In this example, though, we can see the absurd limits of Kant's third level of the imperative seen from a phenomenological point of view. Is there any way to think about the dialogic dimension of the "individual law," in Simmel's sense, in a way that does not fix itself outside the context of immediate social action? This is only one difficulty of arriving at a version of a dialogic ethics of everyday life. Another issue we have hinted at is that while Weber is indebted to Kant's epistemology he also subverts Kant's philosophy by stretching his arguments to their logical limits. I want to argue though that Weber does not go far enough and that we need a more radical revision of Kant's theory of action. The addition of the fourth postulate (defined in chapter 4) is the key to breaking through to a more dialogic ethics.

Bakhtin: The Fourth Postulate and Body-Dialogue

The young Bakhtin gives us a definition of action similar to Kant's, Weber's, and Habermas's in that it is also defined as a process of taking responsibility to be yourself, but Bakhtin's understanding of action also differs from theirs. His twist is that ethical action is more than submitting to duty, obeying the law, and overcoming inclination as with Kant. It is also more than following a calling or choosing from rational, emotional, or traditional value orientations as with Weber, and it is something other than Habermas's mutual understanding through communicative actions. The ethical act or deed is more than rational for Bakhtin, *it is also answerable.*

Like Weber, Bakhtin follows a path that is flanked by early-twentieth-century neo-Kantianism but unlike Weber he is also influenced by the linguistic turn in the twentieth century. He was in fact one of the first thinkers to join the critique against both Humboldt's "individualistic subjectivism" and de Saussure's "abstract objectivism." Previous chapters demonstrated that Bakhtin, in fact, steers a narrow analytic course between the philosophies of consciousness and of language in the twentieth century—touching base in both but belonging to neither. His critique of linguistic formalism accompanies his shift away from Kant's ethics to a more existential position. In his first writings he develops the related problem motifs of the personalist ethics of being yourself in the context of the growing relativity of values; of the aesthetics of the self-other or author-hero relation in everyday life and in works of literary art; and of the dialogic work inherent to the whole sphere of culture and action. Before concluding I want to comment further on each of these motifs and situate them in his more radical revision of Kant's epistemology and ethics.

As chapter 4 argued, Bakhtin's assumption regarding the fourth postulate comes out of the larger neo-Kantian context. A central snag in both Kant's and Weber's epistemologies is that we can never know all of the object we are studying, but only those parts of the object that are most significant to us. In other words, we can never know the thing-in-itself. We can only construct a concept of what it should be or might be like. The fourth postulate argues for the necessary faith in the existential animateness of other egos and the possibility of knowing the in-itself. What I want to argue is that it follows from this postulate that the theoretical approach to understanding social action takes on a series of implications that are dialogical and ultimately transcultural. Each of Bakhtin's problem motifs can be seen as an attempt to deepen these dialogic and transcultural implications, which in turn shift the emphasis away from a transcendental synthesis of knowledge and analytic concept formation to a need to address the creative side of any ethical action. The fourth postulate rejoins the spheres of ethics and aesthetics because it poses as a criterion a direct engagement with the other. Bakhtin no longer limits the aesthetic to Kant's problem of the judgment of taste but he still defines it through a philosophical anthropology that seeks to shape parts of objects into wholes. In one of his very last works, Kant also proposed a philosophical anthropology that would allow moral privilege to the other, but he conceived of the problem in strictly formalist terms (1978a).

Bakhtin differs fundamentally from Kant and Weber in that he shifts the whole problem of the will to the plane of answerability. Kant's question, what can I do? becomes for Bakhtin, how should I act toward this other "I"—this other emotional-volitional orientation— and in what aesthetic form can we consummate this action? In other words, Bakhtin asks: How should I act, not because of rules or the expectation of a duty founded in my own subjectivity, but from my own will, my own striving; not, then, because of an a priori interest that orients my actions but rather: *how should I act given the imaginary, but not fictional, subjectivity of another who can answer me back?* It is hard to overstate the importance of this argument for Bakhtin's version of a strong voluntarist, yet postmetaphysical, ethics of alterity.

In *Toward a Philosophy of the Act* Bakhtin presents a philosophy of Being as an event of answerability in which the actor must take personal responsibility to be herself or himself and thus resist pretending to be someone else. This notion comes close to Weber's idea of finding your daemon. Also like Weber, Bakhtin suggests that humans must overcome all kinds of value diversity and relativity in order to become themselves. With Simmel, he defines Being as singular and once-occurrent and so the event-of-Being is also seen to precede any kind of essence or identity thinking. In existentialist jargon, this means that race, sex, gender, or ethnicity are cultural essences that are only constructed after I act from my non-alibi in Being. Bakhtin puts it this way: "It is only my non alibi in Being that transforms an empty possibility into an actual answerable act (through an emotional-volitional referral to myself as the one who is active)" (Bakhtin 1993, 42).

Unlike Weber and Kant, however, for Bakhtin taking the responsibility to be myself through others is the same process in art as it is in life. This does not mean that Bakhtin follows Nietzsche's and Scheler's path to theorize a politics of resentment or the aestheticization of life. Nor does it mean that he reduces art to the status of a mere reflection of the social. Like Weber, the young Bakhtin is keenly interested in the unique character of cultural meanings and the processes that bring them to fruition. Bakhtin also takes up an axiological or "point of view theory" he calls exotopy, or the theory of an excess of seeing. Where Bakhtin differs from Weber is over the meaning of the relation between the points of view and how they exist both through and outside one another. The way in which the self conceives the other, or the author creates the hero, is always from a position outside the other. This "outsidedness" gives the advantage of an excess of seeing that accounts for the crossover or doubling process of the self-other relation. The self-other relation is doubled in the sense that each of us sees the Other from outside and each of us has the advantage of a point of view above and over that which the Other might have on herself or himself.

We need to remember that for Bakhtin action requires something more than simply taking into account the behavior of others. Again, action involves a normative dimension that is emotionally and volitionally orientated toward another axiological position that can answer back. An understanding of the creative dimension of the act, which the young Bakhtin is reaching for, can only be achieved by balancing the need to consummate or complete an interpersonal act between two or more individuals with the unfinalizable principle of self-other relations. To achieve this he considers a whole series of crossover or transgredient relations. In other chapters we have encountered examples of transgredient relations that Bakhtin works with across his writings, including the gift of the soul to the other, the whole sphere of transgredience between self and other, and between inner and outer body images that come from the excess of seeing. It is this last relation that I now want to compare to similar ideas in Weber and Kant.

Bakhtin's early discussions of the body dismiss sexual inclination as being either problematic or as being interesting from the point of view of aesthetics or ethics. He considers the sexual approach (carnal desire, pleasure, gratification) to the other's body as aesthetically nonproductive. In such a case the other's outer body is simply appropriated in the inner body. "This merging into one inner flesh is an ultimate limit toward which sexual attitude tends in its purest form." On the other hand, for Bakhtin, there is no pure sexual inclination that is not "complicated by aesthetic moments." In his later work on carnival, he privileges a pre-Socratic shift to an ethics of bawdy, scatological instincts rooted in Dionysian traditions. In *Rabelais and His World*, he demonstrates how such actions are confined to a specific and unique time and tradition in the culture of laughter.

In both his earliest writings and in the Rabelais book Bakhtin understands the inner-outer body relation as a form of deep sociability. He sees the relation between the inner and the outer body as transgredient in the same sense as the self-other relation. "My own body is, at its very foundation, an inner body, while the other's body is, at its very foundation, an outward body" (1990, 47). When we see our outer body in the mirror "we invariably attitudinize a bit . . . giving ourselves one expression or another that we deem to be desirable" either according to our own value judgment or according to our anticipation of the other's evaluation and what we might feel about what they might think. "We evaluate our own exterior not for ourselves but for others through others" (1990, 33). In the same vein, when I touch my exterior body it is not the same as when someone else touches it. "It is only the other who can be embraced, clasped all around, it is only the other's boundaries that can all be touched and felt lovingly. . . . Only the other's lips can be touched with our own" (1990, 41). This is the living space "that has the character of an aesthetic event . . . the outward image of a human being can be experienced as consummating and exhausting the other, but I do not experience it as consummating and exhausting myself" (1990, 42).

Bakhtin ties his examples of body doubling to an ethics of responsibility that begins with the individual struggle to be herself or himself but always in a relation with another. This is an important difference from Weber's ethics of responsibility, which sees the individual as striving for authenticity in the inauthentic world of instrumental reason. For Bakhtin, the individual actor is somewhat decentered and always in an intersubjective relation.

Bakhtin's philosophy of the act has a much stronger phenomenological orientation than one finds in Weber's sociological definition of social action. At the same time, Bakhtin arrives at his understanding of action by taking the critique of Kant's formalism to a new level without dismissing the latter's original postulates regarding immortality, the existence of God, and individual freedom. On yet another level, Bakhtin extends Weber's theory of social action by taking into account not simply the behavior of others but the answers that other actors might give should one act in a way that is consistent with his or her own once-occurrent Being.

I have shown that Weber's sociology goes beyond Kant by being more Kantian than Kant. He argues for value-free explanations of action but, unlike Kant, his argument problematizes the subjective valuation of the actor. Following the fourth postulate and Simmel's individual law, Bakhtin takes Kant's universal question, "How should I act?" and transforms it into the question, "How should I act given the animated existence of other imagined but not necessarily fictional actors who can answer me back?" Bakhtin problematizes the larger question of answerability so as not to lose sight of the ontological grounds on which action unfolds. Weber has one hand on the ontological pulse of the social actor and one on the brake of the determining interest. He is mainly focused on how actors overcome irrational ontic experience through objective understanding. In contrast, Bakhtin proposes a general outline of culture as a dialogic process that builds on the practical problems associated with answerability.

Bakhtin and Weber, in different ways, both remove the wedge that Kant drives between knowledge and experience. Bakhtin challenges what he calls the "theoreticism" that results from the separation of the spheres of knowledge, ethics, and aesthetics and argues that all acts must be understood as being carried out from within the emotional-volitional or axiological positions of acting subjects and not from transcendental or analytic categories. Understanding the other's coeval and equal existence, from Kant's point of view, can only be a formalist understanding of how it should be, or what it should be like. With respect to Kant's formalism, Bakhtin argues a much stronger critique than Weber is prepared to make, for in Bakhtin's eyes Kant's theory of action can only ever be an abstract and normative understanding of how, or what, action should be.

Bakhtin suggests that cognitive psychology is another example of this kind of theoreticism. While psychology purports to study the uniqueness of a subject's experience of an object, the experience itself is not studied from its axiological position. It looks to get the "inner experience to another state of yet-to-be health" (Bakhtin 1990, 114). By extending Bakhtin's examples of theoreticism we could characterize much of *verstehen* sociology as seeking to explain how the self, or ego, steps over to the significant and generalized other, or superego (the group), without explaining how the self then returns back to the I-for-the-self to complete interpersonal consummation. Weber's sociology relies on deepening the paradox of the already-made social actor as a type that has no existence outside of social construction. In this respect, Weber's theory of knowledge is yet another form of the transcendental argument. In other respects, however, neither Weber nor Bakhtin reads society as being founded on an ultimate ideal unity. On the contrary, both understand society as a site of polyphony, conflict, and domination whose unity is that which is always "yet-to-be-attained." This thick dialectical inversion of the real and the possible redirects normative theory to a focus on the always illusive creative dimension at the heart of the act.

Eros and Action Today

Because Eros is linked to both objectification and sociability—the capacity to maintain intimacy through association—it is seen as a principal element in the construction of uncertain relationships among modern individuals, society, and culture. Simmel defines sociability in the following: "While all human associations are entered into because of some ulterior interest, there is in all of them a residue of pure sociability or association for its own sake" (Simmel 1949, 186). For Bakhtin, this residue of pure sociability is itself a transgredient process and a creative result of the "gift." In this duality, the value that sociability possesses through the answerable act (in realms ranging from the erotic to the economic) has the potential to shape our critical and creative relation with the world around us (Pinter and Nielsen 1990).

Social scientists have been working on the shifts in sociability for over a century. What happens to cultures when one society comes into contact with another? Or, when the foundations of a peasant social structure disappear into contemporary formations? Or, when the traditional can no longer hide in the cracks of modernity because of the cynical folklorization of the last trace of its value? Shifts from *gemein-schaft* to *gesellschaft*, from mechanical to organic solidarity, from rural to urban, from symbolic to sign-based cultures, and from face-to-face contact to serialization are only a few of the concepts addressing the questions of sociability and the place of intimacy and Eros in cultures in transition.

There appear to be signs everywhere pointing clearly to the uniqueness to our own time. This uniqueness derives, in part, from a peculiarity evident in the thesis that our society, as a whole—with all its loopholes, appears less capable of maintaining intimacy between and amongst its members. Given this, Kant's solution to the dilemma of ethically consummating a sexual association via the marriage contract has become as foreign to many modern people as many modern values would be for him. On the other hand, even the most telling feminist critiques of the objectification of intimacy and eroticism in contemporary culture, often only indirectly address its presence in "once-occurrent Being" (Nussbaum 1999). The erotic is defined relationally: a political horizon is used in an explanation of eroticism (Warneke 1999). Is this not yet another form of transcendental theoreticism? Defining the erotic as a form of power or as a field of reification misses an immanent understanding and so risks dismissing eros by reducing it to instrumental interest. Both Weber (1995a) and Simmel (1984) were opposed to defining the erotic in relation to the political, and ultimately to the moral and ethical economies of culture. The erotic must first be located in its specific practice, and in its creatively dialogical relation to emancipation and to domination, as well as its immanent ability to construct dynamic practices. Asking what is good about objectification and what is bad parallels the question about good and bad power. This means that the autonomy of erotic forms is open to analysis apart from gender and sexuality and from the political horizon accompanying it.

Eros today is a principal element in the construction of uncertain relationships; its meaning is vague and subject to ceaseless variation. It is, in other words, implicated in the modern crisis of disciplines that claim to be able to reflect accurately on the integrity of individual and collective life in the everyday world (Pinter and Nielsen 1990). I want, now, to retrace how the specific modernity of this crisis can be better seen through a comparison of the complementary and contradictory theories of the subject put forth in George Herbert Mead's and Bakhtin's theories of action.

6

Reflexive Subjectivity

(Mead-Bakhtin)

Interest in a systematic and comparative discussion of Bakhtin and George Herbert Mead has been growing in recent years as Bakhtin's elaborate interdisciplinary scholarship and special place in Russian intellectual history becomes better known and as Mead's place in American philosophy and sociology continues to be better understood (Koczanowicz 2000; Joas 1997). As we have seen in previous chapters, Bakhtin's project shifts from a personalist ethics of action to an aesthetic theory of self-other relations as a problem of authorship and to a general dialogic theory of language and culture. Mead's project begins in an encounter with idealist philosophy out of which he helps contribute to the founding of American pragmatism and goes on to build a sociological theory of the self in opposition to behaviorist psychology. The issue of authorship for both Mead and Bakhtin remains complicated from the point of view of the systematic study of their texts. The most influential of Mead's books, *Mind Self and Society,* was put together from students' notes. At least three books written by members of Bakhtin's circle are claimed by some to have been written by Bakhtin himself. Despite these thorny debates over authorship, I want to examine how, on certain points at least, their approaches can be thought through in a mutually reinforcing manner.

My argument is that while Mead and Bakhtin differ in terms of disciplinary and philosophical orientations, and while neither is known for his contribution to political theory, their respective theories of reflexive subjectivity, or of how the subject recognizes itself by looking back on its actions, are mutually reinforcing and, as such, provide an interesting theoretical opening for a discussion on the dialogic nature of the political subject—a theme I propose to develop in the final chapters of the book. Each approach is built on the concepts of sympathy and dialogue, which are in turn rooted in both libertarian and communitarian traditions. For Mead, the self becomes itself by learning to put itself in the place of others. For Bakhtin, the self steps across to co-experience the other's subjectivity and then returns to its own interior position to consummate the act. For Mead, the "I" becomes a "Me" by internalizing the general attitudes of others. For both, the community is a source of solidarity and a threat to individuality; and only the community can provide the linguistic resource for a symbolic or dialogical understanding. From their positions, to say that the self is social, or that the personal is political, risks an error of the most vulgar sociological reductionism if the social and the personal are not defined as processes occurring through dialogue. As Bakhtin says, "[O]nly a dialogic and participatory orientation takes another person's discourse seriously, and is capable of approaching it both as a semantic position and as another point of view" (1984a, 64). The community is the source for a variety of points of view but it can also fuse the word of the one with that of another and become closed off, monologized. The search for a balanced understanding of the community, as a source of political difference and as a source of solidarity, underlies Mead's theory of radical democracy and informs the background assumption of Bakhtin's signature concept of dialogism, that is, the hybrid semantic infrastructure that comes out of the clash of different voices or points of view.

Mead's and Bakhtin's projects can thus be seen as making a unique contribution to the reflexive theory of the subject as an actor in a political community that remains useful to contemporary theorists, provided that three kinds of problems are taken into consideration: 1) looking back on the subject of the subject or historically situating the problem of subjectivity is itself a theoretical position that needs to be clarified; 2) looking back on the subject also suggests that the experience of the subject can only be referred to as something that has already happened and yet remains unfinished; and 3) this same aspect of unfinalizability needs to be theorized when looking back on the subject of the political. This chapter focuses on a presentation of the first two problems and develops the latter in the final chapters.

The first problem refers to the assumption that not all aspects of classical theories are coeval or transgenerational and that, therefore, we need to describe something of the contemporary theoretical sensibility around the concept of the subject and make an argument regarding the appropriateness of joining this sensibility with Mead's and Bakhtin's work. The second problem refers to the various difficulties related to theorizing the subject's immediate experience. The second section of this chapter compares how Mead and Bakhtin theorize reflexivity. Put another way, looking back on the subject is the only way one can become aware of one's own subjectivity and that awareness in turn is rooted in shared solidarity or intersubjectivity. To explore this question of reflexivity and intersubjectivity I show how each thinker might analyze a fictional narrative regarding murder, confession, and the paradox of the individual-community relation from Dostoevsky's *The Brothers Karamazov*. This is done to facilitate a comparative discussion of the way each thinker defines how the subject comes to be self-conscious. The story of Father Zosima's encounter with the confessor is summarized, followed by a discussion of how each thinker might explain the story. But before presenting this comparison a few preliminary remarks concerning the disciplinary and philosophical differences between Bakhtin and Mead need to be stated.

Philosophical and Disciplinary Orientations

In considering the different philosophical backdrop of each theorist's position it is helpful to keep in mind that pragmatism and phenomenology traditionally share a common interest in bringing theory closer to the subject's experience on both the real and imaginary planes (Rosenthal and Bourgeois 1980). On the other hand, the two approaches tend to differ over how to go about constructing an explanation and understanding of experience. Where Mead constructs explanations of practical experience by emphasizing cognitive solutions, Bakhtin does so by emphasizing ethical and aesthetic solutions. He asks the question: How should I act? given the imaginary but not fictional subjectivity of another who can answer me back—however radically different that subjectivity might be from my own? The question, What should I do? becomes for Bakhtin, How should I act toward this other "I," this other emotional-volitional orientation, and in what aesthetic form can we consummate this action? Mead defines action as thinking through practical problems by using significant symbols that elicit the same response in the other as they do in the self. The question, What should I do? becomes for Mead, How do the I and the Me (the interiorized attitudes of the group) think through this action and how might we find agreement between the self and the other regardless of subjective experience in order to consummate the act?

Both Bakhtin and Mead present arguments against Kant's a priori formalism. Mead argues that concepts are not dependent on a priori conditions of the mind itself. Conditions of space and time, ethical postulates, aesthetic judgments, and the categories of quantity and quality that allow thought to occur in a wide variety of modalities (possibility, necessity, etc.) are not dependant on transcendental forms. Following the romantic reaction to the Enlightenment in general, and Hegel's response in particular, Mead situates thought in the unknowable in-itself place of sensuous experience. Forms work out solutions in experience rather than the other way around. "Logic as the romanticists conceived of it," says Mead, "was a dynamic not a static affair, not a simple mapping-out of judgements which we can make because of the forms which the mind possesses, but a process in which these very forms themselves rise." For Mead, thinking is a response to immediate experience. The normative logic, the emotional-volitional content of thought, and the ethical significance of experience is found in the act alone. Intelligence, or thinking, is seen as an interiorized dialogue in which "the passage from percept to concept, is by way of attentive selection and the source of this attentive selection must be found in the act. Knowledge predicates conduct, and conduct sets the process within which it must be understood" (1956a, 4).

Hence, the definition of the subject who is conscious of his or her immediate experience is ambiguous. As Mead says many times, the subject only appears to itself as an object. A key question for Mead, then, is how does the subject become self-conscious? His response is that the subjective "I" can only be grasped as an objective "Me" (Mead 1964, 132). The "I" can only be known after an act is already carried through. The "I" turned into a "Me" is discussed as a theoretical concept and not the actual experience. For Mead, the subject can only be known by referring to action.

In his essay "The Author and the Hero in Aesthetic Activity," Bakhtin presents the cognitive image involved in the shift from the perception of an object to the formation of a concept as a key aesthetic problem. The condition of exotopy is a practical condition in which it becomes possible for us to offer a loving axiological position to another; a teacher to a student, a father to a child, a friend to a friend, a lover to a beloved, an author to a hero (1990, 34). Aesthetic value is derived from the synthesis of the inner and outer body and its external appearance and actions. The synthesis is seen in the creative value that constitutes the self-other gift relation. Only a gift derived from a sympathetic understanding of the hero's "forward looking life" can free the hero so he can experience his I-for-himself.

A sense of creativity is also fundamental to Mead's approach but he does not theorize the question of aesthetic value. For Mead, creativity lies in the intelligent solutions derived from the tension between the I and the me in a given situation. For both Mead and Bakhtin thinking cannot be separated from the body. In his 1903 essay "The Definition of the Psychical," Mead argues against voluntarist, individualist, positivist and "materialist psycho-physical" approaches in nineteenth-century psychology as being rooted in flawed versions of the subject-object and mind-body dichotomy. He points instead toward a theorization of the subject and object of consciousness in terms of corporal, emotional, volitional, and mental reciprocity. His solution is derived from a revision and synthesis of William James' argument for the inverse relation between experience ("soul-theory") and physiology ("brain-theory") and John Dewey's argument that the psychical is a moment of consciousness that constitutes and reconstitutes its object rather than a passive response to stimulus. Mead's social theory of subjectivity begins in the dissatisfaction with one-sided physiological and voluntarist varieties of psychology, and goes on to posit subjectivity in terms of the evolution of the organism or body as well as its formation through symbolically mediated communicative action.

It thus bears repeating that although Mead and Bakhtin see the fact that we can abstractly distinguish our self from our body, neither develops a mind-body dualism. For Bakhtin, a solution to the self-other relation can never be fully achieved as there is always the loophole created by subjectivity. One can never be co-natural with objects. Mead's social definition of the self helps explain how a subject becomes a subject, which is to say, how the subject becomes an object, but it does not get at the aesthetic proceess of "authoring" that Bakhtin pursues.

Between Consciousness and Language:
The Ambiguity of Experience

Keeping in mind the differences in emphasis and in philosophical orientation I would like to turn attention to the first problem proposed in the introduction. This problem has to do with looking back on the subject from the point of view of theorists who did not have to face the radical erasure of the concept that has today become common-place. Poststructuralism is often credited with the original pronounce-ments concerning the death of the subject. The paradox, though, is that studies in the archeology of knowledge, discourse, and power al-ways return to theories of subjection *(assujetissement)*. Yet this theory of subjection assumes the prior existence of a subject who acts as a conduit; otherwise power could not be exercised. Niklas Luhmann ad-dresses this paradox in his critique of the concept of intersubjectivity. He speaks of his embarrassment with this "dead end way of thinking" and questions all those who continue to speak of intersubjectivity when there is no longer any empirical basis for a theory of a unified subject (1995). Luhmann accounts for reflexivity in the subject-object model relation by substituting the terms systems theory for the subject and environment for the object. The theoretical ability to reduce com-plex environments is characterized as a systemic achievement. The au-topoietic ability of systems to reflect on their own structures and produce change within their own unity is the way in which systems react to the complexity of environments. Yet, like poststructuralism's critique of subjection, Luhmann still speaks of the "dehumanizing" aspects that result from dysfunctional systems integration.

Critical theorists continue to use the concept of intersubjectivity but argue that the modern subject is decentered. Habermas (1992) suggests that modern social divisions overburden individuals with con-flicting demands leading to the disintegration of conventional identity, creating both the condition for emancipation and the loss of self. Michael Walzer (1994) argues that we need to contrast thick hierar-chical theories of the self developed in moral philosophy, psycho-analysis, and social criticism with thinner, less stratified theories that problematize the subject as internally divided by its interests and roles, different identities and ideals and values that belong to each of its parts. Charles Lemert (1994) presents an equally compelling plea for a dark and light distinction in the theory of the self so that new kinds of subjectivity might be brought into the view of sociological analysis.

Mead and Bakhtin theorize a dialogical relation between subjects according to a subject-object model that was posited in the early phase of the linguistic turn. Consequently, their theories of the subject, and of action, maintain a relation to the philosophy of consciousness that makes contemporary social theorists nervous. Strictly speaking, Mead and Bakhtin rarely used the word *subject* and never used the words *in-tersubjectivity* or *identity*. Although the term *practical intersubjectivity*, as Hans Joas points out, is not used by Mead, it is the term that perhaps best characterizes "the core of his thought" (1997, 14). Bakhtin's term for intersubjectivity is the co-being of being or *sobytie bytiia*. Bakhtin's and Mead's works can thus also be seen as rooted in the postmetaphysical transition in which contemporary theorists are engaged in that both contributed, at an early stage, to an understanding of a subject constituted in and through language. They are both thinkers who helped provoke a clear break into the philosophy of language (as Habermas, Joas, and Honneth correctly argue in the case of Mead), but they are also thinkers who could still listen much more intensely than their contemporary interpreters to the arguments and theories that defined the nineteenth-century philosophy of consciousness. After all, Mead thought he was adding a theory of the self to a sociology that was underdeveloped due to the dubious start Comte gave it when he skipped over psychology in defining the stages of scientific development—skipping, as it where, from biology to sociology. Although Bakhtin is not a sociologist, his theory of culture, and of the self, provides a potentially important support to sociologists who seek to continue an in-between kind of theorizing. Both developed a theory of the subject that could be thought of as falling between the decentered-thin-light version and the centered-thick-dark variety. Following William James, Mead unpacks the definition of the self, showing it to contain an "I" and a "Me," while also adding his concept of the generalized other. As we saw in chapter 1, Bakhtin's complex definition of the self includes the I-for-the-self, the I-for-the other, and the other-for-me, to which he later adds the concept of the super-addressee (generalized other). Both understood that the subject takes on multiple roles or identities as he or she becomes herself or himself in a particular community or across different communities.

There are, however, some important differences between Mead and Bakhtin regarding the development of their respective concepts. Where Mead posited a theory of the self that could be distinguished from the body, even though it is of the body, Bakhtin preferred the Latin word *subiectum* (as did Kant) precisely because it does not distinguish between the soul and the (inner)body. To some extent Mead is most famous for his adaptation of the thick Hegelian argument that the subject becomes an other to itself in becoming conscious of itself. He succeeds in synthesizing this idea with pragmatism and posits an original sociology of intersubjective communication (Honneth 1996). Again, Bakhtin follows a path flanked by philosophical idealism and the linguistic turn. His interests shift from an early engagement with philosophical anthropology, ethics, and aesthetics, to a study of the polyphonic novel, a theorization of the social stratification of discourse, or heteroglossia, a study of carnivalization, or the transposition of popular culture into art and a general dialogic theory of the utterance and of speech genres. It helps, then, to keep in mind that Mead and Bakhtin were part of a generation that steered a narrow path between the philosophies of consciousness and those of language, touching base in both but belonging to neither. Yet because both of them develop their theories of the self within the philosophy of consciousness, a second problem has to be addressed.

I am referring here to the difficulty of analyzing the unmediated content of consciousness as experience other than through a description of its most peripheral external aspects. Both thinkers solve this problem by situating the question of consciousness, and its content, in a philosophy of the act rooted in discourse or gesture. Both Mead and Bakhtin caution against theories of experience that do not take seriously this distinction between consciousness and discourse or gesture into consideration. Both argue that the subject cannot be directly represented or communicated in its actual state of experience.

This is an important point, and in order to explain what I mean more clearly I now introduce a comparative discussion of how each theorist might analyze how the subject becomes reflexive in the story recounted by the elder Zosima in Dostoevsky's *Brothers Karamazov*. Thinking through how both Bakhtin and Mead might interpret this story allows us to explain the ways in which each theorist thought about the place of the subject in the community. Dostoevsky's stories often lend interesting insights to the paradox regarding the individual-community relation. Is the murderer's personal and moral crisis about an individual act or is it about the community's inability to create a good subject? Mead helps us understand the impossibility of directly knowing the subject and how the murderer in the story comes to an intense level of self-consciousness. Bakhtin, on the other hand, explains how the character comes to know himself by maintaining his outsidedness to the community and by finding a threshold that allows him to become himself and a member of his community simultaneously.

Bakhtin is drawn to Dostoevsky's art because it provides a sophisticated example of how to create a self-conscious hero, however radically deviant his subjectivity might be. According to Bakhtin, Dostoevsky's small Copernican revolution was to create a hero who could be completely separate from the author. In Dostoevsky's novels not only does the hero have an opinion on the world but on himself as well. It is not possible to create this kind of character by abstracting out elements

from types of personalities. The self-conscious hero absorbs the surrounding socio-characterological features. He looks at himself through
other people's worlds. The other's consciousness is not merely a prop
that lies alongside the hero. The author and hero are not part of the
same representation but they are represented on different noncoinciding planes. The self-conscious hero *must* have the final word on himself:
"All the stable and objective qualities of a hero—his social position, the
degree to which he is sociologically or characterologically typical, his
habitus, his spiritual profile and even his very physical appearance . . .
'who he is,' becomes in Dostoevsky the object of the hero's own intro-
spection, the subject of his self-consciousness; and the subject of the
author's visualization and representation turns out to be in fact a *function* of this self-consciousness" (Bakhtin 1984a, 48).

Murder, Confession, and Community

In Dostoevsky's novel *The Brothers Karamazov*, Zosima, the elder
monk, tells the story of his life as a young man in the army and the
event that inspired him to choose a religious life (Dostoevsky 1990).
The event includes the realization of his own humility and a choice he
makes for life over death. After making a public confession in which
he breaks all codes of conventional military honor—he deliberately
misfires in a duel and places himself at the mercy of his opponent—
a man in the crowd is so moved by the act that at its resolution he
comes forward to ask Zosima if he will agree to see him in his quar-
ters, so that he too may confess his secret.

That night Zosima receives the mysterious guest and the story he
tells gets very involved. Very slowly, over the course of several
evenings, Mikhail tells the story of how he killed his beloved after she
chose another man and what has happened in his life since then.
Slowly, Zosima is convinced about the credibility of the story as the
details begin to outweigh his doubts. And he is struck by the idea that
"crimes committed with extraordinary boldness are more likely to suc-
ceed than others" (305).

The night of the murder, Mikhail climbed up the back of the
house. He knew the servants to be lazy and suspected they would forget to lock the door inside the house that he could access through an
open window. He snuck across the garden, climbed over the fence,
crawled up the back of the house and along the roof until he entered
the attic window. From there he quietly, without making a sound,

walked down the narrow staircase to the unlocked door. He was right about the servants. He entered a hallway leading to her bedroom. The two maids had gone to a party without their mistress`s permission. Mikhail found her asleep alone. With each step he took toward her, his rage overtook him, and finally he plunged a dagger into her heart.

He carefully arranged the evidence in the room so the servants would be suspected. He took only trinkets a servant might take, leaving more valuable items untouched. Her male servant was immediately suspected because the mistress had made it known that she intended to send the servant to the army to fill the quota for the manor. This was assumed to be the motive. The servant had also been seen falling down drunk in the street in front of the house that very night. The police arrested the servant but shortly after he died in prison.

Mikhail was never suspected and now no one ever could suspect him. He gets away with murder but has to live with the fact that the woman he loves is dead. He feels no remorse for the murder but does feel remorse for the servant, and for the trinkets he stole to make it look as if the servant was the murderer. Some time passed and Mikhail married a much younger woman and had three children. He also became a highly successful member of the community, well known for his acts of philanthropy and participation in civic affairs. But he began to have fears about his ability to love his children given his secret. Gradually he has fallen into a deep remorse for the crime. As each year goes by he thinks more and more about the horrible act. Then he begins to have a recurring dream of publicly confessing the crime. Finally, one day after his talks with Zosima, and roughly fourteen years after the crime, he attends a public gathering of his town's citizens and blurts out a confession of what he did. But none of the authorities believe him. They could not imagine how such an upstanding, longtime fellow member of their community could possibly have committed such an act. He comes back to see the assembly again and shows them the artifacts he stole from the murder scene to make it look as if the servant did the deed and convinces them that only the killer could be in possession of such things. Finally, the authorities agree to a trial that will review the case. But Mikhail dies of natural causes five days after the proceedings begin.

Why the Subject Is Behind Us

What is the story about? Is it about the personal, moral crisis of the murderer? Is it about the community's ability to create both a good and an evil subject? Is it an allegory of alienation? Is it about the legacy of the most horrific elements of patriarchy? It could be argued that if Mead and Bakhtin were here with us today, they would argue that Dostoevsky's story is about all these issues. For both Mead and Bakhtin we could say that the murderer is a deviant whose act is possible because he has momentarily lost sight of the generalized other of the community, or the "Me" that acts as a representative of his community. The pure violent impulse of his "I" is only part of the subject of experience. Mead argues that subjectivity also includes the organized response to the community or the "Me." But as we discuss the "I" in Mead's sense we are discussing a theoretical concept and not the experience of the "I." We can only have sympathy for the murderer's moral suffering by putting our self in the place of the murderer and his life history. This is part of what the story is about. The murderer's "I" came to be after his act. We know little of his history other than his motive for murder. The story is about what happens in the act and what happens during and after the act as a way of revealing the character's life history. His "I" cannot be a habit any longer because it is caught in the moral struggle between the "I" and the "Me" to such an extent that his very presence now leaves the moral order of the whole community in doubt. How could such a community not have a procedure in place that would protect its innocent members from such harm?

For Mead, understanding and explaining moral crisis and crime are not fundamentally different because the ethical self is not a neutral self but social and even political. The "Me" disciplines the "I" by holding it back from breaking the law of the community. But the law of the community is not a transcendental universal. The self interiorizes the attitudes of the generalized other across the stages of its development. The shift from playing light games to darker adult forms of interaction involves developing the capacity for sympathizing with the other's position. The good in the act is derived from a practical situation not a transcendental norm. Each act needs to be seen in terms of the mutual conditioning between the individual and the community. "The good does not depend on transcendental ideals of perfection of the self," writes Mead, "nor on the sum of happiness for all, but on the effectiveness of the actor's deeds in the community" (Mead 1968a, 77). For Mead, there are only two possible solutions to an ethical dilemma. Either the subject adapts to the cues in the situation or creates a new solution. The interpretation of an ethical act is found in the practical situation. While the "I" and the "Me" are never actually separated here, it is the creative "I" that acts against the generalized other or the community.

For Mead, looking back on the subject means looking after the act is achieved. The murderer comes to see himself gradually as he looks back on his action. At a certain point in the story it is clear that each moment the murderer does not commit to an act of confession, his conscience—his awareness of himself as an object—refuses to allow him to act out of habit. But if he chooses to confess, his children and wife will be destroyed. Action and non-action are intimately connected. The act is the "I"'s response to the organized attitudes of the group that constitutes the "Me." The non-act is the "Me" thinking about the yet-to-be committed act. As Mead put it in one of his lectures: "If you ask where directly in your experience the "I" comes in, the answer is that it comes in as an historical figure. It is what you were a second ago, that is the "I" of the "Me." It is another "Me" that has to take that role. You cannot get the immediate source of the "I" in the process" (1934, 175). Hence, we only look back on the subject from the point of view of a second "I," a slightly removed "Me," a spokesperson for the self as a type of other.

Action Inside and Outside the Subject

As was seen in chapter 4, Bakhtin's ethical theories are drawn, in part, from Georg Simmel's radical replacement of Kant's universal absolute (Categorical Imperative) with an absolute individual law. Simmel argues that the ought does not come from a universal subject but from the individual I. While Mead and Bakhtin share the common neo-Kantian suspicion of Kant's doctrine of the inability to ever know the thing-in-itself, their reactions to Kant's theory of practical reason are quite different. Both distance themselves from *lebensphilosophie* and other intuitivist approaches and yet, like Simmel, both reject outright the formal notion of the "ought" *(sollen)* as having a status that transcends interpersoanl relations. Both Mead's and Bakhtin's works can thus be read as an attempt to move beyond Kant's formal theory of practical reason. Again, though, their steps differ in important ways.

For Bakhtin, we also look back on the subject from a second position. On the other hand, Bakhtin sees the ambiguity of consciousness in the space between corporal ontology, ethics, and aesthetics rather than between cognition, logic and corporality. Action is more than an intelligent reasoned response to a problem or situation. The act or deed has the two-sided form of answerability. This is a dimension that is very familiar to, and yet also distinct from, Mead's discussion of answerability. Recall that for Bakhtin the two-sided form of answerability includes both a reference to its uniqueness as an event and a more general moral reference. It follows from the fourth postulate regarding faith in the animateness of the other that for Bakhtin, the murderer's suffering could be defined as a result of his inability to reconcile the horrific uniqueness of his act with any general moral reference.

For Mead, too, the murderer suffers because of the struggle between the self and the community, or the "I" and the general attitudes of the group carried by the "Me." But this is not derived from the fourth postulate. In the last instance, the values of the community are the most important force of social adaptation. This is not necessarily the case for Bakhtin. His assumption of the fourth postulate, and the triadic definition of the self, helps explain that, at another level, the murderer's moral suffering is about his inability to join the uniqueness of his act with the general moral content for his overall life history. As a result, he can only join the superaddressee or the chorus of the community in a superficial sense. In the community the I lives "in the other and for the other. . . . In my lived life, I participate in a communal mode of existence, in an established social order, in a nation, in a state, in mankind, in God's world" (1990, 120). In each of these contexts, Bakhtin argues, the I lives life in the category of the other: "I experience, strive, and speak herein the *chorus* of others. But *in a chorus* I do not sing for myself; I am active only in relation to the other and I am passive in the other's relation to me" (1990, 121).

Acts are performed in a context that is relative to day-to-day life, to a universe of social and political values, and to aesthetic and ethical values. Self-consciousness is derived in these contexts but is not reducible to them. Self-consciousness is both the part of the self that seeks autonomy and the part of the self that longs to join the "Me" (I-for-the other). The I-for-the self seeks to be an other for others, as Bakhtin puts it, and "to cast from itself the burden of being the only I in the world" (1990, 116). This is a distinctly Hegelian moment in Bakhtin's phenomenology as others have pointed out (Côté 2000). In *Elements of The Philosophy of Right* Hegel writes:

> Love means in general the consciousness of my unity with another, so that I am not isolated on my own [*für mich*], but gain my self- consciousness only through the renunciation of my independent existence [*meines Fürsichseins*] and through

knowing myself as the unity of myself with another and of the other with me. . . . The first moment in love is that I do not wish to be an independent person in my own right, and that if I were, I would feel deficient and incomplete. . . . The second moment is that I find myself in another person, that I gain recognition in this person [daß ich in ihr gelte], who in turn gains recognition in me. (1991, 199)

This is an internal relation of subjectivity that Mead appears to withdraw from in developing his theory of self-consciousness as the subject reflecting on itself and becoming an object. In other words, for Mead the "I" is an immature version of the "Me." Bakhtin, though, has a way of including both the externally objective and internally subjective relations so as not to reduce the one to the other.

Remember that in Bakhtin's I-for-myself, the I sees an object from the standpoint of a future inner experience. But the I can never see itself except through the mediation of the I-for-the-other or through the other-for-me; that is, self-consciousness is only possible in light of how I think others might look on me or how I might want them to look back on me. The murderer sees the woman he murdered through an objective calculation. For him, she is gathered and fitted as a whole into her outer image, as an object. He responds with rage at her outward actions (her marriage to another). In the beginning, he has no guilt for the act he has committed, only a heartbreak from being separated from his beloved. Seeing another come forward and confess his secret gives the murderer the ethical clue to come forward and begin to transform his I-for-himself into an other-for-others. The act of confession momentarily releases him from moral suffering but it also engenders a new moral dilemma in that he is well aware that harm is going to be visited on his new wife and children because of his act. Here, the murderer experiences his own exterior image through the community (Bakhtin's superaddressee; Mead's generalized other). Yet, he cannot experience all of himself as an object of his community. His outward image cannot be completely cleansed because he cannot join his own life history to a general moral content. In other words, his I-for-himself is not co-natural with the world.

Bakhtin links the cognitive image involved in the shift from the perception of an object, or an action, to the production of aesthetic value. The latter is derived from the synthesis of the inner and outer body as well as external actions and appearance. The inner body is the site of a complete self-conscious awareness whereas consciousness of an external image remains incomplete given that it relies on others to measure an aesthetic value. "The plastic value of my outer body has been as it were sculpted for me by the manifold acts of other people in relation to me, acts performed intermittently throughout my life: acts of concern for me, acts of love, acts that recognize my value" (1990, 49). The I-for-the self resides in the inner body, which "represents the sum total of inner organic sensations, needs and desires that are unified around an inner center" (1990, 47). The I-for-the-self looks back on its "inner center" from the point of view of another. As Bakhtin puts it: "I am not alone when I look at myself in the mirror: I am possessed by someone else's soul" (1990, 33). The murderer gradually comes to look back at his "inner center" from the point of view of the community and his self-consciousness is transformed into self-hatred. In the end, his self-conscious I seeks to be annihilated by the generalized other-for others (the law of the community).

If we withdraw from our analysis to a more general level, a series of convergences and differences between the two approaches to reflexivity are easily identified. For both Mead and Bakhtin, the "Me" is the ethical dimension of the self. While both might agree on this point, each draws quite different conclusions. For Bakhtin, an act is seen to include any thought or deed or sign that is both a once-occurrent and an open-ended event. Mead, on the other hand, is concerned with explaining the process in which symbolic action seeks to provoke the same response in the addressee as it does in the self. While Bakhtin argues, "[W]e must not love others as ourselves, we must love each other and remain ourselves" (Morson and Emerson 1989, 21), Mead suggests: "[W]e cannot be a self without being an other. The human individual is a self only insofar as he takes the attitude of another toward himself. Insofar as this attitude is that of a number of others, and insofar as he can assume the organized attitudes of a number that are co-operating in a common activity, he takes the attitudes of the group toward himself, and in taking this or these attitudes he is defining the object of the group, that which defines and controls the response" (Mead 1956b, 290).

Both are right, given their respective definitions of the self-other relation and thus they offer mutually reinforcing ideas about a self that is built on the concepts of sympathy and dialogue. Mead constructs explanations of practical experience by emphasizing cognitive solutions. Bakhtin asks the question: How should I act given the imaginary but not fictional subjectivity of another who can answer me back? Mead defines action as thinking through practical problems by using significant symbols that call forth the same response in the other as they do in the self. The question "What should I do?" becomes for Mead, "How do the 'I' and the 'Me' find agreement between the self and the other regardless of subjective experience?" Mead argues that thinking and emotional-volitional attitudes do not seek the same kinds of responses. "Thinking, he says, "always implies a symbol which will call out the same response in another that it calls out in the thinker." The emotional part of the act does not always call out in us the response we seek. As Mead puts it: "[T]he person who is angry is not calling out the fear in himself that he is calling out in someone else. . . . We are not frightened by a tone which we may use to frighten someone else" (Mead 1934, 139). The paradox, for Mead, lies in the assumption of the innocence of reason in thought and its capacity for undistorted communication. For Bakhtin, the paradox lies in the relation between the absolutely individual character of the act and its universal moral significance.

Up to this point, I have tried to flush out and contrast Mead's idea of reflexivity as an objectification of the subject and Bakhtin's idea of two-sided answerability as a non-finalizable externally objective and internally subjective process. I began this chapter by trying to limit the discussion of the subject and of subjectivity in terms of two problem motifs. I argued that looking back on the subject of the subject means, in part, that what was appropriate for theorists in another context may or may not be appropriate for us. Next, I considered how the definition of an actor's awareness of his or her subjectivity is a result of looking back on the subject of action. The choice of the Dostoevsky story as an example of reflexivity admittedly biased the comparison toward Bakhtin. Perhaps it was because of his personal circumstances as a thinker out of line with a totalitarian regime that Bakhtin preferred stories about morally corrupt or ethically dubious characters. In contrast, Mead preferred analogies to American baseball when developing his theory of reflexivity.

Although Bakhtin remained apolitical throughout his career it could be argued that his approach is compatible with a particular version of politics. Mead's preference for direct democracy and mutual transnational forms of recognition can be seen to accommodate Bakhtin's concept of two-sided answerability and the ongoing mixtures of multiple, simultaneous values that modern individuals, as well as groups, must navigate. The next chapter looks to extend their positions and considers a third problem regarding the theoretical implication involved in the shift from the micro level of reflexivity to a societal level. Here I propose a dialogic theory of the relation between the particularities of *ethnos* and the universality of *demos* as opposed to their reduction into discrete opposites. I argue that when we look back on the subject of the political we find traces of the same paradox we met in the self-other relation; that is, we find that the relation needs to be thought through as open-ended or unfinalizable.

This brief imminent study and comparison of Mead and Bakhtin reveals that neither develops the theoretical shift from the level of re-flexivity to a normative politics. The value of imminent criticism, how-ever, is not to demonstrate what a theory does not do, but to show what it does, and to suggest how it might be taken a step farther. In the third problem we see that the general theories each thinker develops within his own disciplinary and philosophical orientation direct us to a much needed dialogic theory of the open-ended relation between *ethnos* and *demos*. This is a relation that contemporary debates about citizenship in postnational democracies have tended to separate. Let us move, then, to a discussion about citizenship, national identity, and the nation as we proceed to our third problem motif.

7

CITIZENSHIP AND NATIONAL IDENTITY

In these final chapters I want to move into questioning the way a social theory situated between Bakhtin and Habermas might theorize
an ethics of citizenship and national identity in the contemporary era
of postnational democracy. Whereas Habermas has written extensively
in this field, Bakhtin has left us neither a text on political theory nor a
definition that would clearly demarcate the fields of culture and politics.[1] This means that I will be less focused in the following chapters
on reconstructing Bakhtin's approach to ethics and aesthetics and more
engaged in contrasting it with Habermas and others who argue for a
separation of culture and politics when defining citizenship, national
identity, and especially the nation.

The meaning and parameters of a two-sided form of answerability between the individual's culture and his or her political community have been debated throughout the history of Western and non-
Western societies alike. Citizenship is usually defined in terms of the
relationship an individual has to a political community, or *demos*. Citizenship, however, has also developed another *telos*, which is that membership in a polity also involves sharing and participating in a common
project or identity that has a historical and cultural specificity or
ethnos.[2] Modern civil, political, and social definitions of citizenship
were developed in the West during the eighteenth, nineteenth, and
twentieth centuries respectively (Marshall 1963). Liberal democracies
developed throughout this period under the assumption that the state,
and especially the judicial system, should remain a neutral arbitrator
and force recognizing citizenship as a universal category that privileges
no specific cultural meanings, religious practices, or lifestyles. The

question of the neutrality of the state is one of the most important subjects of debate in contemporary political theory given that in the twenty-first century structures of governance are increasingly having to come to terms with pressures and demands for sustaining cultural identities in an emerging postnational global constellation of political, economic, and social powers. As a consequence, the neutral role of the state as administrator and arbitrator of universal citizenship rights is being reconsidered. In this emerging constellation, nation-states are increasingly forced to share their sovereignty with other global, regional, and transnational institutions; for example, through international and trans-statal adjudication mechanisms and regional agreements such as the European Union and NAFTA.[3]

There is another striking and haunting problem linked to the paradox of citizenship and the neutrality of the state's role in managing postnational identities. Only 20 percent of the world's economic activity takes place in the context of globalization. Most exchange of this international capital occurs accross large metropolitan areas away from peripheral areas inside developed countries and "outside the so-called developing countries all together" (Diekhoff 2000, 23). And yet the cultural and political effects of globalization reach far beyond these confined zones. For the last two hundred years, through the Euro-centered colonization process, almost all formerly non-state societies have been fully encapsulated into a state polity (in the First World, the Second, and the Third). This, as a rule, was done against their will.[4] As a result, most present-day nation-states have to confront the fact that they have imposed a citizenship on non-state peoples and other conquered minorities. Due to the effect of globalization, will the weakened sovereignty of each nation-state continue to provoke a reawakening of the formerly non-state cultures and national minorities now present in their midst? In what form will these new polities emerge? Should we encourage and support movements toward a political re-fragmentation and re-mapping of the world that would better fit its cultural diversity? In what name should the unity of contemporary nation-states and related citizenship rights be preserved, and should it be done against the will of many minority nations in the world? Could it be that the existing federal polities should stop trying to conceive of themselves as constituting nation-states and start to reinvent themselves as more flexible entities? Finally, how could any form of citizenship that does not coincide with the existing cultural fragmentation of the world, not be responsible for some diminishing cultural diversity?

Various aspects of the contemporary discussion on postnational democracy, citizenship, and new national pleas for recognition can be understood using a social theory situated between Bakhtin and Habermas. In order to get a sense of how this might be done, however, I first need to explain the logic for a shift in levels of abstraction from the norms of answerability, which operate on the plane of self-other relations, to those operating on the plane of the *demos* and *ethnos* of nation-states. Addressing the ongoing mixtures of multiple and often contradictory values that modern citizens and nations must navigate is the last and most difficult theme of this book because it requires shifting between very different levels of dialogue: the interpersonal and societal.

Transculturalism is a midlevel concept that helps us bridge the interpersonal and societal and to analyze the shift proposed here. My argument in the first chapters was that if we link the concept of transculturalism to both Bakhtin's ethics and his concept of dialogism and to Habermas's concept of communicative action and discourse ethics, we would be in a position to pose a much broader set of questions regarding national politics and social justice than would be possible should we approach either theorist's position separately. Cultures or representations of cultures enter into contact with one another and take on elements from each other without ceasing to be themeselves on both the interpersonal and societal levels. At the interpersonal level, for both Bakhtin and Habermas, discourse offers the only ethical form of conflict resolution. Different norms are understood by both as different rules of action that actors voluntarily enter. Habermas argues that the transformation of different norms is possible only when procedural access is guaranteed to each other's traditions for criticism and reform. For Bakhtin, norms are a two-sided form of answerability that require both a unique creative moment and a universal moral one. His philosophy of dialogue understands most words as belonging to the "other's" lifeworld, but also as potentially belonging to a community, or communities, of unique individuals. It is worth repeating his argument that when two social discourses meet that are "equally and directly orientated toward a referential object within the limits of a single context [they] cannot exist side by side without intersecting dialogically" (Bakhtin 1984a, 188–189).

Unlike Bakhtin, Habermas argues for a clearly demarcated and normative theorization of the politics of the nation within his equally clarified theoretical definition of society as system and lifeworld. Like many other contemporary political theorists, Habermas argues rigorously against culturally specific, or ethnic, definitions of the nation for both theoretical and historical reasons. This is especially clear in his writings on citizenship and the emerging postnational constellation of nation-states, as we will see further in chapter 8. As chapter 1 demonstrated, although Habermas develops a dialogic approach to communication and the construction of social bonds within lifeworlds, his theory of communicative action quickly evolves out of the space of intersubjective dialogue and into a theory of procedural forms for introducing norms that are guided by fixed rules regarding fairness and justice. His separation of *ethnos* from *demos* is argued against the background of expanding the postconventional moral values that define universal human rights and a purely civic sense of belonging to a political community.[5] He expresses numerous objections to ethnonational conceptions of popular sovereignty that would define the nation in terms of a dialogue among "the people." Synonyms that link "the people" to "the nation" are rejected on the grounds that the political community needs to be organized around a legal, binding constitution that citizens voluntarily adhere to regardless of cultural tradition, kinship, or ethnicity. Any definition that roots national sovereignty in "the people" puts the rights and obligations of all those who do not belong to "the people"—either through kinship ties or common ethnicity—in contradiction to the rights and obligations of their fellow citizens (Habermas 1998a and 2001).

Bakhtin, on the other hand, retains a philosophical anthropology and a theory of discourse that counter Habermas's more one-sided stance on the separation of *ethno*s from *demos*. Earlier chapters demonstrated several pressure points in Habermas's ethical, sociological, linguistic, and aesthetic theories, and led to a deeper examination of the influences on Bakhtin's ethics of two-sided answerability and his shift toward a philosophy of dialogue. Seen through the lens of various critiques and revisions of Kant's transcendental philosophy and ethics it is clear that, for Bakhtin, neither a transcendental definition of the political nor an entirely immanent theory of culture could sufficiently explain the dialogic at a societal level. For in a manner similar to Weber and Habermas (chapter 5), Bakhtin sees society as a decentered site of polyphony and heterglossia whose unity is always "yet-to-be-attained." Finally, I also argued in the last chapter that Mead's pragmatism (and I might add his preference for dialogue through direct democracy and mutual transnational forms of recognition) could be seen to accommodate Bakhtin's earlier concept of two-sided answerability. Still, the question of political theory and a societal level of dialogic analysis remains underdeveloped in both Mead's and Bakhtin's approaches.

The goal of this chapter, then, is to outline the practical grounds for thinking dialogically about the shift that occurs from the analysis of interpersonal relations within culture to the analysis of citizenship and national identity at the societal level. As in the level of interaction where both a unique expression and a universal response are anticipated by the actor, the societal level of interaction also encompases a two-sided answerability that occurs between *ethnos*—the specificity of an historically constructed autonomy of a people or nation—and the *demos*—the multiplicity, diversity, and contingency of the people as a political community in the world of nations. I argue for a dialogical way of thinking about the autonomy of *ethnos* within the *demos* of the nation and for a theoretical logic that does not separate these two spheres into monological opposites. I expand on the shift in analytic levels of abstraction between interpersonal and societal dialogue in the first section and then develop definitions of the concepts of citizenship, identity, and the origins of the nation. My strategy is to proceed from definition of concepts, to a review of well-known sociological and historical definitions of the origins of the nation and nationalism and finally to a demonstration of how "national identity," as a form of *ethnos,* is negated through an overemphasis on *demos* in these latter definitions. Although I completely disagree with ethnic "purity" definitions of the nation, I do argue that civic definitions cannot be entirely separated from ethnic ones because modernity is not absolutely discontinuous with the premodern, and that social constructivism cannot completely replace primordial explanations when defining anew the nation and national identity. I attempt to rejuvenate a qualified theoretical status for *ethnos* by showing how its presence is unavoidable in a dialogic analysis of the nation. *Ethnos* is redefined as a weak way of imagining the nation in ethnic, premodern, primordial terms, and is contrasted with a stronger way of imagining its civic, modern, constructivist form. In other words, I propose a convergence between such definitions rather than a separation of the main conceptual couplets.

On the Dialogue Between *Ethnos* and *Demos*

What would a dialogical approach to citizenship, and to the culture and politics of the nation, look like today? Despite being societal, administrative, or public, as opposed to being interpersonal, existential, and private, political events can in and of themselves be understood as dialogical insofar as they conclude deliberations between groups in society while at the same time open up new questions and in turn anticipate new rejoinders. In this sense, societal dialogue carries the same paradox found in Mead's and Bakhtin's approaches to the self-other relation, that is, the paradox between a pure form of undistorted communication (instituted among its various organizational parts) and the universal moral consequences of creative individual (instituting) acts. If, then, the political is conceived of as dialogical, political acts cannot reasonably be decontextualized in the name of a rational order (juridical or otherwise). In Dostoevsky's story, a man kills his beloved but later becomes an outstanding member of his community. How is this possible? A dialogical theory of the political cannot universalize *demos* by eliminating the particular pathologies of *ethnos*. The specific uniqueness and autonomy of a people needs to be understood as if it were in dialogue with the multiplicity, diversity, and variety of individuals and groups that cohabit the political community. Dialogical theory would argue, then, for a thicker mix between *ethnos* and *demos* as opposed to their further thinning out into monologic opposites. Dialogism, or the as-yet-unknown political and cultural accommodation that might be created from the clash of utterances in the encounter between *ethnos* and *demos,* can only be accomplished by recovering some of the cultural specificity Habermas's political theory dis-integrates.

What I am suggesting here is that theorists engaged in a dialogical understanding of societal events need to adjust for a change in the conceptual status of terms such as solidarity and the lifeworld when engaging in macro explanations. These terms always need to be understood, at least partially, under the umbrellas of both culture/*ethnos* and politics/*demos.* If not, then social solidarity, and the decentered subject's lifeworld, risk being reduced to a mere function of civil and political society or to an essentialist cultural characteristic of the lifeworld. This is not an argument in favor of cultural politics wherein identity claims are seen as synonymous with ethical definitions of action but is, rather, an attempt to better balance the two-sided norms of answerability.

From Bakhtin to Simmel to Cohen, Weber, Mead, and Habermas, the social actor is seen to anticipate rejoinders from an animated other. Learning to dialogue intersubjectively is about learning a two-sided form of exchange that includes a reference to the uniqueness of an individual subject of action and to a more general one that situates emotional-volitional orientations toward action in a political and moral community. Dialogue includes not only a normative orientation to the idea but also to action so the question, "How I should act?" is not resolved by deferring to the ideal expectations of my community (superaddresee, "generalized other") or to legal definitions of the political subject via citizenship alone. Like the murderer in Dostoevsky's novel, the question, "How I should act?" needs to be worked out with the reflexive knowledge that I act according to both my own imaginary but not fictional subjectivity as well as to my image of another's subjectivity. However radically different the other's experiences may be they can respond with answers that are potentially harmful or supportive.

The question of how I should act toward others who commit evil acts is not the same as how I should act when I encounter citizens who are not like me, those who do not share my lifestyle, traditions, values, and norms. In Bakhtin's notion of two-sided answerability the problem of comprehending another is transgredient with moral judgment, not prior to it. When I encounter strangers, the question becomes, How should I act toward this other unique axiological position and how can we gain access to each other's traditions, languages, or lifestyles in order to consummate an interpersonal encounter? Dialogue is situated in heteroglot contexts that are stratified both socially and linguistically but this does not mean dialogue is "scripted" or automatically coded by power, and a most important assumption is that actors have the ability to respond in non a priori ways. In dialogue the response of another is anticipated, and, in this sense, included in the reflection of the actor who speaks and acts. Unlike in monologue, where I assume I have the last word, in dialogue there is no final word. Rather, I must adjust myself to ideas and to concepts as they present themselves.

At a societal level, a dialogic approach to the culture and politics of the nation carries forward several important assumptions from the level of interaction but also requires conceptual adjustments or shifts. An important reason that structures such as the nation persist as a form of community, social organization, or society (even though some of the most horrific kinds of criminal violence and genocide have been committed in its name) is that it is not possible for a social actor to learn to dialogue without having been socialized. Of course, people do learn traditions, lifestyles, and languages outside or across the societies they live in but only by drawing on cultures that have been nurtured within some *ethnos*.[6] Taking the dialogic definition of identity to mean how we imagine others might see us as well as how we image ourselves reflexively, I argue that *ethnos* develops within the nation-state and transculturally, across nation-states, in a similar way. *Ethnos* can refer to both the universal definition of a particular people, as in the American, German, or Swiss *"ethnos,"* and to the collection of different national and ethnic identities that contribute to its character—African-American, German-Turk, Swiss-Roman, etc.

A second assumption is that however it is constructed or imagined, the relation between *demos* and *ethnos* needs to find coherence in the actor's lifeworld. As Alexander Motyl puts this, "to ask about the origins of national identity is to ask about the origins of lifeworlds" (1999, 71). Seen only in the dimension of *ethnos*, all national identities are exclusive. On the other hand, *ethnos* cannot be isolated from membership in a wider *demos* given two generally acknowledged facts: 1) almost all contemporary nation-states include a variety of national minorities or immigrant cultures within their *demos;* and 2) transnational migration, and the increased exposure to the global culture of contemporary media, means it is no longer possible to isolate or "cleanse" national cultures from contact with at least the images of other society's cultures outside the *demos*.

A final and more important point in moving to the macro level is that the relation between *ethnos* and *demos* can be considered dialogically to the extent that their internal differences can divide actors into various camps when public deliberations between distinct communities cannot be resolved. At the same time, the tension generated between groups can also be thought through dialogically in that such tensions become the reference point for new ways of posing questions as well as for developing new kinds of solutions to problems that in turn require new responses. For example, if questions of "fellowship," of peace and good government, and of international cooperation were pressed solely on the grounds of accommodating the "imaginary" *ethnos* of the national society, without separating the political framework of its *demos*, new conceptual tools would be unavailable for actors from different traditions to enter into trannscultural or transcivilizational exchange. On the other hand, if we were to insist on overdetermining *demos*—enforcing a world government for defining citizenship, for example—we would risk a democratic deficit that would lead to the misrecognition of the cultural dimension of nations, regions, and peoples. When defining an approach to citizenship and national identity it is important to keep these two extremes in mind, not in order to carve out a conceptual middle ground, but for practical, dialogical reasons.

Identity

Whereas national identity has been a hotly disputed topic for more than two centuries, debates over citizenship and membership "in the city" have been going on in a variety of forms for more than twenty-six centuries. The political community, which may be larger than the nation in the ethnic sense of the term, is unified within the nation-state, which in turn receives support through the mutual recognition between nation-states in the greater world system. Citizenship guarantees a number of rights (individual, social) but also carries certain obligations (e.g., to pay taxes, to learn to read and write a language or many languages, to obey laws, to serve in the military) that are backed by the rule of law. On the other hand, the political community is not simply a legal constitution or social contract; it is also defined through its cultural and narratological specificity, or *ethnos*. Citizenship is about membership in, and the juridical significance of, a nation as a political entity that also has a normative or ideal dimension that encourages virtues of public-mindedness, patriotism, practices of deliberation, display, and dialogized self-reflexivity. Although citizenship is about membership and participation, the meaning, components, and procedures of each of these features differs considerably from country to country and from epoch to epoch.

It would not be an exaggeration to say that today there are as many different definitions of citizenship as there are national identities, recognized nation-states, and regional organizations. Even if we did a comprehensive textual analysis of the legal definitions of citizenship defined by all nation-states recognized by the UN we would still not be able to understand the diversity of the values these definitions express without studying them from the perspective of the deeply dialogized background contexts from which they evolved. On the other hand, such an analysis might suggest that citizenship be pictured as a protective shell: an outer body as Bakhtin might describe it.[7] The external body carries the *demos* that surrounds and protects an *ethnos* or inner sense of specificity and identity. The first layer of the *demos* protects the core and includes "suffrage and basic civil and political protections" as well as lesser political, economic, and cultural rights that make up the outer, softer layers. "For those potential members who have overcome the considerable barrier of admission to a country, the outer softer layers are easily penetrated, but the resistance becomes ever greater as one moves toward the centre."[8]

Debate around the struggles for recognition in democratic states coincides with the progressive weakening of unifying forces in the sovereign nation-state that have traditionally given legal definition to citizenship. In this process the *ethnos* of the political community has shifted focus away from any singular narrative or voice of cultural and historical representation. Emerging and unprecedented global immigration and technologies of communication increasingly render problematic any sense of a unified national culture as representing citizenship. A strong cultural turn has thus come about in the social sciences to try and explain the polyphonic character of *ethnos* and the political community and the emergence of multiple discourses of power, norms of identity, and different values or objects of desire that are contested issues previously absent from the debate on citizenship and national identity.

The multiple, conceptual dichotomies that surround the discussion of citizenship, the nation, and national identities demonstrates a lack of theoretical consensus. Under these circumstances it is difficult to offer a common definition. Still, it is possible to sketch a preliminary definition that is appropriate for a dialogical approach but with a very important proviso. Tom Narin argues that nationalism was born in the ambiguity of a "modern Janus." On the one hand, every population in the world scrambled toward progress through urbanization and industrialization. On the other hand, to have access to modernity meant cultural and political independence and, hence, a capacity to define "backwardness" and overcome it. The Janus face of nationalism means it can be either a positive expression of identity or an ethnocentric and violent expression of imperial force ("arrogant, homogenizing and armed to the teeth" [Narin 1997, 71]). I have argued the first principal of a dialogic approach is that disputes be solved through discourse and not violence. Although this may serve other purposes as well, from the dialogical point of view nationalism needs to be understood as the multifaceted, intersubjective way in which people envisage their identities and interpret their worlds (Tamir 1993; Miller 1995; Walzer 1997; Calhoun 1997). As a sociological phenomenon, nationalism combines ideas, values, and experiences from which emerge actual practices, including the way in which argument, or discourse, is carried out and positions are stated (Brubaker,1999). Nationalism carries political, economic, and moral argument and expression. Thinking dialogically about national identity permits us to attend to the manner in which the elements of its discourse emerge from lifeworlds that intersect with each other.

The term *identity* is in some ways even more difficult to define than the term *nation*.[9] Identity is our understanding of who we are, with whom we identify, and how we expect other people to treat us (Nielsen 1997). If I identify myself to others as a doctor, doing so tells people certain things about me and how, under certain circumstances, we will interact with one another. But identity is also our understanding of who and what we are not, and from whom we are different. Ukrainians from the west of the Ukraine, for example, see themselves as different from Russians, and part of their Ukrainian identity is this historical sense of being different. The same is not true for eastern Ukrainians, who identify themselves as Russian. On the other hand, most Ukrainians are also not the same as Spaniards or Danes, but those differences are not part of what Ukrainians typically see as relevant to their identity. What becomes relevant to people, what becomes a part of their identity, and especially their national identity, has to do with the social relationships through which they deal with those "others" they consider the same as themselves and with those "others" whom they consider to be different.

In a way, our identity is a claim about ourselves whereby we tell others what makes us distinctive. This claim is validated when it is recognized, that is, when others acknowledge us and accept us as being what we claim to be. Being "ourselves" becomes difficult when our difference is not acknowledged. When Americans say Canadians are pretty much the same as them, Canadians become surprised and sometimes a little angry at such a failure to recognize the distinction. After all, if Canadians cannot be different from Americans, who can they be? The failure to recognize one's distinctive identity, then, is a challenge to our sense of who we are. Such misrecognition generates resentment, frustration, sometimes anger, and it certainly threatens the ongoing social relationships among people.

Perhaps there really is no satisfactory definition of what exactly national identity means. Too rigid a definition risks unfair exclusion. After all, it is possible to live in a country without taking on its identity. On the other hand, sociologists have argued for at least a century that either too weak or too strong an attachment to national identity risks destroying the solidarity needed to maintain a society. Given that there is still no alternative to the nation-state, one must admit that social disintegration brought on by the strengthening of proto-national solidarities is still a very real danger, as recent events in Central Europe show. Disintegration need not follow only as a consequence of social control breaking down when loyalties are too strong and identities are too exclusive. It may also be a consequence of a lack of attachment to a nation and the absence of a strong collective identity. The more widespread the apathy concerning a sense of belonging to a country, the less citizens are willing to participate in the democratic process and the greater the risks to that country of social disintegration (Taylor 1991).

Citizenship, and the sense of belonging to a larger collectivity—a "We"—is an important dialogical component of identity. In this respect, the national minority "We" and the national majority "we" are very different. Though one could consider oneself a descendant from either a national majority or minority and still not subscribe to either of these positions. The national minority identity is that of a people who are seen to have a unique history, a common memory, a common language (though not always), and a dream of founding a nation-state. A stronger version of this definition is one that sees the national minority as an oppressed or colonized people who remain distinct from the majority. A national majority can also carry such an *ethnos* vis à vis other dominant majorities but, as stated above, multicultural societies challenge the idea (of both national majorities and minorities) that any single *ethnos* can center the definition of citizenship. (Angus, 1997) Immigrant minorities struggle with the loss of their own traditions and the gains of their new host cultures until an assimilation process is finally completed. Other transnational or diaspora identities are more complex. In the weak version, they might be seen to be rooted in diverse histories, many languages, and possible so many cultures that no single one can be identified as the original source. This identity might acknowledge the national and immigrant, or ethno-racial minorities and majorities, as only some of the many groups of people that flow into the make-up of the world citizen (Nussbaum 1996). The strong version James Clifford describes would define diasporas as groups that have struggled against structural forms of prejudice to maintain something like a national identity with a strong attachment to an imaginary homeland but without the dream of founding a state. "Peoples whose sense of identity is centrally defined by collective histories of displacement and violent loss cannot be 'cured' by merging into a new national community" (1994). Though, again, one could consider oneself a cosmopolitan and not subscribe to this definition either.

This may seem confusing if one forgets that these definitions of identity are ideal types. They are useful definitions because they help us to understand some of the contradictory aspects of difference between national minorities and majorities, as well as between ethno-racial and immigrant groups. But these definitions of identity do not explain why politically and morally we should recognize a nation as sovereign or unique. In this sense, ideal type definitions of identity carry the same limitation found in the analyses of the nineteenth-century French sociologist Emile Durkheim. Durkheim tried to show that if individuals were not integrated enough, or if they were too well integrated, into the collective identities of their societies, they would suffer, and eventually the societies themselves would be weakened. The problem with an approach such as Durkheim's is that the exact balance of integration and difference cannot be determined. For Durkheim, identity was what he called a "social fact." This means that one's identity is formed by external forces such as ethnicity, religion, social class, race, or gender; it is explained as a function of some other determining cause and cannot be explained from within its own *ethnos* (Durkheim 1966).

In Durkheim's theory social order should be maintained regardless of how identities may evolve or how people's understanding of their identity may change. Yet the world around us today is filled with change as new countries come into being and old nations fall apart. Ignoring the dynamic of such change in favor of some abstract notion of social order poses the risk that change, when it comes, finds us unprepared, which can generate violence, misery, and chaos for the people involved. This raises an important challenge for the dialogical approach to citizenship and national identity. Can this approach help determine how to decide when a new country should be created? In other words, how can the claim to nationhood be judged except by understanding the evolution of an identification toward some form of "We" from its own point of view? This question returns us to the familiar but even more difficult problem concerning contradictory claims that are made by different groups, with distinct identities, who occupy the same *demos*.

Durkheim's sociology was developed toward the end of the colonial period as European societies were becoming increasingly aware of other cultures and different identities. The large-scale migrations of the twentieth century are an unparalleled historical phenomenon. A broad consensus has been growing that the best kind of country is the one that looks for ways of sharing as many different individual and collective identities as possible (Rawls 1999; Tully 1995). At the same time, however, it remains an unavoidable fact that nations or countries continue to exist. And if a nation is to exist, it cannot simply be a collection of multiple individual and group identities, for such a collection is not a nation. To be a nation means to have some common identity and *ethnos* that can serve as a reference point for all members of the *demos*. But what exactly constitutes a nation is the subject of a great deal of disagreement.

For and against the Nation

Contemporary discussions that address the question of the nation rarely look to demonstrate how well the nation is doing. On the contrary, most of the literature is concerned with the "problem cases" and with the need to renew theories of the nation in light of a rapidly transforming world order. Every national framework has more and more difficulty facing global competition and reducing the growing democratic deficit created by the transfer of sovereignty to regional and global institutions. It may well be that a political response to the challenge of the emerging disorder is so huge it is almost impossible to know where to begin to look for an answer. Evidence for the increasing irrelevance of the nation-state can be found in Europe's plan to expand membership to countries through the perplexing complexity of a two-track approach, potentially leaving the future of any specifically national identity in doubt. Ironically, North America is traditionally much better known as living with identity crisis. The former "New World" is now struggling to catch up via NAFTA and the FTA, and may well pick up the pace as Mexico works its way through democratic reform.

Evidence for the increasing importance of nation-states can be found in the fact that they are still among the primary players in defining the terms for the new federations and institutions, even as their ability to be self-governing is displaced. Further evidence is seen in the proliferation of new nation-states since 1989 and the intensification of self-determination movements in countries with large historical, cultural, and territorially fixed national minorities such as the Québécois, Scots, Welsh, and Catalonians. My point is simply that nation states *are* still among the key players in making globalization work politically. The question of whether or not citizenship will, or should, be more regionally or globally determined is on the horizon for anyone who looks to understand postnational identity in the present context—not because forms of shared sovereignty are new but because they appear likely to become more common.

Much of the discussion on the nation can be divided into three general options: 1) pro-nationalists who defend the nation as a modern liberal form of social solidarity; 2) antinationalists who attack the nation as a dangerous, destructive illiberal force of modernity; and 3) globalization theorists who predict that the state structure that supports the nation is becoming irrelevant due to the ever-increasing deevolution of the state's power to regulate capital flows and legal and cultural institutions within its own territory. In the remainder of this chapter I focus on the example of the second tendency in relation to the third, whereas a comparison of pro- and antinationalists is discussed in more depth in the next chapter.

Whether nationalism is seen as an illiberal or liberal force, its analysis is increasingly carried out in an earnest attempt to grasp the effects of change unleashed by massive and often overwhelming forces of globalization. In the process, the debate about the nation shifts from historical and sociological definitions, to the issue of whether or not the emerging context of globalization will weaken the state to the point of disappearance or contribute to its further growth and mutation (Sassen 1996; Held and McGrew 1999). As a counter to the position that the nation-state will disappear, Narin poses the following dilemma:

> For the first time in human history, the globe has been effectively unified into a single economic order under a common democratic state model—surely the ideal dreamt-of conditions for liberal or proletarian internationalism—[but] these conditions have caused it to almost immediately fold up into a previously unimaginable and still escalating number of different ethno-political units. . . . Why has globalization engendered nationalism, instead of transcending it? (1997, 63)[10]

Against Narin's observation of a surge in the creation of new nation-states, it is argued that there are many more ethnic groups than there are nation-states, and that the idea that each one might aspire to forming its own state is not feasible. This argument is commonly raised against nationalists who argue for the right to self-determination. Although it is true that there is no argument that demonstrates that a nation must inevitably become a nation-state, does it necessarily follow that the right to self-determination should be forever silenced? There is no acknowledged social science measure for determining how many nation-states the world can support, and international law is at best a rough guide that is often only invoked after the fact. Indeed, Narin's observation is difficult to refute. The dramatic increase in the recent birth of new nation-states seems to indicate that the number of nation-states may well continue to expand in the current phase of globalization.

The question of whether or not citizenship should eventually be determined more by international organizations than through the absolute sovereignty of the nation-state is beyond the scope of our present discussion. Nonetheless, it is certainly a question on the horizon for anyone who looks to understand the question of national identity. For the present discussion, however, as long as the system of sovereign nation-states exists, the question remains what kind of criteria are needed in order to distinguish liberal claims for national self-determination or, at least, enhanced autonomy? Along with the nagging and far-reaching questions

of just how much sovereignty should be given up to international organizations, this question has of late been a source for much violent con-
frontation. Recall that the NATO intervention in Kosovo was ostensibly
undertaken to protect the human rights of national minorities and not
to recognize a separatist movement, while intervention in East Timor
was explicitly justified in terms of protecting a referendum on independence. In cases such as these (the recent accord in Northern Ireland
being another example) it may be that any distinction between liberal
and illiberal claims is so enveloped in violent and monologic circumstances that any postnational solution that stops the violence has to be
employed for none other than humanitarian reasons.[11]

In other cases, claims for nationhood occur across decades of
public, nonviolent debate and remain within the control of the nation-state, even though their solutions ultimately require some new
form of shared sovereignty. Democratic and peaceful neonationalist
movements such as those in Quebec, Scotland, Wales, and Catalonia
need to be clearly distinguished from their violent, antidemocratic
counterparts in, for example, Northern Ireland, the Basque country,
and Corsica. Similar distinctions concerning stateless nations can also
be made in the growing variety of postcommunist nationalisms.
These are necessary distinctions not only for analytic reasons but in
order to make political and moral judgments on which "We" plea to
listen to and under what circumstances the plea should be supported.
Creating a new state for any of these movements means the secession
from larger states, and hence the question: How do we know to whom
we should listen? Anti-violent and democratic principals regarding
citizenship remain the fundamental criterion along with respect for
universal human rights. To paraphrase Bakhtin: "When dialogue
stops, you're dead."

Establishing criteria for distinguishing between good and bad
nationalism is a common feature in the area of the contemporary sociology of nationalism. Jean Cohen argues that such theoretical distinctions have reemerged in recent years as "a response to the resurgence of
ethno-, racialized and very illiberal or anti-democratic versions of na-
tionalist-communitarian identity politics" (1999, 253). There is no
commonly held definition of the nation and national identity but oc-
casionally new ways of describing old definitions reemerge only to be
once again put into doubt. A good example would be the neat definitions that would separate nationalism into the good "civic," "territorial," or "patriotic" kind that defines citizenship according to universal
categories versus the bad "ethnic," cultural, or separatist variety that

defines citizenship according to "the imagined blood relation," or other particularistic categories.

Anthony Smith draws a strong distinction between civic-territorial (political) and the ethnic-genealogical (cultural) origins of nationalism. For Smith, nationalism is as much about national identity as it is about political instrumentalism. He defines nationalism as an "ideological movement for attaining and maintaining autonomy, unity and identity on behalf of a population deemed by some of its members to constitute an actual or potential 'nation' " (1991, 72). The "core doctrine" of nationalism is deliberately separated from the state in this definition. Smith argues that not all nationalisms need be aligned with a state tradition nor does nationalism necessarily fix the founding of the nation-state as its ultimate goal. "Nationalism is an ideology of the nation, not the state" (Smith, 1991, 74). Nationalism is a political ideology but it is more centrally a cultural doctrine. The cultural doctrine is not posited here as the inner speech of the subject in a lifeworld but as a transsubjective relation that is reinforced by the group's use of language and symbols.

Smith defines territorial anticolonial nationalisms as mainly civic in the pre-independence phase. They tend to reject foreign symbols and leaders and seek to replace them with a new nation-state. Here the political forces of independence are strong enough to bring in a new symbolic order that will eliminate its previous "other." In the post-independentist phase, the new political community becomes "integrationist" and is composed of a transcultural mix left over from the previous regime. Smith defines ethnic nationalisms as those that "seek to secede from a larger political unit . . . and set up a new political ethno-nation." Here again, a lifeworld accumulates sufficient political power to break from its other. After independence the political community constructs itself by recovering its ethnic kinship outside of its own territory or by "forming a much larger 'ethno-national' state through the union of culturally and ethnically similar ethno-national states; these are 'irredentist' and 'pan' nationalisms." While Smith admits that this typology does not account for all possible forms of nationalism, he argues that it does allow for a comparative study of nationalisms that stem from the diversity of cultures that coexist within a single social system. What should be remembered is that the nation, as an investment into identity, itself exists both before and after the state is put in place.

The dichotomy between civic and ethnic nationalism appears to have held currency for a while only to have retreated into confusion since the events of 1989 and the intensification of the still as yet unknown effects of globalization. One obvious shortcoming of the civic definition, be it of the French or American variety, is that even once achieved, a particular language and common set of procedures must be observed in order to sustain the state institutions that in turn support the definition of the nation. Even in the most tolerant, so-called "postethnic" immigrant societies, languages and some features of ethnicity are officially or unofficially excluded from public communication and so the idea that the civic nation is more inclusive is at best a relative approximation.

A second set of dichotomies grafts the civic-ethnic couplet onto the premodern and modern definitions of the nation. Ernst Gellner is best known for his argument that the complexity of modern nationalism is itself a product of modernity (1983). Nationalism is bound up in the shift from agrarian to mass society and in the fundamentally different forms of social division that each type of society has produced. Proto-nationalism is, for Gellner, grounded in the agrarian model while the turn to a more ethnic or civic nationalism depends more on how local elites establish their relations to nation-state "building" in the modernized metropole. Agrarian society is founded on an "organic solidarity." Members submit to common oral traditions, accents, and costumes. Social division depends on a particular hierarchy that separates the larger isolated peasant society from a political class composed of overlapping layers of authority. The religious, military, and administrative personnel are recruited from a limited number of educated members of a small ruling class. Gellner isolates the accessibility to education and power as key factors in determining the type of nationalism that might emerge in opposition to such a social division.

A major consequence of the transition to industrial society is massive democratization and a new accessibility to education, power, and, we might add, communication. This new mechanical solidarity is built on a more complex division of labor than was necessary in agrarian societies. Ideally, members no longer submit to tradition, common accent or language, and costume as the distinguishing marks of identity. The societal consensus, or solidarity, is mechanical and abstract rather than organic and concrete. The distinction between culture and *Kultur,* or high culture, is no longer the code that allows members to move from one sector of the society to another. Theoretically, members are henceforth potentially owners of enough cultural capital to allow safe passage across what, in agrarian societies, were impassable divisions. For Gellner, cultural capital is much more important than economic capital in determining the type of nationalism that might emerge.

In the modernist argument, nations do not simply have histories; they themselves are the outcome of modern history and nation building. Thus, before modernity, the study of nations and nationalism can only be a study of proto-nationalism or of tribalism, which are not the same thing. But does the coherence of such designations not belong more to the retrospective glance of the historian/sociologist and anthropologist than to the phenomena themselves? On a more practical level, a similar question is raised against the modernist typology by stateless first nations or indigenous peoples who refuse the imposition of a Western philosophy of history on their own experiences and traditions (Guibernau 1999). However deeply the premodernist-modernist dichotomy can be seen to ground current definitions of the nation it does not enjoy a full consensus.

A third distinction, built on the premodern-modern couplet, occurs around the difference between primordialism and constructivism. Eric Hobsbaum takes issue with the primordialist argument that situates the birth of the nation with languages. His argument, though, is ambiguous. On the one hand, he contests a top-down approach that explains the nation as a manipulation of elites over a citizenry. Initially, he argues for an approach that looks at the history of the nation from the point of view of the people at the bottom. While he prefers such an approach he leaves it aside for two reasons. First, a large part of the history of vernacular culture is not written. Therefore, the past cannot be traced through the written documentation of the everyday. Second, after a brief description of the nature of nationalist writings and manifestos, he concludes that such materials are, in the end, suspect because they are too imbued in the myth-making process of the nation itself. He argues that national languages are "almost always semi-artificial constructs . . . virtually invented. They are the opposite of what nationalist mythology supposes them to be, namely the primordial foundations of national culture and the matrices of the national mind" (Hobsbaum 1990, 54).

According to Benedict Anderson, the vernacular languages and "creole" cultures of the New World that developed in the movement against European imperialism as early as the sixteenth century, led to the first sense of nation-ness as a problematic of identity. National identities are concomitant with the possibility of imagining the nation, a perception made possible through the widespread availability of printed materials. Anderson's definition of the "imaginary community" has a double meaning. It is imaginary in the primordial and anthropological sense in that it is about how humans come together to confer a creative sense on the world and it is imaginary in the constructivist sense. Given that the people the community holds cannot all have interpersonal relations, and thus can only have an imaginary sense of who and what they might be together, the image of the community is invented, or constructed, by institutions organized by elites. Stressing the second meaning of the term, Anderson argues that the precondition for the "imaginary community" is found in the print technology that creates a historical record and a new state-centered administrative culture: "[T]he very conception of the newspaper implies the refraction of even world events into a specific imagined world of vernacular readers; and also how important to that imagined community is an idea of steady, solid simultaneity throughout time" (Anderson 1983, 62).

Hobsbaum and Anderson sever language from its living contexts in order to provide a non-ontological explanation of the nation. Ethnicity is also argued to play a qualified role in the life of the nation. For Hobsbaum, there are simply too many exceptions to the claim that the common polity of nations is held together on the basis of ethnic affiliation alone. With the exception of China, Japan, and the two Koreas, he maintains that nation-states that occupy large territories are always heterogeneous in their ethnic makeup. Ethnicity does play an important role in distinguishing "us and them" but at the same time ethnic differentiation occurs both horizontally, between nations, and vertically, within nations. In both cases, "visible ethnicity tends to be negative, in as much as it is more usually applied to define 'the other' rather than one's own group." Negative ethnicity and religio-ethnic identification are ultimately irrelevant to proto-nationalism "unless they can be fused with something like a state tradition" (Hobsbaum 1990, 66). The "historical nation," the idea of belonging to a political tradition, becomes one of the overriding factors in determining the nation. This reasoning points back to the administrative and political cultures that manage the nation's social divisions.

No one argues that language and ethnicity are without importance to national identities. At the same time, for Anderson and Hobsbawm, they are not the foundation of the nation. Their choice to approach the history of language from the point of view of politics and linguistics demotes the status of language as a living aspect, or utterance, of culture to a secondary plane. Here, ruling elites and new technologies establish the functional prerequisites from which the politics of language and the nation emerge. The reduction of the imaginary to a mode of communicative production negates the initial anthropological meaning that promises a more interpretive understanding of the nation in terms of its relation to a lived "imagined community." To get a more balanced understanding of the "imaginary community," language has to be understood as a living form of dialogue that arises from the diversity of lifeworlds that coexist within a given modern society. Defining "official" language as an artificially elite-driven system deals neatly with the set of historical deductions they make but it ignores the especially problematic modern role of language in the formation of identity. If we were to retreat to Hobsbaum's first position, that is, to a consideration of the nation from the bottom up, or at least from the point of view of the actors who have given and claim to give it birth then a much more appropriate starting point for analysis would be the points at which national struggles over the meanings and explanations of language and ethnicity have taken place. Similarly, if we were to recover Anderson's provocative meaning of the "imagined community" from its reduction to the constructivist explanation (the political economy of print capitalism), then a focus on the dialogized utterance in civil society is the place to begin to search.

The dichotomies ethnic/civic, premodern/modern, and primordialism/constructivism demonstrate that it is not easy to define what we mean by the terms *nation, national identity,* and *citizenship.* These conceptual divisions explain part, but not all, of the dynamic involved in the culture and politics of the nation. Hobsbaum, Anderson, Gellner, and Smith all recognize a distinction between a positive concept of citizenship related to state-patriotism and a negative citizenship rooted in popular nationalism, and in this sense each tends to look for a way to separate off the *ethnos* from the latter and promote the *demos* of the former. All reject extreme primordialism that assumes nations and national identities are a naturally occurring form of human community that transcend history and are not affected by institutional arrangements.

A weaker and more dialogic version of primordialism would argue simply that nations are human communities wherein social actors come together to creatively consummate self-other relations. I have argued that such a Bakhtinian postulate could be extended to define the nation as a form of two-sided answerability wherein *ethnos* and *demos* are unconsummated in the sense that their relation is never finalized but is rather in a process of historical becoming. In the weaker version of primordialism it could also be admitted that such communities existed well before the modern state came into being and that they could also decline, cease to exist, or reappear through all kinds of loopholes. In other words, the mark of the weaker version is the admission that nations are bound by history and institutional arrangements. Nations are neither outside history nor are they absolutely historically determined. The core assumption of extreme constructivism is that nations are discursive practices coded within institutions that invent or imagine the national community in the interest of reproducing regimes of power (Motyl 1999). A weaker and more dilalogic version begins in the first meaning of Anderson's "imaginary community" and is about how humans come together to confer a creative sense on the world through dialogue.

Nation-states and federations that are looking to counter nationalist movements evoking extreme primordialist arguments often counter with extreme constructivist arguments but when promoting their own identities will retreat into whichever argument best opposes the movements against them. Most theories of the nation, and most comparative empirical case studies, conclude that secession from larger federations (and nationalistically driven social policies that accompany the regional political expressions of such movements) is a pathological consequence of nationalism. But exaggerated "gloom and doom" descriptions of nationalist movements are just as often countered by what Rogers Brubaker describes as the "architechnonic illusion": "the belief that the right 'grande architecture', the right territorial and institutional framework, can satisfy nationalist demands" (1998, 273). Both extremes need to be guarded against in discussing national identity or the culture and politics of the nation.

With Brubaker (1998) I want to argue that approaching national identity dialogically means that the category "nation" should not be defined as a vessel for a group's ethnicity as if it were a closed-off and enduring cultural block. He argues that a more fruitful approach should focus on the nation as a "category of practice and not of analysis, [on] nationhood as an institutionalized cultural and political form, and [on] nationness as a contingent event or happening, and refrain from using the analytically dubious notion of 'nations' as substantial enduring events " (1999, 21). On the other hand, I cannot follow his extreme constructivist postulate that "nationalist conflicts are in principle, by their very nature, irresolvable" (1998, 273). Are nations and their citizens real or are they simply interpellated by already institutionalized and coded discursive structures? As David McCrone points out, deconstructing the nation means we never actually "get down to analyzing what happens on the ground" (1998, 4). For my purposes, extreme constructivism means that we never get to a dialogical understanding of the culture and politics of national identity and citizenship and we never make a non a priori judgment about the "We" claim.

Understanding the nation as a two-sided form of answerability means we also need to understand its investment in the event or creation of unique identities: of "nationness." In other words, the nation takes on an emotional-volitional orientation, which is implicated in an event-of-being. This does not mean that such identities are fixed or noncontingent, nor that they need to determine the norms of answerability. The dialogic approach is well suited for thinking about the eventness or contingent, creative dimension in nationalism. To put this in Volosinov's language—as a neutral exterior sign, the nation always has the potential to become part of the "inner speech" of identity. Here the nation cannot be neutral. The potential of the nation to become the "semiotic material of inner life" is a proof of its dialogicality; of its capacity to anticipate rejoinders from the imaginary but not fictional other. The dialogic openness of the nation means it is a potential public resource for all citizens. On the other side of answerability there are all kinds of events where the narration of the nation in the form of nationalism demands very clear-cut closures, definitions, cautions, and restrictions. These are the themes of the next chapter.

8

A DIALOGUE ON THE NATION
IN POSTNATIONAL TIMES

Nations and nationalism are not going to disappear with globalization, nor are the conflicts they engender. If this is the case then we need to know more about what kind of nations and nationalism might be imagined dialogically and democratically in the context of an emerging "postnational constellation." To explore this question this chapter employs a version of the methodology and social theory situated between Bakhtin and Habermas, which I have endeavored to outline in earlier chapters. My strategy is to isolate some fundamental oppositions between different theoretical positions on nations in the postnational era and from these positions, or "parts," to consummate a "whole" in the form of a mutually supportive theory that could take into account the problem of two-sided answerability—even within the context of increasingly decentered societies. Thus, this chapter sets aside direct discussion of Bakhtin's work and instead enacts his theories through a dialogue with a group of contemporary thinkers (including Habermas) who can be seen to mutually reinforce each other's positions despite what appear to be irreconcilable differences.

The dialogic way of imagining opposite positions that carry legitimate differences is easily seen in the argument that cosmopolitanism and liberal nationalism are not incompatible and that they can in fact be held simultaneously (Tamir 1993; Miller 1995). By this I simply mean that there is no inherent contradiction in joining the ideal of the universal citizen with the particular identity of the city dweller. Echoing Bakhtin's two-sided normative approach to answerability, Kai Nielsen argues that in moral philosophy it is crucial to "see the universal in certain particulars, so a cosmopolitan may be intensely partial to a particular nation or group while at the same time having committed to the whole of humanity. We must refuse to put the interests of our country before wider human interests. Still this does allow us, and arguably requires us in certain circumstances to support liberal nationalism" (1999, 8).

To be sure there are many historical reasons to be wary of nationalism. On the other hand, condemning all forms of nationalism as inherently xenophobic is a serious empirical and theoretical mistake—as is the assertion that "nationalist conflicts are in principle, by their very nature, irresolvable," to again cite Brubaker's provocative position. More moderate positions argue that the question of liberal nationalism needs to be addressed through constitutional reforms in the context of the politics or struggles over recognition. Charles Taylor (1994) galvanized this position in his argument for a balance between a procedural model for individual rights (Liberalism I) and a second-level model that would guarantee collective rights for Aboriginal peoples and a French-speaking national minority in Canada (Liberalism II). Habermas joined the debate on recognition with a special reference to the Quebec question and a critical response to Taylor's two-level formulation of liberalism (Habermas 1994). Will Kymlicka continues to provide one of the most dynamic additions to the debate on citizenship and multiculturalism and has made important contributions to the debate over Quebec (1995; 1998). Although the Quebec case is cited in almost all comparative studies of contemporary nationalism, its own theoretical understanding of itself is not well known or understood given the linguistic divide in North America wherein French-speaking Quebec intellectuals are rarely heard from.[1] Introducing two of Quebec's best-known social theorists, the late Marcel Rioux (1919–1992) and Fernand Dumont (1927–1996), whose ideas contradict and complement positions taken up by Habermas, Taylor, and Kymlicka, is one way of balancing the scales.[2] They differ from these latter thinkers in the sense that while neither pursues an extreme primordial definition of the nation, each theorizes *ethnos* over *demos* when defining the nation as a sociology of culture.

Thinking dialogically about the counterpoint between the legitimate differences on both sides of the national question in postnational times leads me to push the approach to recognition farther than its original authors would perhaps want. Intellectuals caught within the tension of an immanent critique of constraints imposed by surrounding postcolonial structures, and the affirmation of their own interior discourse—in itself often divided between the voices of utopia and those of pragmatism—find themselves in a spiraling counterpoint. Unraveling this counterpoint is a key to the comprehension of its dialogical form. As was seen in earlier chapters, dialogue, in the sense of counterpoint, encompasses more than the usual formalist or pragmatist definition of dialogue in language; more than an exchange of utterances between speakers in a conversation that may be formally decoded according to the axis that splits language from speech, the word from its accentuation, ideology from its interest. This is only the superficial manifestation of a much broader phenomenon that exceeds direct referentially ordered discourse to permeate everything that has meaning and value in human interaction. Understood in the broader societal sense as the production and exchange of meaning within social discourse, dialogical phenomenon develop within a variety of contexts (institutional, ideological, cultural) and across a series of social categories (groups, classes, regions, nations).

Critique of the dialogical form in the social imaginary demands reflection on the immanent nature rather than the determined representation of cultural production. Hidden or interior discourse founded in the oppositions between the multiple codes of cultural production are only discernable through immanent understanding. Hence, as is the case with many neonationalist scholars, one finds in Rioux's and Dumont's interior discourse an intense response to an imagined *other*, a response that refers to the conditions, as well as the reality, of cultural domination. The others' words at the center of this imaginary are heard as if expressed in a series of imagined voices. In the neonationalist imaginary, dialogical form confirms the internal relation between the author of the discourse and the solidarity with an audience by a sustained distancing from the other. Paradoxically for the Quebec case, this deep sense of otherness is consummated in a North American identity. As the French sociologist Edgar Morin once remarked:

> Basically the thing that strikes me is the sort of double identity, the double consciousness. On the one hand, a ferocious will to safeguard a French Québécois identity and on the other the fear of adventure and the bond of I would say, a globally North American identity. There is a conjunction of a need to live one's life with the fear of suddenly breaking the bond, which means to live one's life and to dominate one's fears. Thus it is basically an internal struggle, a struggle which is carried out within. (Rioux and Morin 1980, 15)

Although neither Rioux nor Dumont employ the concept of dialogism their basic definitions of culture, as that which instills meaning in everyday life and as that which retains the potential for overcoming the restraints of domination, can be seen to fit well within the broad contours of Bakhtin's philosophy of dialogue. At the same time, like Habermas, they both distinguish between a primary culture or lifeworld and a secondary one that operates across a complex set of divisions and decentered societal institutions. As much for their dialogical point of view, then, as to understand the application and procedures of their own approach to the nation as a sociology of culture, my reading of their works is at once a critique of the social imaginary of Quebec society and an introduction to two unique North American thinkers.

I argued in the previous chapter that studies of the nation and nationalism often tend to misdiagnose the politics of difference by overcoding *demos*. More and more contemporary societies have come to define themselves as having a multicultural and multi-narratological *ethnos*, by which I mean that they imagine themselves as constituted by many societal cultures, ethnicities, languages, and lifestyles such that no singular culture or narrative can sufficiently define the specificity of the political community. The different civic definitions of the nation implied in the work of Habermas, Taylor, and Kymlicka all seek a political framework that would transcend these differences. After placing their positions in dialogue with Rioux and Dumont's neonationalist theorization of the Question, I argue that their positions need to be revised in order to better explain how the Québécois national minority is itself sociologically constituted within a fully modern, complex, multicultural, and multi-narratological civil society. On the neonationalist side the tendency is to overcode the singular genealogy of its *ethnos* and misdiagnose the problem of plural identities and narratives when constructing an imaginary reference to the nation. Consequently, the imaginary reference to *le peuple*[3] *Québécois,* as it comes to us through Rioux's and Dumont's sociologies of culture, and as it is used by the political class in Quebec, needs to be revised through a political philosophy of "recognition" (Taylor) that allows for a more "decentered" (Habermas) theory of society and a contingent (Kymlicka) definition of the imaginary nation. I conclude that the plea for self-determination and associational sovereignty will become more commonplace in the context of an evolving continental public sphere. My gamble is that the convergence of diverse theoretical concepts derived from immanent readings of each position will lead to a new cosmopo-

litical definition and thus to the new modernity of the national question within the North American context.

As previously argued, the Quebec case is comparable to several
other neonationalist movements aiming for various forms of shared
sovereignty that have emerged since World War II. Scotland, Wales,
Catalonia, and Quebec have each evolved democratically defined self-
determination strategies driven, in part, by new economic structures, on
the one hand, and by important changes in political structure and cultural norms and values, on the other.[4] In Quebec, neonationalism has its
roots in the combination of an emergent middle class, which evolved
out of a boom in industrialization, and a major cultural revolution that
washed away the more traditional lifestyle values of the pre-1960 era.
This phase in the development of modern Quebec society set the stage
for an identity politics over the choice of remaining French-Canadian
within the existing Canadian state or becoming Québécois in a newly
independent state. The political compromise between these two extremes would be a form of cultural and political sovereignty for Quebec
within the NAFTA context and a new set of institutional associations
within Canada. As these three positions have developed, the intersection
of class, culture, identity, and neonationalism in Quebec has continued
to merge with issues of globalization, immigration, and an evolving
multi-narratological *ethnos*.[5] Further, NAFTA created what might be
the beginning of a postnational condition for shared sovereignty in
which neither Quebec, Canada, Mexico, nor the United States can continue to define their national politics without reference to each other.

Taken by itself, Rioux and Dumont's definition of the nation as a
sociology of culture only partially contributes to explaining how cosmopolitan and liberal nationalist identities are imagined dialogically. It
is an approach that focuses on the autonomy, specificity, and potentiality of national culture rather than on its relation to the foundational
principles of membership in a political community composed of local
and cosmopolitan political subjects. Both "libertarian" and "communitarian" traditions point to the need to establish a political community
that would transcend different cultural referents within the same state.
Taken separately, though, neither tradition offers a conclusive philosophical and political strategy for achieving such a goal in every case.
An understanding of the transgredient processes of democracy is
needed in order to bridge sociological, philosophical, and political definitions of the nation in postnational times. Toward this end I return
to a more detailed discussion of Habermas's two-leveled theory of
society as system and lifeworld and discuss his political philosophy vis

à vis the positions set forth by Taylor and Kymlicka. The works of each of these thinkers overlap, complement, and oppose one another on a variety of levels. To retain a certain degree of coherence, and in the more modest hope of shedding light on this debate, I will restrict myself to indicating some of the weaknesses in each approach and conclude with some suggestions for how their strong points might be brought together in a mutually reinforcing manner. Each thinker has written on Quebec nationalism and each draws different conclusions, but the reference to this case allows me to interpret their positions from a common platform.

I begin by introducing the Quebec case and Rioux's and Dumont's approaches to the nation as a sociology of culture. Next I discuss Habermas's contrary approach to the *demos* and demonstrate how he derives an ideal definition of the nation as "subjectless" communication. Finally, I review Taylor's politics of recognition and situate the role he plays in the Quebec context. Before concluding, I examine how Kymlicka's distinction between national and ethnic minorities takes a step toward the sociology of culture discussed in the first section but also how both Taylor and Kymlicka end with a definition of the nation as a politics of concession.

The Nation as a Sociology of Culture: The Quebec Case

There are risks in suspending the well-trodden comparative method widely employed in sociological and historical studies of the nation and nationalism in order to explore the specificity of the Quebec case. For one thing, such a departure presents a dilemma given that my presentation could very easily slip into an index of parochial facts or historical interpretations that are of considerable importance for understanding local dynamics but would draw us away from the subject of a dialogue on the nation in postnational times. My strategy is to proceed with a reconstruction of the most instructive theoretical elements of Rioux's and Dumont's mixture of weak primordialist and constructivist approaches to the Quebec case. Their neonationalist approach evolved out of a critique of the dominant ideology of ethnic nationalism that dominated Quebec cultural and political institutions in the period following World War II. They are part of a whole generation of intellectuals who rose up in opposition to the conservative inward-looking ethnic nationalism of the 1945–1959 period and who would go on to become among the most important architects of the early arguments for outward-looking sovereignty-association or shared sovereignty. Understood as a societal project, they define the Quebec nation as an ideal of self-determination that presupposes the existence of social solidarity in the genealogical sense. Their definition suggests a weak primordial argument but also the constructivist idea. As Dumont explains it, "[I]f the Québécois nation is not endowed with a sovereign State, in contrast, the literary institution, memory and the collective utopia have long existed" (1993). For Rioux and Dumont, the nation as a societal project presupposes that the Québécois ethnos can be rescued from the colonization effected by the subsystems of administrative power and money that are located more or less in the hands of the Canadian state, and inside the larger phenomenon of American continental preeminence.

Combining weak primordialism and constructivism fits well with the dialogical approach to national identity I sketched out in chapter 7. Focusing on a presentation of Rioux and Dumont's definition of the nation as a sociology of culture illustrates the need to negotiate a shift between primordialist and constructivist types of analysis and, further, to build a bridge to other disciplines that are necessary supplements to this approach. But before discussing their ideas more directly we need to introduce the Québécois national minority identity in the North American context.

Until recently, many observers have persisted in viewing the development of Quebec solely within the context of ethnicity and ethnic nationalism. Québécois nationalism is most often reduced to either an extreme primordialist variety of separatism or to the extreme political expression of a homogeneous ethnic group whose political identity has been misrecognized by the political and administrative apparatus of the Canadian state. Analysis of the Quebec case is most likely to begin with the assumption that Quebec is a region or province within the Canadian federation that has suffered from unequal development and reactionary antidemocratic impulses due to its roots in a conservative cultural and linguistic resistence to modernization. What gets overlooked in this misreading is that Quebec is a complex, modern multicultural society with a fully developed civil society that emerged hand in hand with one of the first post-Enlightenment forms of democratic government in the Western world.[6]

The recent intensification of the *differend* between Canada and Quebec needs to be situated against the background reception of this misunderstanding. It also needs to be placed within the emerging context of globalization where, like other OECD countries, the Canadian state has witnessed a decline of the political and economic powers traditionally at its disposition.[7] Although Canada has proven itself capable of defining a multicultural policy that for some is the envy of the world, it has never been able to solve the fundamental pleas for self-determination that have come from Aboriginal and French-speaking populations, nor the pleas for better political representation in the federal government from its peripheral regions (McRoberts 1997). In this sense, the Native and Québécois national minority experiences, rightly or wrongly, have sometimes been compared with the subaltern experience of black Americans (Kymlicka 1995).[8]

Although a very similar dynamic is also unfolding in other neonationalist substates, the Quebec case has a North American specificity that has to be considered. The explanations of political divisions within the *ethnos* of Quebec society are complex but tend to fall back into the above stated assumptions concerning the embededness of its ethnic or homogeneous character. There is a great deal of evidence supporting the hypothesis regarding the lag in transforming and integrating traditional, agrarian, Catholic Quebec institutions into a fully urban and modern society. However, there is little agreement on the significance of delayed development for either extreme constructivists or primordialists. In the weaker version of the delayed development thesis, Quebec's case is seen as similar to several other societies that have undergone a late transformation from a rural to an urban formation. On the other hand, Quebec is a unique case in that it is the only territory in North America where a language other than English is politically and legally defined as the "only official language." At stake for nationalists, and for those that oppose them, are questions regarding the transfer of powers from the Canadian state that would allow further control over Quebec's civil society, economy, and international relations. To date, there is little consensus within Quebec's political culture for the establishment of absolute sovereignty. There is, however, considerable support within Quebec's political culture for shared sovereignty through a new partnership with the rest of Canada—an option that is aggressively opposed by the present Federal government. The place to begin trying to understand the weaker constructivist argument for a postnational arrangement is in the period of transformation called "the Quiet Revolution"—a period in the 1960s that saw a sharply accelerated change in cultural values and the transfer of powers from institutions managed by the Church to those managed by the Quebec provincial state.

Fernand Dumont argues that from the onset the Quiet Revolution was itself a fundamentally "cultural revolution where an intelligentsia had tried to stage a social revolution" (1981b, 309). He indicates that in the cultural movement of the era, the new demands for the redistribution of economic and political power emerged parallel with identity claims. Marcel Rioux, in a similar vein, had already defined the debate in terms of recognition and redistribution, as Charles Taylor would also later do. Rioux, like Charles Taylor, tried to show how the historical demands for recognition call into question forms of cultural domination. The more that identity demands were heard, the more the demands for redistribution were also heard. Conversely, Dumont and Rioux maintain that demands for redistribution focused on structural forms of inequality and were posed in terms of class but they also agreed to pose them in terms of gender and ethnicity (Dumont 1996). Since the implicated groups were fundamentally interested in legal and cultural recognition for a new and sovereign nation-state, demands tied to gender, and to sexual orientation, were also linked to questions of redistribution via the national question. Similarly, demands tied to social class and ethnicity were also directly concerned with redistribution. The modern concept of the nation and nationalism in the Quebec case took root in dimensions of both recognition and redistribution. It is important to keep this duality in mind, but let us examine the theoretical dimension of the *ethnos* that Rioux and Dumont develop. The Quebec case was introduced to the world in Rioux's 1969 best-selling book *Quebec in Question*, in which he writes:

> In the era of great world superpowers, common markets, the increasingly spurred unification of the means of communication, at the hour of the conquest of space, is it not outrageously anachronistic to raise the problem of a people made up of six million individuals, who do not know the tragedies of war nor the pangs of hunger, and who live reasonably comfortably in North America, the continent of stability and of a high standard of living? It is a question that has been asked for a long time, paradoxically it has come out of a flagrant modernization; it encompasses interpolations which coincide with those of contemporary decolonization and contestation. (1978a, 3)

Rioux's affirmation of the modernity of the national question in Quebec remains coherent today only if we consider the advancement of globalization, as well as the transformation of national identity around the politics of recognition and redistribution—politics that have evolved out of the former Cold War context of superpowers, the emergence of the European and North American common markets, postcolonialism, and the push for worldwide expansion of the human rights procedural model of justice. In addition to considering this new context of globalization, three other considerations arise from the dialogical approach outlined in the previous chapter. First, is the movement for an independent state in Quebec nonviolent and democratic? Second, if it is democratic, is it an ethnic nationalism, and hence exclusionary, as the critics of primordialism charge, or is it a civic nationalism, and hence inclusive, as its defenders hold. Third, do its policies contradict the human rights model, as its appellants have claimed, or would they hold up to the scrutiny of international tribunals?

There has been no political violence over the issue of separation in Quebec since 1970 despite the failure of three referendums, since 1981, to bring about a constitutional solution to the claims of Quebec nationalists. The last referendum, in 1995, saw an extremely close vote against sovereignty and a new partnership with Canada. Although police came out to separate the two sides on the evening of the vote, no political violence was reported. Past human rights challenges at the international level, against provincial language laws, have been resolved through legislation and have won partial political and legal consensus. Today there are no outstanding legal challenges before international courts. However, minority groups continue to protest restricted access to schools and signage laws through the provincial courts. This continued protest suggests that the democratic process is working according to the rule of law and in this sense the existing provincial state apparatus has responded in a responsible and inclusive way. In addition, the Canadian Supreme Court recently ruled that a unilateral declaration of Quebec independence would be legal if a clear majority, to a clear referendum question, were to be achieved. Under such circumstances the Canadian government would be obliged to negotiate the terms of secession.

The question of whether Quebec nationalism is an ethnic or civic variety is an issue that overlaps with the wider theme of democracy and the rule of law but needs to be thought through in sociological and not legal terms. Rioux begins his analysis of the Quebec question by asking how, in an age of global superpowers, common markets, and the forms of unification resulting from communication technologies, is it possible to raise the question of Quebec's specificity? In the context of globalization and the growth of transnational forms of identification within modern nation-states, nationalist projects that even hint at primordial categories are easily dismissed as illiberal. In strictly economic terms, globalization has compromised the internal sovereignty of nation-states, while on the level of political expression nationalist movements seem to contradict the neoliberal model of individual freedom and formal democracy.

As Mark Lajoie points out, it is precisely the anachronistic appearance of the national movement within Quebec that Rioux argues lies at the heart of the Quebec question. Why, Rioux asks, "against the backdrop of globalization and the promotion of the neo-liberal atomization of the citizenry realized in terms of formal rights, should the question of Quebec's existence and persistence as a nation and as a society be posed?" (Lajoie 1999). Rioux argues that the Quebec question is a very special instance that needs to be considered outside the ethnic and civic models of nineteenth-century nationalist movements. The latter are seen to have stemmed from bourgeois revolutions, whereas the former is seen to have its origin in a 1837 peasant or *habitant* rebellion. For Rioux, then, Quebec nationalism does not share the same genesis in class interests that categorize other European and North American nationalisms. On the other hand, he recognizes the rapid rise of a new economic class in Quebec following the Quiet Revolution and warns that the time frame for such a model will quickly run out.[9]

Echoing Gellner's argument, Rioux formulates his analysis of the Quebec question along the lines of a critique of the transition from rural to urban social structures. Three ideological phases emerge from a series of historical cleavages. The first phase is an agrarian based conservative mentality of *survivance* that lasted from the defeat of the 1837 Rebellion to the end of World War II. After the British crushed the rebellion, and put more pressure on the clergy to better control the population, a more traditional Catholic and patriarchal mentality set in as a strategy to survive English hegemony. Traditional lifestyles, as well as a self- understanding of French ethnicity as a race rather than a culture in North America, is paramount to this mentality. By the 1950s, resistance against modernization eventually gave way to a new mentality of trying to catch up to the rest of North America, and to overcome the long accumulated cultural and, even more so, political and economic, lag. This transition is contained in a movement toward a neonationalist model with a self-understanding of French ethnicity as a secular, cultural minority, rather than as a race. The emerging urban industrial working and middle class is from the onset split between an independentist movement that would transform the secular self-understanding of itself as a national minority into a new Québécois nation-state and those who continue to search for solutions that would keep French Canadians within the Canadian Federation. Much of today's political discourse in Canada evolves around attempts to either accommodate or check these two ideological camps (McRoberts 1997).

Despite Rioux's constructivist assumption about the relation between class and nation, the problem raised by his argument about Quebec's *ethnos* is that it assumes a primordial reading of Quebec's pre-1960 past. Rioux and others argue that the late modernization of the region was due to the institutional reproduction of the conservative, Catholic, rural-dwelling peasant population. Rather than looking at political economy factors as determinant to the development of a modern Quebec as a North American region, Rioux's generation of intellectuals (said to have been influenced by both the French and the Chicago schools of sociology) tend to look to cultural homogeneity as a primordial or determining factor. Rioux's point is that cultural resistance to modernization created a margin to maneuver development of a new kind of global society, in North America. It is important not to confuse his definition of the Quebec *ethnos* as uniquely composed of its French speaking, formerly Catholic majority. Although he is referring to the French-speaking Québécois identity, he is not proposing an extreme primordial ethno-racial nationalism. He defines the nation as a sociology of culture and never proposes an ethnic definition for citizenship along "imaginary blood lines." On the contrary, for Rioux, Québécois identity is constructed from its institutions and traditions and is therefore deeply rooted in social structure (Thériault 1998).

Rioux's sociology of culture distinguishes between the real and potential social imaginary (1978b). The importance he accords to the potentiality of the imaginary dimension of culture can be seen in one of his earliest essays in philosophical anthropology where he writes: "Human culture appears to us as an acquired nature, a second nature which is super-added to the innate nature of man, and which permits him to develop his potentialities." This approach rests on the classical distinction in anthropology between primary and secondary culture. Primary culture, or *ethnos*, includes "the mass of ideas and the primarily implicit emotive reactions from which the group derives its lifestyle" (Rioux 1950, 315). Secondary culture, or *demos,* designates the actions of individuals in a given society as well as the material objects and political structures used by the group. The important constructivist point Rioux makes from this distinction is that the specificity of a culture is not defined by its moral, legal, or political edifice, nor even in its oral tradition, "but rather in the putting into practice of the normative ideals at stake in these representations" (1955, 7).

What is striking across Rioux's work is the importance he attributes to the specificity and potentiality of the primordial imaginary dimension of *ethnos,* and how he de-essentializes it by stating that what counts is the "putting into practice of the normative ideals at stake." *Ethnos* is an affective base from which the social imaginary is deployed on the normative institutional level. *Ethnos* is thus an enigmatic field of study for the human sciences in that the instituting social imaginary is also linked to the *demos*—the political-historical structures—but it remains autonomous. Rioux's definition of culture is an attempt to renovate the dimension of the *ethnos* and surpass its social determinations, but it also includes the idea of a transmission of traditions. This is paradoxical though. Given his statement concerning the potentiality and the creative utopian-like quality of the social imaginary, how can it be tied to something as seemingly embedded as tradition. The same paradox is made even more explicit by Rioux's colleague Fernand Dumont.

Dumont's more philosophical sociology of culture rests on a series of concepts that have been described as constituting a highly original approach (Weinstein 1985). Indeed, he is currently described by some as Quebec's most important intellectual (Warren 1998). His sociology of culture also deals with the distinction between primary and secondary levels. In its simplest definition, the master concept of culture is also couched in a weak primordial argument. For Dumont, culture refers to an actor's attempt to confer sense on the events of social life. To confer meaning, or sense, on an event is to explore both an absence and the shift to a new absence (Dumont 1968). In its more abstract and general form culture is also said to include the disciplines that seek to explain it, which in turn suggests that any approach to culture also needs to be reflexive. As Dumont puts it, "[A]nthropology is a reply to culture " (or *ethnos*), whereas ideologies are the "properly collective attempts at interpretation," in an attempt to articulate *demos* (Dumont 1981a, 11).

Dumont defines culture sociologically, as a set of discrete practices that operate dialogically in four overlapping zones of narrative (1981b, 129–153). In the first zone, he identifies a distinction between *culture savante,* which absorbs the categories proper to primary culture, but according to specialized perspectives and the different integrative institutional practices such as law, business, education, government, the church, administration, and the economy that operate in a second zone. This second zone of institutional practices can adopt the model of *culture savante,* but not its programs of action, given their role in the management of secondary culture. A third zone, popular culture, undergoes the effects of organizational stratification, but it adapts according to its own logic. Finally, the fourth and most archaic zone— the discourse that carries imaginary belonging, alterity, and memory— resides in the traditional practices of culture that maintain themselves in narratives either in isolation from, or alongside, the other discursive zones. These traditional pockets of meaning are appropriated, reified, or even folklorized by organizations. But they can also survive in the cracks, as it were, and live to reappear as sources of mobilization, and change.

This somewhat simplified presentation of Dumont's disciplinary approach to culture informs his definition of the genesis of Quebec society in a way that compliments Rioux's. For both thinkers understanding the genesis of Quebec society requires placing it in the context of European imperialism and colonialism. World views and forms of discourse conceived in the context of the world system have a definite impact on the origin of Quebec society but both its *ethnos* and *demos* are seen as being marked by Quebec's internal struggle to adapt to the imperatives of modernity via a stubborn resistance from its conservative elites. For Dumont, opposition between world views and forms of discourse turned toward the past and the maintenance of traditional values and those orientated toward progress and the personalization of the individual over the collective subject is the fundamental conflict at the birth of the French North American social imaginary. The Quebec *ethnos* is carried in the imaginary reference to the French-speaking people of North America for whom Quebec would become the territorial center. Reference to the imaginary collectivity is derived from historical events and the "written conjugation of utopia and memory" through literature and historiography (1993, 320). Dumont insists that the study of references to the nation's *ethnos* is not a study about nationalism but of the resources on which nationalism might draw.

Rioux and Dumont's concept of the nation as a sociology of culture thus anticipates many of the arguments found in the history and sociology of nations and nationalism discussed in chapter 7. The genesis of Quebec society is not the degree-zero of either an ethnic or political definition of the nation in the sense that Anthony Smith develops his typology. These Quebec sociologists are well aware that the majority of humanity does not and will not live within a nation-state composed of only one reference to a people. Their contribution to the literature on the nation is to provide a study of the way in which *le peuple* is imagined. This is a famous research path pointed to by

Anderson in the first chapter of *Imagined Communities,* but abandoned in order to take up a political economy explanation of the rise of nationalism, which is not the same subject. Hobsbaum argues that the historiography of the national imaginary cannot be studied because the day to day levels of society, or popular culture, were for the most part not written and therefore have not left the necessary documentation. Yet Dumont's *La genèse de la société Québécois* and Rioux's *Quebec in Question* are able to demonstrate the specificity of the national sentiment in the zone of *culture savante* as well as in organizational, popular, and traditional zones. Both Rioux and Dumont argue in these works that the founding narrative for the imaginary is above all a hybrid political culture that comes out of the failure of the European dream to find the Northwest Passage. Its genesis, they argue, is in the polycultural organization of New France; that is, the mixture of aboriginals and peoples with diverse ethnic backgrounds. Quebec's polycultural makeup developed in a long series of oppositions that gave birth to parallel institutions of French-Canadian and eventually Québécois historiography and literature that would carry the reference to *le peuple* or the nation.

Rioux and Dumont conceived their arguments for a modern form of Quebec sovereignty-association according to weak primordial and constructivist arguments. As we have just seen, their definitions of the nation rest on a sociology of culture that distinguishes multiple levels of institutional discourse and identities. It is clear that both privilege an ethnographic, and to a certain degree ethnological, approach to culture but they do not make either an ethnic or a civic argument for nationalism and so the question of whether or not such a definition risks defining citizenship primordially or as a pre-political, homogeneous ethnic group remains ambiguous. Does their approach exclude reference to other sociological communities that have contributed to the building of a civil society and economy in Quebec? Or does it provide a broad platform for negotiating a political community that would form a future postnational state?

Quebeckers have been divided now for a generation between the status quo and negotiations for a new partnership with a sovereign Quebec state that would include a shared monetary union, common passport, and possibly a host of other overlapping confederal-Canadian institutions. Most minority groups within Quebec have demonstrated that they do not want a sovereign Quebec. Paradoxically, though, we have to remember that these minorities have also been active participants in both Quebec's and Canada's societal cultures and therefore can be defined as being both Québécois and Canadian. Like most minorities in Quebec, it should also be underlined that the majority of *independentists* do not seek to break all ties with Canada but rather seek shared sovereignty or sovereignty and a new partnership with Canada. Indeed, many Quebec liberal nationalists opt for federalism and see no contradiction in defining themselves as both Québécois nationalists and Canadian. There is a margin of maneuver here for thinking dialogically about the relation between *ethnos* and *demos* in Quebec that needs to be explained more clearly in sociological terms.

Any imaginary referent to Quebec national identity should be prefaced by a full discussion of the main sociological communities and multiple national identities that now constitute a decentered Quebec society. At least four such communities are readily identifiable both in terms of their self-definitions and possible negotiation strategies: 1) a French-speaking majority within Quebec (5,700,150 whose mother tongue is French out of a total population of 7,045,080) which is also a conquered national minority within Canada, and a minority within North America; 2) a potential English Canadian national minority within Quebec (586,435) which is also part of a national majority within Canada and a minority within North America; 3) Quebec minority immigrant communities with linguistic origins other than French or English (657,580) who are also minorities within both Canada and North American; and 4) national aboriginal minorities (71,415) within Quebec who are also minorities within Canada and North America.[10] Each of these communities would need to be approached in terms of both their specificity *(ethnos)* and in terms of the recognition of each community's contribution to a possible new political society *(demos)*. Thus, the definition of le *Québécois* as citizen would need an inclusive assumption (in the civic sense) and yet also be flexible regarding the recognition of differences (in the cultural sense).

Unlike the civic and ethnic models of the nation, the dialogical definition of the nation I would like to propose has the advantage of directing theoretical strategies toward both the recognition of difference between communities (by according institutional rights, for example) and toward the development of an inclusive political community (individual rights derived from the convergence of various sociological communities). If we agree that Quebec is a modern, complex, multicultural society, and not a homogeneous one, then any argument that might entertain an extreme primordial definition of the Québécois *ethnos* has to be rooted out and critically examined. In this sense, Rioux's and Dumont's definition of the nation as a sociology of culture (an imaginary

reference to *le peuple*) needs to be revised toward a more political definition that would recognize a plurality of peoples who live inside its
demos and participate in its institutions. Caution is necessary here not to
simply repeat a purely civic definition of the nation, because such a definition risks misrecognizing the French-Québécois identity, or end in
a pretense to universality that is itself exclusive.

The idea of becoming a "normal nation"—an aspiration pro-na-
tionalist politicians and intellectuals in Rioux and Dumont's paradigm often articulate—needs to be clearly understood as one that
lends a broad and open-ended definition to the imaginary community
of the *demos* as a hybrid of complex overlapping sociological communities. It is important to stress that admitting the lack of unity in such
a reference to the *demos* does not entail opposing some form of shared
sovereignty arrangement between Quebec and Canada in the future,
in favor of a renewed federal Canada under the banner of some abstract constitutional accommodation—so-called asymmetric federalism. Rather, this admission requires asking how the sovereignty of a
people actually constituted by cultural and political diversity can be
instituted—a position that should, therefore, admit the contingent
nature of the referent and of the need to share sovereignty itself. I will
come back to this argument after further discussing the politics of
recognition and the discourse theory of democracy via the debates
among the antinationalist political philosophies of Habermas, Taylor,
and Kymlicka.

Habermas: The Nation as Subjectless Communication

Habermas's recent writings on the nation and democracy offer one of
the strongest counterarguments to the cultural and ethnographic approaches of thinkers such as Rioux and Dumont. He wages perhaps
the most stubborn critique against one-sided culturalist arguments in
the defense of a highly rationalistic theory of democracy. Arguing
against the "neo-Hobbsian" philosophy of Karl Schmitt, in particular,
and the German tradition of the "imagined blood relation," in general,
he proposes a normative theory of democracy that is derived from a
complete separation of *ethnos* from *demos* (1998). I do not propose to
argue that Habermas's position should be taken up as a better way of
getting to a postnational definition of the nation—given the dialogical
definition of the *ethnos-demos* relation. Instead, I try to indicate how
one of his key theoretical concepts—the "decentered society"—can be

utilized to correct the overemphasis on *ethnos* in the definition of the nation as a sociology of culture. A brief review of his approach to the two-level concept of society is offered before proceeding more directly to the discourse theory that directs his approach to the *demos*.

In his earlier two-volume work on *Communicative Action* Habermas treats the development of a sociological theory of society as a process that has led to "the unmixing of two paradigms that could no longer be integrated into a two-level concept connecting system and lifeworld" (1987, 202). He argues that systems theory fails to distinguish between systemic and social forms of integration, while interpretive sociologies replace the explanatory capacity of concept building in favor of "methodological descriptivism." Interpretive sociologies are orientated uniquely toward intersubjective meaning, whereas systems theory defines meaning as a function that reduces "the complexity peculiar to social systems" (McCarthy 1991, 122). If we see society only from the point of view of systems integration then we reduce it to its structure of domination, of equilibrium management, or of self-regulation, and hence social actors cease to be seen as creatures who create mutual understanding. On the other hand, if we define society only as the social integration of meaning in lifeworlds, then the material and symbolic reproduction of society can only be seen from the point of view of the actor in limited situations. Consequently, we give up the claim to be able to explain society as a whole. Systems "have to be gotten at hermeneutically, from the internal perspective of the participants." Entities subsumed under systems "must be identified as the lifeworlds of social groups and understood in their symbolic structures" (Habermas 1987, 151). While the steering media of money, administration, and power colonize lifeworlds, it is the lifeworld that is the ordering principle of society according to Habermas.

System and lifeworld should not be confused with macro and micro levels. As soon as a speaker enters language he or she also enters a lifeworld as well as a mediating subsystem. Habermas connects the seemingly opposite conceptual strategies of systems and lifeworld by introducing the concepts of communicative action and discourse ethics, as was seen in chapters 1 and 2. These concepts, in turn, explain the grounding of the public sphere in democratic societies. Although it is constantly pressured by steering systems of administration, power, and money, the public sphere is understood to be on the side of the lifeworld and civil society. Habermas argues that in democratic societies, public communication processes should work toward operating in relatively unconstrained conditions given that the sphere itself is derived from differentiated interpretations of the same symbols by distinct lifeworlds.

Habermas's concept of communicative action, and the corollary procedure of discourse ethics (discussed in chapter 1), defines the mixing of lifeworlds as a process of rationalization. Giving up the burden of dialogue to systems integration puts pressure on the public sphere that, in turn, responds by producing new means for deriving mutual understanding. The legal institution becomes the "drive belt" on which the systems equilibrium is generated (1996a). Returning to the question of national identity, we can better understand why Habermas argues that constitutional patriotism and social solidarity need to rest on levels of communication that get uncoupled from primary culture and not on the level of the imaginary reference to the community. Since the diversity of lifeworlds and their discourses demand normative expressions on the part of "decentered" subjects who are bearers of multiple traditions, Habermas contends that the parliamentary and legal forms of communication that constitute the nation must be "subjectless." In other words, the nation itself is subjectless in the sense that its reference must be derived from sources beyond all particular traditions so it can represent all members who live under its constitution.

In developing his position on the nation, Habermas draws elements of an innovative discourse theory of democracy from a synthesis of liberal and republican models that is worth reviewing in order to get the full effect of his argument (Nielsen 1998b). For liberalism, he argues, society is a network of private interactions. Government must conciliate the diversity of these private interests. Elections, and the formation of public opinion and of political will, are at the source of a decisional rationalization of the administrative apparatus controlled by laws that apply to all citizens. The rationalization of discourse is more than a simple way to respond to the problem of legitimacy in the liberal sense, but it is not the political force that fashions society, as the republican model would have it. When the administrative apparatus of the state entrenches itself in public reason, it must equally adjust its positions in relation to this public. Popular opinion creates an influence that initially transforms itself into a communicational force and later, on the basis of legislation, into an administrative force. "Even when it is acquired, popular sovereignty must conform to democratic procedures and to communicative presuppositions in order to itself become a force" (Habermas 1996c, 28–29).

For liberalism, the state is understood as the administrative apparatus of political power that manages the plurality of interests of civil society. A certain separation of state and society is demanded, but the principle force of integration of interests resides in society rather than the state. What is important is that the state does not upset the pluralist equilibrium. The process of forming a political opinion thus includes the alliance between diverse interests for or against the administrative apparatus, which must in turn react. Liberalism defines democracy as a process of compromise between a plurality of interests derived from fundamental rights. The individual citizen is the bearer of these rights. Habermas's discourse theory argues that liberalism's reference to the formation of political will must be normatively reinforced, but without going as far as the republican model (1996c, 1996a).

In the republican model, society is understood to be formed by a multiplicity of communities which, through a process of political deliberation, become normatively conscious of one another. Rights are conceived in a positive rather than a negative manner since they consist less of protecting the citizen than of favoring his or her participation in public debates on the common good. This capacity to communicate is the source of power upon which society as a whole is founded. The rights of citizens do not exist by virtue of the transcendent principle of reason, as in liberalism; they are rooted in the formation of political will through dialogue in the public sphere. "Politics is conceived as the reflective form of substantial ethical life, namely as the medium in which the members of somehow solitary communities become aware of their dependence on one another and, acting with full deliberation as citizens, further shape and develop existing relations of reciprocal recognition into an association of free and equal consociates under law" (1996c, 21.) The political paradigm thus flows from dialogue and not from the market.

Habermas criticizes both liberalism and republicanism as resting on a unitary conception of society. For liberalism, the whole of society is in the reference to the individual, while for republicanism the whole of society is in the reference to the community. For the discourse theory of democracy, society is defined as decentered because of the increased rationalization of the lifeworld (the dissociation of "culture," of "society," and of "personality") and the increased capacity of the social subsystem for self-regulation. Lifeworlds and subsystems uncouple when the effects of mutual engagement *(bindungseffekt)* are no longer produced in an endogenous manner, but are incumbent to different spheres of the processes of intercomprehension. For modern societies, the creation of public space rests on an increased rationalization of conflicting lifeworlds. The unity of this space is in turn mediated by the regulatory mediums of money and power. The politics of recognition, the postulate of the inherent cultural autonomy in the lifeworld, increase the pressure on the public space that must, at the same time, absorb the forces of rationalization of the system as well (1987).

The discourse theory of democracy privileges the formation of public opinion, but it also demands a constitutional framework, which is understood as a guide for the instutionalization of opinions expressed in the public sphere. For Habermas, the institution of deliberative democracy and state neutrality (liberalism) is preferable to the collective action of the citizens (republicanism). The liberal approach to elections is considered to be more reasonable because it reinforces constitutional patriotism without compromising the separation of legislative, executive, and judiciary powers (Habermas 1996c, 29). The democratic unity of society must rest on a "constitutional patriotism," a result of the process of rationalization in the legal and political domains and this, even if the sources are profoundly cultural. Habermas argues that the unity of society should derive from the legal rules that link together the diverse ethical and cultural communities within the same structure, but which permits each an autonomous development.

As I have stated, it is important to retain Habermas's concept of the "decentered society"as a corrective for the reference to the imaginary nation. On the other hand, the idea of "subjectless communication" (the neutrality principal of the state) needs to be nuanced while "constitutional patriotism" should be challenged on the basis of its implied monologization of the *ethnos-demos* relation. The weakness in his discourse theory of democracy stems from its exaggerated contention that an equilibrium between administrative powers, economic powers, and social solidarity could, in fact, achieve mutual reciprocal adjustment (Joas and Honneth 1991). On this point, the criterion of universality in the search for systemic equilibrium goes too far in that it risks cutting politics off from all cultural forms of expression. From this position Habermas concludes that the separation of federal countries unified by diversity (of which Canada is a prime example) must be avoided and that it is preferable to not precipitate the unification of countries separated by conflicts (Germany was an example, and Korea remains one, along with the new divisions in the Balkans). As he argues, it is preferable to envisage a postnational future in order to avoid the pathologies of *ethnos* and preserve a more universal *demos* (1996b; 1998b; 2001).

Here we have returned to our point of departure. There is no way to make a judgment about "We" claims in the extreme constructivist versions of the civic nation, only this time, the argument is couched in a juridical and not historical model, as with Hobsbaum and Anderson. To paraphrase Alexander Motyl's criticism: "Even constitutional patriotism can appeal only to the speakers of a given language who enjoy a certain kind of historicized relationship with a well defined deified basic law" (1999, 78). Constitutional patriotism insists too much on the *demos* and not enough on the *ethnos* to be able to think their relation in dialogical terms. As Bakhtin states: "It is only in a dialogic perspective that the discourses of one and of the other are taken seriously, as propositions endowed with sense and as points of view." Habermas's uncoupling of *ethnos* from *demos* thus risks eliminating the analysis of collective identity altogether.

Taylor: The Nation as a Politics of Concession

In contrast to Habermas, Charles Taylor's approach to democracy is often described as "communitarian," though he himself does not find the term appropriate (Horton 1998). He derives his approach to the politics of recognition from a reflection on the ethical sources of mutual respect, dignity, and especially the individual quest for becoming an authentic modern self. The quest for individual and social identity is seen as deeply rooted in the recognition gained from open-ended and "non-scripted dialogue." Recognition thus has a tendency to take on a hetroglot or asymmetric form that places stress on individuals and groups looking to achieve equal dignity. In the sphere of private intimacy, very much in sync with Bakhtin and Mead, Taylor says the stress is placed on the dialogue between significant others wherein each person depends on an increasingly smaller circle for recognition in order to discover who he or she is, and often what he or she wants. In the public sphere, stress is imposed in terms of a clash between particularistic politics of equal dignity and the universal politics of procedural forms of equality based on the principle of the freedom of the individual. "Nonrecognition (in either sphere) or inadequate recognition can cause suffering and constitutes a form of oppression, by imprisoning some in a false, deformed or reduced manner of being" (1994, 25).

The search for recognition thus takes the form of a quest for identity and a critique of the structures of exclusion proper to the dominant society. The historically oppressed culture demands reparation for the injustices that prevented the authentic expression of its narrative, of its images of itself, of its language and its customs in the public sphere. It is through linking the search for recognition and identity that a space where the individual can realize his or her subjectivity in its deepest expression can be modeled. The search for recognition thus often implies a need for reparation through the granting of asymmetrical rights. Identity demands are in this sense paradoxical, because they are directed, at the same time, to a politics of influence and a politics of inclusion: such demands envision, at the same time, a defense of particular interests, including the autonomy of a lifeworld, and equitable representation for all in the context of a social system that colonizes them. The more the unity of culture is defined around an essential difference proper to it, the more it risks making itself exclusive. And the weaker this definition of unity, the more culture is subject to disintegration.

According to Habermas, the main weakness in Taylor's proposed politics of recognition is that it endeavors to combine feminism, multiculturalism, nationalism, and the struggle against colonialism and Eurocentrism into an ultimately reductive single frame of reference. Taylor's other mistake, according to Habermas, is that embedded in this reduction of different social struggles to a singular politics of recognition, is a false opposition between the rights of individuals to equality, and the need to protect collective identities. According to Habermas, Taylor maintains that in the conflict between these two forms of rights, one must take priority over the other. Habermas argues that Taylor's truncated reading of liberalism is most mistaken with respect to the meaning of the universal rule that says that all individuals have a right to equal treatment. He contends that this founding idea of justice does not forcefully demand blindness to difference, as Taylor contends, but rather that justice is sensitive to the fact that the autonomy of the private sphere is as important as the autonomy of the public sphere. Individuals only have autonomy if they can exercise it as citizens, and if it is possible for them to understand that certain sectors of the population can suffer from inequality. According to Habermas, blindness to difference disappears as soon as liberalism integrates the argument that bearers of rights are intersubjective beings. The human subject, exactly like the legal subject, cannot become an individualized subject except though a process of socialization. "The politics of recognition do not demand that we let the universalism of rights fall in favor of an alternative communitarian model. It simply consists in applying the system of rights as they evolved in civil society in a coherent manner" (Habermas 1994b, 123).

Although both thinkers have addressed each other's political terrains, Habermas's position on the national question is formulated mainly through his European, and especially German, experience, whereas Taylor's discussions derive more directly from his engagement with the political cultures of Canada, and particularly Quebec. Both Taylor and Habermas are antinationalist in that they tend to categorize claims for associational sovereignty as vaguely transformed versions of ethnic nationalism. The resolution of the Quebec question, for Habermas, would thus consist of a reciprocal adjustment aiming for legal compromise within the Canadian system. Writes Habermas: "[I]f I am not mistaken, in Canada, the debate is not about the principle of the equality of rights but about the nature and extent of the state powers that should be transferred to the Province of Quebec" (1994b, 128). For Habermas, the limited application of a politics of multiculturalism in the Canadian case, in contrast to nationalism, does not have a very important structural impact and has only a small influence on the identity of the majority of the citizens. On the other hand, in a federation such as Canada, nationalism and secessionist movements could have a very broad structural impact on people's identity.

There is a contradiction in Habermas's argument that needs to be pointed out. On the one hand, he claims that we should entertain a contextual and historical understanding of the legal culture in the sense that it might evolve toward a consensus concerning the recognition of certain groups' rights. An example would be the pluralist argument for affirmative action, wherein groups may temporally receive special compensations because they can be shown to have been historically discriminated against by the state or the dominant culture. On the other hand, Habermas categorically refuses to attribute rights, such as language rights, to groups based on the argument that such rights are necessary for the groups' cultural survival. Cultures, he argues, cannot be protected like animal species. Either they have the will to survive and flourish, or they do not.

The difference between Taylor and Habermas on this point is quite instructive. Taylor understands that there is at least a partial consensus in Canadian law and society that the French culture and language should be protected. In a sense, he assumes Habermas's argument against his own separation of individual and collective rights. Habermas, on the other hand, assumes that the Quebec question is nothing more than the transfer of state powers. Given Taylor's theoretical orientation toward recognition, his position on "the Quebec question" is more ambiguous. This may be due, in no small part, to his well-known identification with, and sense of belonging to, Quebec; and to his life-long fight to gain recognition for a special status for Quebec in the Canadian federation. On the other hand, Taylor resists defining Quebec as a national minority in the political sense, and instead prefers a cultural definition—at least in part because he knows that the political definition threatens the continued existence of the federation (Seymor 1999a). For Taylor, Canada, in fact, needs Quebec's recognition in order to secure its own sense of identity. Taylor's solution? Canada needs to concede a legal definition of the distinct status of Quebec within Canada so that Quebec will be assured of its future existence; and Quebec needs to give up its distressing tribal claims.

Taylor argues that Quebec and Canada have each developed different political and legal cultures, especially since the repatriation of the Canadian constitution in 1982. In part, Taylor argues, misrecognition of Quebec by English Canada stems from an accelerated absorption of the American model of liberal-individualism and the equality of states version of federalism. The procedural definition of justice in which the rights of individuals take precedence over the rights of collectivities seeks to guarantee each person the same rights by making sure the law treats individuals with exactly the same procedures. Taylor argues that Québécois and aboriginal identities are examples of a collectivist quest aimed at securing protection for language and culture. Such protection was only partially secured in the British North America Act of 1867. The collectivist approach to group recognition is an example of how the politics of recognition can clash with the universalist model of individual rights.

Taylor's position on Quebec has not shifted much since he broke his alliance with nationalists looking to found a new social democratic party during the Quiet Revolution.[11] Taylor recognizes the French Canadians as a founding nation and does argue for an asymmetric form of rights, but he does not recognize *les Québécois* as a national minority whose rights may be best achieved through some form of shared sovereignty. He thus retains the definition of Quebec as a homogeneous cultural or ethnic nation while English Canada is seen to be a diverse, heterogeneous, and, hence, more fully modern society (Seymor 1999a).

It may not be as difficult to move from Taylor's position toward a more modern, complex definition of Quebec society as some would suggest. Taylor and Habermas provide a rich definition of the relation between the moral and the political that could also be applied to a postnational scenario. As Habermas argues, the realization of rights occurs in the context "of the political discussion which bears on the shared concept of the good life." This political discussion of the good life includes the demands of citizens in a given country, region, city, or district; it includes the identity of the inheritors of a culture, the choice of traditions they want to retain or transform, the official language, or the teaching program in schools, for example. Disagreement is not provoked by the neutrality of the juridical system, but results from the fact that "the democratic process for the realization of fundamental rights is from the outset saturated with ethical questions" (1994b, 112–113).

Although he has never taken a middle-ground position, for his option has always been antinationalist, Taylor remains one of the most important dialogical thinkers to interpret both sides of the debate on Quebec over the last thirty years. He draws a sympathetic audience from Quebec pronationalists who perceive him as one of the rare contemporary intellectual figures not to reject outright the principle of Quebec sovereignty-association. When discussing in French with francophones he is able to show his immanent understanding of the advantages of Quebec independence. On the other hand, his writings in English reassure anglophones of the moral, and especially economic, impossibility of separation. Despite the apparent inconsistency of presenting such different tones of argument, there is no dishonesty in advancing one side of this subject to anglophones and another to francophones. As Taylor himself points out:

> One too easily falls prey to the habit of speaking separately to the audiences who define themselves as distinct. Since each of these audiences has its own perspective, its own key terms, and its own premises; the starting point of the discourse is different in each case. In former times, Canadian politicians were often accused of saying different things in Quebec than they said in English Canada. In fact, it is almost impossible not to do so, even when there is not the slightest intention of trickery. I do not pretend that our politicians were never dishonest. Far from it. But I do maintain that a rigorously honest discourse cannot be identical in both contexts. (1993)

Moreover, Taylor persuades an *independentist* audience to enter this dialogue largely because he is able to convey the message that he is will-

ing to admit a space for a "maybe" regarding the question of sovereignty-association. It is important to recall that this is a message few involved in liberal federal political culture are able to formulate in
Canada. Given a linguistic barrier, English Canadian intellectuals are
not always privy to Taylor's more conciliatory positions on Quebec independence, but are often stiffly reminded of the political and cultural
specificity of Quebec's ethnic or cultural nation. This audience appreci-
ates the insider knowledge he smoothly and masterfully delivers. They
also read the federalist message behind his talented juxtapositions of
ideological differences within Quebec and within Canada. Both "cultural readerships" are drawn to his work with the added knowledge that
he entertains a worldwide audience. On the other hand, Taylor is also
known as a vigorous opponent of so-called hard-line separatists. In
some respects "hard-line separatist" is an ambiguous term which has
become coded to instantly categorize anyone who thinks the only solution to the Canada-Quebec impasse is sovereignty-association. In fact,
no political party promotes an absolute version of sovereignty and the
percentage of respondents who favor outright independence is consistently minuscule. Leveling political opponents is a tactic that works
well in the heat of debate but is hardly the stuff of recognition, nor can
it be seen as part of a dialogic approach to *ethnos* and *demos*. This kind
of classification designates gradations of the nationalist project that are
meant to remind listeners of the slippery slope one inevitably slides
down, in primordial ethnic definitions of the nation that are, in turn,
understood as a major source of violent confrontations in world history.
Many neonationalist intellectuals and politicians promote strategies for
cultural survival that get confused and mired in definitions of ethnic
purity. In attacking these strategies aggressively, Taylor reveals a political position that sometimes cuts him off from serious exchange with
neonationalists who wonder how anyone adopting such a hardline position against "separatists" could possibly pretend to a politics of recognition (Bariteau 1998).

Taylor joins the argument against the emerging identity claims of
Quebec francophones who seek recognition for a new nation and ask
to be identified as Québécois and not French Canadian. This question
of identification is a very interesting problem in the Canada-Quebec
dialogic impasse, one that leads to a number of misunderstandings
around political definition and which, therefore, prove irresistible for
an astute and sophisticated theorist like Taylor. Taylor is aware that a
major source of confusion over the recognition of Quebec within
Canada relates to the interpretation of history—and particularly to the

reluctance on the part of anglophone Canadians to accept the importance of the Conquest of New France by the British in 1759. While
this was undoubtedly a founding moment of Quebec's political identity, the Quebec "nation" is in fact much older and its culture, traditions, and sense of a strong collectivity can be traced back to New
France at least a century or more prior to the Conquest.

The word *Canada*, which means village, comes from a language
group belonging to the Huron and Iroquois whose ancestors migrated
to Canada more than 20,000 years ago. *Quebec* is a word that comes
from another linguistic family whose speakers include the Algo-
nquin—a native North American tribe that inhabited the region before the Huron and Iroquois. The word *Quebec* signifies a passage, or a
strait, like the Saint Lawrence Seaway which runs in front of Quebec
City. For more than a century before the British Conquest, the inhabitants of New France referred to themselves as *Canadiens* in order to
distinguish themselves from the French. Gradually, as the English and
American settlers in Lower and Upper Canada began referring to
themselves as Canadians, the roughly 65,000 inhabitants of Quebec
(1763) started calling themselves *Canadiens-français*. The term *Québécois* originally referred only to the inhabitants of Quebec City. Its first
reference to the "people" of Quebec appeared about one hundred years
ago (Rioux 1975, 11–13). The term *Québécois* only came into widespread use in the 1950s when it emerged as a term specifically associated with those looking to endorse the will to self-determination or
sovereignty. While most anglophones in Quebec (less than 8 percent
of the population have English as their mother tongue) prefer the
term *Quebecker*, or simply *Canadian*, to describe their national identity (Radice 2000), there are signs among some allophones (less than
8 percent of the population whose mother tongue is neither English
nor French) that their preference could be changing. Ironically, the
term *Québécois* can actually include non-francophones and English-
speaking Quebeckers, and can exclude those *Canadiens français* living
outside Quebec who increasingly refer to themselves in more specifically regional terms as Acadiens, Franco-Ontariens, Fransaskois, etc.

But just what is Taylor's theory of the Quebec *demos?* The folding
of the politics of recognition into a politics of concession can be seen
to occur rather rapidly in his recent two-level definition of the nation
and nationalism (Taylor 1998). Here, he very clearly demonstrates his
willingness to concede the possibility of Quebec sovereignty by weigh-
ing into philosophical debates about whether secessionist movements
such as Quebec's can be considered liberal in a moral and political

sense. Significantly, he does not give any moral and political reasons why this would be the case, other than to admit that *Québécois independentisme* constitutes a democratic social movement. Instead, he locates Quebec nationalism within a literature that is, for the most part, critical of nationalism worldwide rather than locating it within the more conciliatory work that seeks to understand the diversity of cultural and political forms. His article's opening argument provides a taste of the more hard-line position he takes regarding secessionists when it presents a contrast between the self-determination pleas of the Serbs and Croats and those of *les Québécois*. Although elsewhere in this article he condemns the pernicious tendency to "misrecognize" Quebec nationalism, and thus to assume that it will automatically and inevitably lead to the same criminal violence we have seen in the Balkans following nationalist movements. Ironically, though, he makes this admission only to demonstrate that despite some important differences these forms of nationalism are also somewhat alike. "The differences are explained by the first being more extreme than the second; rather than on the analogy of : neat whisky knocks you out, but taken diluted makes you mellow" (1998, 191). It thus seems clear from the outset that he does want to link them to the same source even if, as he says, "[T]he ultimate sources of modern nationalism escape us (Perhaps they always will)." He continues to offer a general theory of nationalism that rests on two levels: that of the struggles involved in organizing the national state; and that which address the sources of "the imaginary community." His synthesis of Gellner and Anderson allows him to bring together his original position on nationalism—as a product of middle-class interests—yet still hold onto a dialogical argument regarding the struggles for recognition within the "imaginary community." Or so it would seem.

What is perhaps most striking about Taylor's position, and as others have commented on as well, is the extent to which he presents French Canada and contemporary Quebec as a homogeneous society comprised of one ethnic group—*les Québécois*—rather than as a diverse, complex, modern, democratic, postindustrial society comprised of diverse cultures and traditions including the dominant francophone culture. The fact that most *non-Québécois de souche*, or, non-old-stock Québécois, continue to identify with Quebec society and continue to live under its civil law and contribute to its societal institutions (despite the fact they want no truck with independence) means that the cultural distinction between Québécois and non-Québécois is not as embedded as he appears to assume. Is not the political subjectivity of the Québécois just as complex, diverse, and multicultural as that of Canadians? Or Americans? Or world citizens? Something seems out of place here.

Kymlicka: On National Minorities

The most sophisticated thinker to revise Taylor's argument about the political status of the Québécois national identity via a theorization on citizenship, multiculturalism, and nationalism is Will Kymlicka. His work on citizenship reduces the gap between Taylor's and Habermas's positions and in so doing comes much closer to a reflection on the fundamentally modern form of the Québécois *demos*. He begins by affirming that the presence of an independentist politics in Quebec does not signal the lack of an already politicized culture in Quebec with all the earmarks of a liberal and democratic society. As we have seen, this is something neither Taylor nor Habermas are quick to concede. On the other hand, Kymlicka concentrates more rigorously than Taylor on recognizing Quebec and the Québécois as a nation within a nation and hence he travels much farther into the liberal nationalist definition of Quebec's origins than either Habermas or Taylor.

In order to integrate traditional republican or communitarian concerns into the liberal model, Kymlicka proposes to sociologically distinguish between ethnic and national minorities. He favors the self-determination of national minorities and the according of certain specific rights within multinational states. Thus, for example, Aboriginals, Puerto Ricans, Hawaiians, or Québécois do not simply constitute ethnic subgroups within a common culture, but distinct "societal cultures." His distinction relies on two different interpretations of the word *culture* that are quite close to Rioux's and Dumont's definitions. On the one hand, it includes a variety of relations—the more or less local and circumstantial multiple affinities and class positions—as well as a series of lifestyles, diverse sexual orientations, social movements, and voluntary associations that include all those groups who seek the recognition to which Taylor alludes. On the other hand, according to Kymlicka—and this is what characterizes nations or peoples through the course of societal modernization—a "societal culture" implies not only shared historical memory and values, but a range of common institutions that can be found in both public and private spheres (Kymlicka 1995, 113). The distinction between national and ethnic minorities, or groups who seek to have their cultural affinities recognized, therefore, does not rest exclusively on a culturalist reading but, on the contrary, refers to institutions and asymmetrical forms of rights. Kymlicka sketches three ways of responding to the demands of minorities in liberal democracies: 1) instituting the right to self-determination for national minorities; 2) offering specific rights that favor the integration of minority groups into society; and 3) guaranteeing the specific rights for better representation in the democratic process (1995, 6; Nielsen 1998b).

To recap, I am arguing that several weaknesses can be discerned in Taylor's and Habermas's approach to the Quebec question. Firstly, as Habermas points out, Taylor does not adequately distinguish the Quebec question from other political struggles. On the other hand, Habermas's discourse theory of democracy ends in an abstract separation of *ethnos* from *demos* and an idealistic plea for constitutional patriotism derived from a subjectless nation. Taylor, at least, remains open to a balance between collective and individual rights but still retains a neutral role for the state. Yet neither Habermas nor Taylor appear willing to acknowledge the existing complex, diverse, and democratic nature of Quebec society as it is already institutionally constituted. Finally, Kymlicka's definition of societal culture and of the national minority is a step toward the argument we saw in Rioux's and Dumont's sociology of culture.

Kymlicka's concept of *les Québécois* as a national minority, endowed with a fully modern societal culture is, thus, a very useful place to begin looking at how to converge the sociology of culture with the political philosophies we have been discussing. However, there is still one theoretical problem to address here. Unlike Taylor and Habermas, Kymlicka's argument for keeping Quebec within the Canadian federation is cast entirely in utilitarian terms. He claims that the constitution and the state policy of multiculturalism offer the legal choice of either English or French language to all citizens, and that because Quebec's aspirations for cultural autonomy are already legally constituted, its aspirations will best be maximized within the Canadian federation. Like Taylor, he does not state a categorical opposition to an associational form of sovereignty but argues simply that it would not be in Quebec's best interests. On the other hand, both argue for an asymmetric form of federalism. The problem with Kymlicka's and Taylor's civic definition of the Canadian nation is that the state has not been able to find an actually existing political agreement in Canada; one that would minimally recognize Quebec as a national minority. I want to conclude my argument by proposing that Kymlicka's position is politically, and especially strategically, limiting. I propose to retain Rioux and Dumont's sociological definition of the imaginary reference to the Québécois as a national minority with the caveat borrowed from Habermas, which is that the imaginary reference to the nation be treated in a "decentered" definition of societal culture. Let me now finally conclude by sketching out what such a definition might look like in a cosmopolitical postnational form.

Associational Sovereignty: A Fourth Way?

From out of a dialogue among numerous thinkers, this chapter has sought to construct a theoretical model capable of addressing the nation in postnational times. I began by reconstructing the dialogical form of the argument made by neonationalists who define the nation as a sociology of culture. Their overemphasis on *ethnos* was corrected in order to provide a definition of the plurality of identities that compose the Quebec question in the North American context. To get at the fuller implications of the problem of plural identities I shifted back to Habermas's counter position on citizenship and national identity and to the criticisms he offers of Charles Taylor's attempt to theorize both individual and collective rights through a politics of recognition. I conclude that overemphasis on *ethnos* or *demos* by either side of the question needs to be readjusted to make room for a cultural and political definition that could converge cosmopolitical and nationalist values.

Contemporary philosophical liberalism has gradually moved away from the principle of absolute state neutrality on cultural issues. The neutrality argument, defended by John Rawls and Ronald Dworkin for example, is rooted in the historical division between church and state. In immigrant societies such as the United States, freedom of religion needs to be respected in order to maintain both liberty and social order. Until recently, the thinking on nations and ethnicity has developed along similar lines. No other ethnicity or national identity than the civic version can be treated as unique or in special need. Since the 1980s, however, a discernable shift has occurred toward a pluralist model that would allow the state to treat some groups differently. The shift toward multiculturalism, once thought of as a strictly North American issue, has now penetrated Europe via globalization and transnational migration. The question I have been pushing is, can we now take the pluralist model to the next level by raising the possibility that the state take the side of some national cultures that are seeking shared forms of sovereignty? Does this take us completely beyond the neutrality principal or does it, in fact, strengthen the principal by opening up the possibility of developing criteria necessary for the state to take sides. In other words, not all nation-states should do this but perhaps some should (Oquendo 1999). This dialogic political problem exists both in the philosophical and sociological sense.

Historically, much liberal and republican theoretical industry has been directed toward legitimating state neutrality. A critique of inward-looking, primordial, ethnic nationalism in favor of a liberal cosmopolitan one that in some cases would include different forms of shared sovereignty deviates from this route. Different forms of shared sovereignty can be seen to be emerging under the banner of de-evolution pushed by "third way" politics (Giddens 1998). In part this can be seen as a continuation of postcolonial successionist movements that gained some international legitimacy in the decolonization period of the 1960s and in part it is also related to new economies (McCrone 1998). Today, pressures for associational forms of sovereignty are showing themselves around the world. The principal of state neutrality is being revised on an ongoing basis in response to such pressures. Emerging ethnolinguistic and racial minorities in the United States and Europe have already established, through affirmative action, that the state in liberal societies should, in fact, take sides in disputes over culture.[12] Although affirmative action is not an example of shared sovereignty, it is part of the expanding political and juridical logic in which forms of shared sovereignty could be argued for in future negotiations within already established nation-states. Another sign that points to shared sovereignty concerns the increase in the ability of political sub-units within nation-states to participate in international agreements—an action once thought to have been the exclusive province of the sovereign state.[13] Multiple danger signals concerning the preservation of national cultures in postnational times are appearing on the distant horizon perhaps, but one wonders how quickly globalization will bring them into focus and how quickly political vision will be able to adjust.

9

CONCLUSION

On Culture and the Political

Citizenship and the nation need to be understood as open-ended, unfinalized, reflexive projects that, on a higher level of abstraction, encompass the dialogic and communicative definition of self-other relations and transcultural exchange. This argument is derived from Bakhtin's definition of two-sided answerability that I extend to a normative theory of the creative dimension of action in a way that counterbalances Habermas's one-sided approach to the separation of culture from politics. Rather than put forward a theory of the nation derived from comments that can be found scattered across Bakhtin's work on the history of the novel, or theorize the political dimensions of the nation from his analysis of language and the public square, I have selected to enter into a dialogue with other approaches to the nation and definitions of citizenship. This discussion led me to argue for a synthetic position situated between the conceptual couplets of the ethnic and civic, premodern and modern, and primordial and constructivist.

Many have commented on the importance of Bakhtin's theory of carnival for political analysis but the connection between this theory and his earlier philosophy of ethics, aesthetics, and dialogue is not always clear. Publication of Bakhtin's early works only appeared in Russian and other languages at the beginning of the 1990s and have yet to be fully theorized within the context of contemporary cultural and political events. Until Ken Hirschkop's recent book, *Mikhail Bakhtin: An Aesthetics of Democracy* (1999), no one had sought to work through a

201

systematic theory of politics from an immanent reading of Bakhtin's early and later writings. Hirschkop provides an important synthesis of recent literature on Bakhtin's neo-Kantian assumptions by comparing his ideas on ethics and aesthetics to Habermas's and Weber's theories of modernity and democracy in a way that complements my argument. Hirschkop's book casts a much-needed light on the aesthetics and politics of democracy but only a narrow beam of this light illuminates the politics of the nation-state—especially through his discussion of Bakhtin's writing on the epic and novel. Bakhtin's primary interest was to solve philosophical problems, which he often attempted through studies of the novel, and as Hirschkop has stressed it is Bakhtin's essays on the history of the novel that are especially important for defining a modernist aesthetics of democracy. Hirschkop's text provides an informative summary of the sequence in which Bakhtin's concepts first appeared and argues that his concepts share a common goal of describing and explaining the complexity of differentiations typical of the modern condition. His study is situated within a synthesis of the increasingly complex Russian debate over Bakhtin's intellectual context while providing sobering warnings against the dangers involved in the prevailing mixture of religious and political tension surrounding the Bakhtin industry's recovery and interpretation of his scholarship.

While sharing many of the ideas put forward in Hirschkop's excellent book it, nevertheless, strikes me that his emphasis on modernity and the novel distracts attention away from Bakhtin's coeval philosophical anthropology and ethics, which have been my central concern. Thus, I have not looked to add to the debate over Bakhtin's intellectual biography, as such, but rather have endeavored to engage Bakhtin in a dialogue with the later Habermas, the Weber of social action, a philosophically oriented Simmel, a communitarian Cohen, and a pragmatic Mead, among others, so as to illuminate some contemporary debates on the importance of national identity in postnational democracies. Given that Habermas's, Weber's, and Mead's approaches can actually be shown to contradict Bakhtin on a series of key points, it might be argued that placing him into a dialogue with this stream of social theory is really an unnecessary digression and not the best way to draw out Bakhtin's special theory of answerability. After all, aren't Martin Buber, Emmanuel Levinas, and Hans Georg Gadamer—all eminent thinkers within the contemporary philosophy of dialogue—much closer to Bakhtin's approach (Theunissen 1984; Trey 1992; Cusson 1999; Sidorkin 1999)? From the sociological perspective my answer is simple: none of these thinkers have contributed directly to the social theory of action. Then why not simply focus on a comparison to contemporary symbolic interactionists and ethnomethodologists from sociology? Again, my reasoning is fairly straightforward: I looked to place Bakhtin's work into a dialogue with thinkers who have focused on the philosophical, cultural, and political dimensions of society. I chose Habermas because he is a rare contemporary thinker who has made significant contributions to both philosophy and social theory through his unique combination of critical theory, philosophical hermeneutics, neofunctionalism, ethnomethodology, and pragmatism; and through his comprehensive engagement with poststructuralist thought. Weber and Mead I chose, not because they articulate a social theory situated between Bakhtin and Habermas, but because they raise some crucial issues that need to be addressed in the construction of such a theory. Weber's problematization of the ethics of conviction, and of responsibility, helps to demonstrate some of the difficulties that arise in positing an aesthetic and ethical approach, when modernity is defined as a process of rationalization that divides spheres of action into increasingly complex and particularized forms. Mead's theory of recognition, how the subject only recognizes itself by looking back on its actions, helps to clarify Bakhtin's architectonic approach to subjectivity wherein consummating the whole from parts must always allow for the loophole of subjectivity.

A core argument linking the chapters of this book has been that a general theory of action derived from Bakhtin's work is one that needs to move across diverse levels of abstraction without leveling one to the other. My concern with these different levels of abstraction derives from contemporary debate regarding the renewal of general sociological theory. I did not aim to reproduce the debate in a comprehensive way, nor to join the search for a new general theoretical logic in sociology. I simply wanted to point out to sociologists the lack of a foundation for reflection on creativity in normative actions and suggest a rationale for encouraging a turn toward interdisciplinary studies, in general, and philosophy and aesthetics, in particular, as a way of renewing the discipline. To those scholars working in the humanities and within other interdisciplinary fields, I wanted to highlight sociology's innovative set of theoretical strategies for moving between micro and macro levels of understanding and explanation.

Following Bakhtin and Habermas, while taking cues from more general sociological theory, I argued that approaching both the normative and the creative dimensions of action means bridging three levels of abstraction: 1) a transcultural level that shifts between transcendental and concrete norms and values within and across lifeworlds; 2) the practical transgrediant and dialogic level of self-other relations, the ethical basis of community, and the specificity of culture *(ethnos)*; and 3) a level of the political community and the universal entitlements of citizenship afforded to members by nation-states *(demos)*. Whereas chapters 1 to 3 develop the philosophical parameters for a transcultural ethics between Bakhtin and Habermas, chapters 4 to 6 discuss the ethics of unique individual-community relations, and chapters 7 and 8 present the logic needed to shift dialogic analysis from the levels of transculturalism and self-other relations to a theory of dialogized societal events. Bakhtin's approach to the practical level of action was drawn out through a comparison with Habermas's approach to communicative action and discourse ethics, which were then traced to their original philosophical sources. The comparison with Max Weber and George Herbert Mead showed more specifically how the dialogic approach to action is drawn from Bakhtin's attempt to build "a philosophy of the answerable act or deed." Finally, I argue that a general theory of the norms of answerability requires that citizenship and national identity be reflexively defined.

The addition of the postulate of a faith in the subjectivity of another as a "time in-itself," the reversal of general law and individual law, and the individual-community relation as a politics of "fellowship," mark some of the core ideas Bakhtin seems to have drawn on in developing an approach of a two-sided norm of answerability. As he shifts from ethics to aesthetics to a philosophy of dialogue, Bakhtin regularly substitutes new concepts for previous ones in an effort to pose the same questions in different disciplines. Bakhtin's concepts of transgredience and dialogism and Habermas's concepts of communicative reason and discourse ethics contribute to the definition of a transcultural ethics. Here, Bakhtin's question, "How should I act towards others who can answer me back?" is combined with Habermas's question, "How can I achieve agreement with others who do not share my values and norms?"

In the last chapter I argued that a social theory situated between Bakhtin and Habermas needs to overcome a separation of culture and politics, but it also needs to account for the increased complexities of decentered societies brought on by the emerging postnational constellation of nation-states. In order to address politics and transcultural ethics from a social theory situated between the two positions, we need to understand rationality as something more than the rational, and creativity as something less than the aesthetisization of life. Defining citizenship as a two-sided form of answerability means that membership refers to both the political and cultural communities of the nation. Politics in this model means something more than the practical administration of power and the abstract constitutional legitimation of justice. But this is not to say that the political is cultural. Yet neither is the political neatly separated off from the unity of the world that individuals and communities create for themselves.

Bakhtin argued in his first published paper that when a social actor is in art "he is not in life and conversely" (1990, 1). In a parallel sense it might be said that, for both Bakhtin and Habermas when an actor enters a political discourse he or she is not in a cultural one and conversely. Political discourse does have a cultural dimension and cultural discourse does have a political one, but Bakhtin's point is that there is no "inner interpenetration" between them in the same sense there is in a dialogism between two different discourses *(ethnos* and *demos)* orientated toward the same object (the nation). What holds an individual together and what holds a culture together—what stops each from simply becoming the "other"—is found in the unity of answerability: "I have to answer with my own life for what I have experienced and understood in art, so that everything I have experienced and understood would not remain intellectual in my life. But answerability implies guilt or liability to blame. It is not only mutual answerability that art and life must assume, but also mutual liability to blame" (1990, 1).

The idea of guilt and the "mutual liability to blame" fall on the side of responding in a moral and universal way rather than on the side of the particularity and uniqueness of an action. Shifting to the level of societal events from the practical level of two-sided answerability and the dialogical relation of interpersonal relations, requires theoretical adjustment and fine tuning. Theorists engaged in a dialogical understanding of the political, for example, need to adjust for a tendency to empty cultural bias from definitions of citizenship and the nation. I have argued that such concepts need to be understood under the sign of culture as well as under the sign of the political while not reducing one to the other. Without such adjustments, the meaning of national identities risks becoming completely uncoupled from citizenship and they are easily dismissed as a private function of civil society rather than as a dialogized transcultural creation. The complexity of contemporary *ethnos* can easily be missed or reduced to a homogeneous expression whereas, in fact, it follows a complex multi-narratological path. In different ways and to different degrees this analytic overshift between the level of interpersonal dialogue and culture to societal dialogue and the political was seen in the case of Taylor's, Habermas's, and Kymlicka's approaches to defining the Québécois case. On the other hand, placing to much emphasis on the side of culture means reducing the complexity of the political, as was seen in the case of Rioux's and Dumont's genealogical arguments about the Quebec *ethnos*.

Shifting from the level of interpersonal to societal dialogue risks obscuring the national question when it ceases, for example, to be explained as a dialogue in social solidarity and transcultural creation and is instead categorized under the purely legal domain in the *demos* or conversely when it is dismissed as an archaic tribal-like pathology of *ethnos*. Genocide, war, and racism are, in some sense, possible only because social actors are able to reduce each other to the status of "just the next man." The categories of the "fellowman," "just the next man," "just the stranger" are implicated in emerging issues and events that need to be understood as rooted in the societal dialogue between *ethnos* and *demos*. In any theoretical shift that posits the nation and national identities in the sole context of a universal *demos* or political community, the fate of nations as a creative dialogue in social solidarity risks being overlooked. It follows from this that concepts forged in the dialogic framework of culture are displaced in a dialogic framework of politics. Thus, cultural specificity and social solidarity become categories of civil society rather than the lifeworld, and the national question gets recast in the juridical arena even though the resolution of the question (the postnational problem of shared sovereignty) requires a convergence of concepts that arise from the exchange between different cultural practices and traditions.

Recall that at the level of interaction, the normative approach to answerability means learning a two-sided form of exchange if one hopes to grow in a creative way when coming into contact with others without causing undue harm. At the transcultural level, this assumption is carried forward in the idea that actors need "thick" cultural traditions in which to develop their identities through their imaginary relations with others. The thinner, less hierarchical and more porous identities of societal cultures need to be listened to in return so the "Great Dialogue" of our time can be heard; that is, if we hope to formulate the kinds of political communities that will care for citizens and foster a world of common fellowship, justice, and "perpetual peace." But the shift from interpersonal to societal dialogic analysis quickly encounters the often difficult, and sometimes painful, adjustments to new norms of answerability that promise to remain with us in the new millennium: the struggles over recognition, redistribution, and shared sovereignty in a postnational constellation; struggles over inclusion and exclusion in definitions of citizenship; struggles over national identities and transcultural communication and over the coexistence of individual and collective rights for different communities that inhabit a common territory. While an attempt to theorize these issues can only ever be partial, my hope is that I have, at least, stimulated others to develop the theories and models I have suggested through the loophole of their own subjectivity.

NOTES

Preface

1. M. M. Bakhtin, *Toward a Philosophy of the Act*, trans. and notes by Vadim Liapunov (Austin: University of Texas Press, 1993), 54. Further references in the Preface are to this edition.

2. For two excellent, very different monographs that deal chronologically with the theological resonances in Bakhtin's texts, see Alexandar Mihailovic, *Corporeal Words: Mikhail Bakhtin's Theology of Discourse* (Evanston: Northwestern University Press, 1997), which is the more insiderly, Russian Orthodox treatment; and Ruth Coates, *Christianity in Bakhtin: God and the Exiled Author* (Cambridge: Cambridge University Press, 1998), which adopts a pan-Christian, even Protestant perspective.

3. Ken Hirschkop, *Mikhail Bakhtin: An Aesthetic for Democracy* (Oxford: Oxford University Press, 1999). Nielsen discusses the relationship between Hirschkop's project and his own more sociological study in chapter 9.

4. The Simmel connection has been discussed in Russian scholarship by the eminent senior sociologist Yuri Davydov, who also observes that Bakhtin begins with philosophical models of the self and, confronted with the question "How is communication possible at all?" gradually expands them into the sociological. See Yu. Davydov, "'Tragediia kul'tury' i otvetstvennost' individa (G. Zimmel' i M. Bakhtin)," *Voprosy literatury* (July–Aug. 1997): 91–125. In his discussion, Nielsen alludes briefly to the most notorious unacknowledged (but verbatim) source for several of Bakhtin's ideas in the carnival realm: Ernst Cassirer. The question of Bakhtin's borrowings, adaptations, and falsifications—which appear to be part of a complex strategy of self-masking and self-fashioning—has become a pressing issue for those working on Bakhtin's biography and on his personal ethics.

5. Bakhtin's lectures on Kant from this period, in the transcription of his friend and colleague Lev Pumpiansky, are translated and annotated in Susan M. Felch and Paul J. Contino, eds., *Bakhtin and Religion: A Feeling for Faith* (Evanston: Northwestern University Press, 2001).

6. Book VI, "The Russian Monk," ch. 2, "From the Life of the Hieromonk and Elder Zosima, Departed in God, Composed from His Own Words by Alexei Fyodorovich Karamazov," (d) "The Mysterious Visitor," in Fyodor Dostoevsky, *The Brothers Karamazov*, trans. Richard Pevear and Larissa Volokhonsky (New York: Vintage, 1991), 301–312.

Introduction: Theory on the Borders of Sociology

1. See Todorov (1981) and Clark and Holquist (1984).

2. This is the term Habermas uses in his debate with so-called Euroskeptics or those who would challenge the democratic legitimacy of the European Community (2001). It describes the effect of globalization on sovereign nations and refers to the process through which nation-states are increasingly obliged to share their sovereignty.

3. Bakhtin's theory of carnival has often been interpreted in terms of political and sociological categories. See for example, Peter Stallybrass and Allon White, *The Politics and Poetics of Transgression* (New York: Cornell University Press, 1986), Craig Brandist *Carnival Culture and the Soviet Modernist Novel* (London: MacMillan Press LTD, 1996), and Ray Morris *The Carnivalization of Politics: Quebec Cartoons on Relations with Canada, England, and France, 1960–1979* (Montreal: McGill-Queens Press, 1995). Bakhtin's relation to the broad outline of Western social theory was introduced by Michael Gardiner in his *The Dialogics of Critique* (Routledge: London, 1992). But until Ken Hirschkop's *Mikhail Bakhtin: An Aesthetics of Democracy* (London: Oxford, 1999) no one sought to work through a sytematic theory of politics from his early to his late work. As I only discovered Hirschkop's book in the final stages of rewriting for publication, I am unable to engage it other than to comment on its simmilarity and difference with my project briefly in the Conclusion. I agree with Gary Saul Morson and Caryl Emerson who were among the first to argue strenuously that Bakhtin's epistemology should not be interpreted as following a path set out by any orthodox historical materialism (1990). On the other hand, Hirschkop's point on Bakhtin's understanding of "historical becoming" through his philosophical studies of the novel, is a very convincing one. It does not necessarily follow, however, that Bakhtin's plan to write on an ethics of politics was conceived in terms of either historical materialism or the tradition of classical liberalism. See also Gary Saul Morson, "Prosaic Bakhtin: Landmarks, Anti-Intelligentsialism and the Russian Countertradition" (1995, 33–78). A middle ground would be to keep in mind a balance of communitarian and libertarian streaks in his work.

4. According to Bakhtin: "Syncrisis was understood as the juxtaposition of various points of view on a specific object. The technique of juxtaposing various discourse-opinions on an object was accorded very great importance in the Socratic dialogue; this derived from the very nature of the genre. Anacrisis was

understood as a means for eliciting and provoking the words of one's interlocutor, forcing him to express his opinion and express it thoroughly" (1984a, 110).

5. Morson and Emerson (1990) were again among the first to argue against Holquist and Clark's (1984a) claim that Bakhtin was the author of a series of essays and books published between 1925 and 1929. The dispute continues to divide researchers in Bakhtin studies as to the question of authorship, especially the three books that are more sociologically and linguistically orientated than his other works. These books include *Marxism and Philosphy of Language,* and *Freudianism,* usually attributed to Voloschinov, and *The Formal Method in Literary Scholarship,* published under Medvedev's name. Much of the evidence of Bakhtin's authorship of the disputed texts is anecdotal. Vadim Kozhinov, Bakhtin's executor insists that Bakhtin confided his authorship of the works while on his deathbed (see Nicholas Rzhevsky 1994). Bakhtin's wife is quoted by Kozhinov and S. Konkin as having complained that she could not remember how many times she had copied the book on Russian formalism published under the name of Medvedev (see Albert J. Wehrle's introduction in Medvedev 1985, XVI). It appears there are more than two sides concerning the interpretation of Bakhtin's work according to whether or not he and not Voloshinov and Medvedev in fact authored these books and essays. Nicoleav (2000) provides the best documented philological accounts of the periodization of the works and suggests a compromise position that Bakhtin may have participated in some kind of oral collective writing project. Still, Hirshkop has the best one-liner on the state of the authorship debate in Bakhtin studies: "For a long time we knew very little about Bakhtin's life. Thanks to the efforts of post-*glasnost* we now know even less" (1999, 111).

6. In 1973 V. D. Duvakin interviewed Bakhtin at length on his life history and work. The interviews appeared in Russian in 1996.

7. Alexander Mihailovic points out a similar state of affairs in his study of the theological influences on Bakhtin's writing. As he views it, many scholars raise the question of theological influences but "like a cat circling a bowl of hot milk, critics interested in Bakhtin's theories have considered the possibility without really approaching it" (Mihailovic 1997, 1).

8. The exception here is the Rabelais book whose 1968 translation was well recieved in anthropology. See Wachtel (2000) on Bakhtin's different reception in English and French.

9. Both philosophy and social theory travel in large circles and while they are concerned with providing rigorous argumentation and sharp analytical tools, neither is as concerned as science with disciplinary boundaries, procedural accuracy, nor the need for precision applications of techniques and first-level hypothesis testing. As Karl Jasper points out, "[P]hilosophy strives to perceive the whole through the whole, not something else, and to understand its own thinking through itself, not through something that went before it." Science, on the other hand (quantum physics and chaos theory not withstanding), needs to eliminate contradiction and paradox as much as possible.

Again, for Jaspers, the difference between philosophical and scientific knowledge is that the latter is oriented toward the whole whereas the former is directed "toward definite objects that confront other objects. Philosophical knowledge strives to transcend all presuppositions in order to preserve its openness to the whole; scientific knowledge derives its cogency from presuppositions and operates in the realm of the determinate" (Jasper 1957, 41).

10. Alexander (1982, 1998) and Joas (1996) reconstruct the general theory of the system of action put forward by the famous American sociologist Talcott Parsons as a prime example of multileveled theorizing (Alexander 1982; 1998; Joas 1996).

11. Social theorists such as William James, John Dewey, and George Herbert Mead looked to "aid human communities in improving their potential for collective action and, in a world that had lost all metaphysical certainty, make a decisive contribution to promoting the solidarity of a universal human community" (Joas 1993, 25).

12. Complex ideological and organizational forces as well as contradictory pedagogies drive interdisciplinarity. Disciplines struggle with and against these forces. A good example is the rapid growth of cultural studies in North America. This approach has helped both sociology and philosophy to open up to interdisciplinarity and some argue that it has given both disciplines a new life (Bernard et al. 1998). The rich debates in moral philosophy around diversity and democracy and the revival of critical sociology as an engaged form of social inquiry have been possible due in no small part to the emergence of cultural studies in the last decade. However, several questions persist regarding the legitimacy of some of the more exaggerated claims and ideological currents in cultural studies. Paradoxically, the survival of sociology as a discipline may very well depend on its capacity to open itself up to nonpositivist and nonempiricist philosophies and yet not be overwhelmed by the ideological requirements of various social movements it wanders into.

13. Here he departs only marginally from Parsons's (1954) earlier plea on this issue by arguing against the synthesis of special theories into one model.

14. Donald Levine concludes his book *Visions of the Sociological Tradition* (1995) by suggesting that of all the ways of recounting the history of social theory, the dialogical narrative (referring to both Buber and Bakhtin) has the greatest chance of maintaining the creative dimension Joas argues for and of absorbing various traditions without damaging them and without committing the kind of unbridled acts of eclecticism Alexander warns against.

Chapter 1. Diversity and Transcultural Ethics

1. As mentioned earlier Michael Gardiner (1992), Ken Hirschkop (1999), as well as my own article (1995) are the only attempts at systematic statements regarding the similarities and differences between their philosophies.

2. I thank Tapaini Laine for the reference and translation from the Russian here (Habermas 1989, 82). Despite the complex discussion around the disputed texts, it would appear Habermas interprets Bakhtin as if he were the author of *Marxism and the Philosophy of Language*.

3. This idea from Bakhtin's early ethics is consistent with his later theory of speech genres where he argues that in entering live speech acts, the speaker becomes, subtly or dramatically, other than what he has been while remaining himself. One cannot claim to be elsewhere while becoming oneself. Indeed, for Bakhtin, one should not become the other. But we can add without contradicting his position that in transcultural acts one does become other than what one was.

4. "The Life of the word is contained in its transfer from one mouth to another, from one context to another context, from one social collective to another, from one generation to another generation" (202). "The living word [is] inseparably linked with dialogic communion, by its very nature it wants to be heard and answered" (300). "To live means to participate in dialogue." In this dialogue a person participates wholly and throughout his whole life: with his eyes, lips, hands, soul, spirit, with his whole body and deeds" (1984a, 293).

5. For Bakhtin, all language carries an anticipation of rejoinder from an addressee. As he puts it: "I live in a world of other's words. And my entire life is an orientation in this world . . . beginning with my assimilation of them and ending with the assimilation of the wealth of human culture." Bakhtin sees a dialogic core in all sociability that is constituted by an active existential response built into the utterance itself (1986, 143).

6. A remarkable sign of their commitment to self-reflexive critique is that each spends a great deal of time explaining the respective dangers of their choice of epistemologies. On one side, Habermas discusses at great length the importance of overcoming the dangers of Kantian and Hegelian rationalism while on the other side, Bakhtin carefully warns of the limits and traps of *Lebensphilosophie*.

7. After surveying the literary genres up to Dostoevsky, he concludes that the polyphonic novel in particular best provides the space for the hero to participate equally with the author (Bakhtin 1984a, 71).

8. Habermas explains the complementary components of the lifeworld by juxtaposing various mediating systems (legitimation, medias of power and money) and processes of reproduction (social integration, socialization, individuation) that are grafted on to the diverse activities of communicative action (understanding, coordination, sociability) in propositional, illocutionary, or expressive speech acts. He distinguishes between "social integration," in the sense of coordinating actions for the collectivity based on "normative consensus and mutual understanding in language" and "systems integration," in the sense of steering mechanisms of money and power that separate economic and political institutions from kinship systems and other subsystems of the

lifeworld. Social formations are distinguished by degrees of complexity and by "the institutional complex that anchors a newly emerging mechanism of system differentiation in the lifeworld" (Habermas 1987, 165).

9. On the other hand, Benhabib and McCarthy do not indicate a resolution for the retreat to relativism that is implied in their positions. Jean Cohen and Andrew Arato argue that the principle of universalizability is defensible but only if its claim to objectivity is shown to be rooted in the structure of the argumentation itself. By returning the debate to self-reflection, a founding principle of critical theory in the Frankfurt tradition, they situate themselves between McCarthy's anthropological explanation of the challenge and Benhabibs's contextualist revision. Without this self-reflective moment, they argue, the distinction between the theoretical and practical meaning of generalizable interests remains blurred. They concede that to escape the charges of elitism, the concept of the universal must give way to the concept of "common identity." The latter "mediates between the metaprinciples and interests of a group, thereby providing the stability and authority of the applications agreed upon, although they also remain open to change" (Cohen and Arato 1992, 372).

10. Habermas's position on ideal speech can also be contrasted to John Rawls's notion of "the original position" and his argument for justice as fairness. Although actors in liberal society speak withouht knowing everything about their interlocutors, that is, they speak through a "veil of ignorance," they can still, at any point enter into discussions about the choice of the "first principles of a conception of justice which is to regulate all subsequent criticism and reform of institutions" (Rawls 1971, 12–13). In this sense the "original position" and "the ideal speech situation" take the place of the state of nature assumption in contract theory. Rawls also argues that the ideal speech situation is a "comprehensive doctrine" and is not limited to the unique dimension of the political (Rawls 1996, 373–434; and Habermas 1998b, 49–101).

11. Willliam Rehg (1994) argues that Habermas's discourse ethics is founded on "a radically intersubjective dialogical concept of moral insight." Cohen and Arato refer to dialogue both as a form of exchange between interlocutors in conversation and as a problem in speech role reciprocity (1992, 351, 355, 358, 357, 387, 402). Benhabib understands dialogue both as part of philosophical conversation and also as a political process: "Public dialogue is not external to but constitutive of power relations" (1991, 353). John Thompson suggests that Habermas's usage of practical discourse "is essentially a dialogical conception" (1993, 186). Yet, it could be argued that at least since his debates with Gadamer, Habermas develops a transcendental-pragmatic and not a dialogic approach to discourse. See the presentation of the two positions in Georgia Warnke (1987; 1992; 1999). For an excellent discussion of the difference between transcendental and dialogic approaches see Michael Theunissen (1984).

12. We will not be able to address the numerous possible criticisms of discourse ethics that might emerge from thinkers such as Alisdair MacIntyre, Charles Taylor, or Bernard Williams, nor the criticisms from Rorty and Lyotard that address Habermas's philosophy of modernity. It is difficult though to think of another contemporary theorist who has so consistently and prolifically responded to his critics. For his response to the questions raised by contemporary ethical and legal philosophers, see Habermas (1993, 19–111). See his original philosophical program for discourse ethics in Habermas (1990, 43–115).

13. The term *transgredient* ("step across, step over") is thought to be used by Bakhtin as an alternative to Kant's concept of the transcendental, which refers to reason as above or beyond experience. In the preface to the French version of Bakhtin's *Art and Answerability*, Tzvetan Todorov defines the transgredient as those elements outside of consciousness that are present in thought and are necessary to its constitution as a whole. See Todorov's preface in the French language edition of Bakhtin (1984, 12). He also uses the term as a synonym of "outsidedness." See his review essay "I, Thou Russia'" (1998). In the English version of Bakhtin's essay, Michael Holquist and Vadim Liapunov identify the source of the concept in the works of the neo-Kantian philosophers including Jonas Cohen and Wilhelm Windelband. Here it is understood as the opposite of immanence in the philosophical sense but not beyond experience. See Bakhtin (1990, 233).

14. Morson and Emerson give the following shorthand cognitive definition: the *I-for-myself* ("how my self looks and feels to my own consciousness"); the *I-for-others* ("how my self appears to those outside it"); the *other-for-me* ("how outsiders appear to myself") (1990, 180).

15. Socrates, Plato, Aristotle, the Stoics, the Epicureans, and the Sophists all differed over the definition of what it means to live a good life. Martha Nussbaum shows how for the Stoics the good is understood as a virtue that carries multiple meanings only because there is a universal logos or reason that each local claim of the good taps into. The highest good is human reason but it needs to be nurtured through dispassionate civic education that allows one to become a completely cosmopolitan world citizen (1996, 7–8). Epicureans, on the other hand, had little interest in politics and community and believed that the highest good was that of the highest possible pleasure. This meant that pain had to be eliminated and which implied in turn that the highest good would be to heal pain (Cicero 1987, 112–113). Epicures thought philosophy should be therapeutic (Nussbaum 1994, 13). The Sophists, like modern day relativists, argued there is no absolute good, nor universal norms. Then, as now, such a position confuses the relation between values and norms. It confuses the relation between ephemeral changing values and fixed ideal rules of conduct (or "techniques of the self" as Foucault would come to call them) that build values, impulses, or desires into good actions or into virtuous public acts.

16. As Rainer Roschlitz points out: "Everyday language is constantly grounded on rational demonstrations. A good argument presented here and now will be valid somewhere else tomorrow" (1993, 75).

Chapter 2. Communicative Action or Dialogue?

1. On his disagreement with Kolberg regarding the natural basis of postconventional development see his "Justice and Solidarity: On the Discussion Concerning 'Stage' 6" (Habermas 1991, 32).

2. Habermas responds by pointing out limitations in the interpretation of the empirical evidence. He claims that Gilligan does not distinguish: 1) "between the cognitive problem of application and the motivational problem of the anchoring of moral insights," 2) "between moral abstraction and ethical practice", 3) "between contextual relativism and postconventional formalism," and 4) "between justice and postconventional contextualism" (1990, 179). Benhabib returns to this theme but does not respond to Habermas on this point in her article "The Debate over Women and Moral Theory Revisited" (1995).

3. For Habermas's response to their criticism see *Justification and Application*, (1993, 153–154).

4. See his discussion on "The Tasks of a Critical Theory" (Habermas 1988, 375–403).

5. See Martin Jay's comments on Habermas's position within the tradition across the collection of articles titled *Force Fields* (1993) and also Helmut Dubiel's response to Habermas in "Domination or Emancipation? The Debate over the Heritage of Critical Theory" (1992, 3–16).

6. For example, in clarifying the history of poetics concerning the centrifugal and centripetal relation of language; see "Discourse in the Novel," in *The Dialogic Imagination* (1981, 271). See also Bakhtin, *Speech Genres and Other Late Essays* (1986, 67).

7. I am using Morson and Emerson's (1985) translation of terms from *The Philosophy of the Act*.

Chapter 3. The World of Other's Words

1. See Hirschkop (1999) and Nicolaev (2000) for more detailed accounts of Bakhtin's context and development of concepts.

2. The Frankfurt Institute of Social Research was founded in 1923 (Wiggershaus 1996). In 1932, Max Horkheimer assumed the direction of the institute and became the editor of its review *Zeitschrift für Sozialforschung* (1932–1941). Under Horkheimer's direction an inner circle emerged that included Theodor Adorno, Walter Benjamin, Leo Lowenthal,

and Herbert Marcuse. Their common interests in aesthetic and literary issues provided an informal bond across their varied projects. Though he did receive some financial support from the institute, Benjamin, increasingly recognized as one of the most influential modern literary critics, was not an official member. He played a seminal role in determining the parameters of debate concerning questions of aesthetics. Benjamin committed suicide in 1939. Hannah Arendt reports in the introduction to his classic collection of essays, entitled *Illuminations* (1969), that Gestapo were about to move in as Benjamin was in the process of fleeing Europe. The rest of the inner circle migrated to the United States before returning to Frankfurt after the war where new students were trained in the 1950s and 1960s that would ultimately carry on the tradition.

3. Horkheimer contrasted his entry into the problem with that of Karl Mannheim's theory of the sociology of knowledge. In his 1929 classic *Ideology and Utopia,* Mannheim argues that truth claims are ultimately considered to be bound to a perspective and that therefore knowledge can only be partial because it is ultimately founded in the social interests that give rise to the perspective. Only déclassé intellectuals, assuming intellectuals may transcend class lines, have the expertise and possibility of detachment from interests that would allow them to derive universal truth claims. Horkheimer argued against Mannheim, as did Adorno in *Prisms.* They argued instead a neo-Marxian position that places the problem of truth claims in the realm of praxis and a theory of social conflict that looks to explore the attempts of groups of social actors to achieve a state of emancipation. Both the concept of *praxis*—the emancipation from or negation of the conditions of domination—and *ideologiekritik*—the critique of the social interests that underlie systems of ideas or ideologies—are mined from Marx.

4. It is important to remember the seminal influence of several thinkers who were not part of the institute but had a wide reaching impact on debates that divided the institute's members. Georg Lukàcs, along with Ernst Bloch and Berthold Brecht, were among those whose aesthetic and literary theories would have the most impact. (Bloch et al. 1977). In their earlier years, Mannheim, Lukàcs, and Bloch were frequent participants at the informal theory seminars on aesthetic and political issues held in the home of Max and Marian Weber. Their influence on Walter Benjamin eventually led to a sharp difference between the latter and his younger colleague Adorno concerning issues in the debate over aesthetics across the 1930s. Benjamin and Adorno represented two extremes that could be adopted within the circle and between which the others would tend to oscillate.

5. Walter Benjamin followed Georg Lukàc's *Theory of the Novel* in developing his approach to aesthetic questions but he combined it with Brecht's theory of political realism which led him to introduce the concept of mediation. On the other hand, and much later in both his *Negative Dialectics* (1995) and *Aesthetic Theory* (1970), Adorno develops the most

extreme version of a critical theory of art in which the complete negation or refusal of the real is seen as the only means of achieving a valid artistic form. In sharp contrast to Benjamin's position, Adorno holds that the validity of art is not in its identification with the social, as in Lukàc's theory of realism, but in its autonomy and ultimately in its refusal of the social. Although Adorno accepted Benjamin's theory of mediation, he rejected his concept of correspondence as a thinly disguised reflection theory of art and literature. Instead, Adorno argued for a theory of mimesis, defined at its best as the repetition of autonomous artistic form that seeks an accidental rupture from its own past in the anticipation of an emancipated unknown future. For Adorno, the autonomy of artistic form makes it the negative knowledge of the actual or real.

6. Leo Lowenthal helped develop a sociology of "Great Literature" that Adorno and others put forth, but never had the commitment to the philosophy of pure critique, the refusal to identify with the real in artistic representation (1961). Similarly, Herbert Marcuse extends the mood of pessimism in his classic critique of modern culture in *One Dimensional Man,* but in his last book, *The Aesthetic Dimension,* published in 1977, he also holds back from Adorno's "negative dialectics."

Chapter 4. On the Sources of Young Bakhtin's Ethics

The section "Simmel's Shadow" is based on an unpublished paper, "Simmel's Shadow," co-written with Tapani Laine and presented at the IXth International Bakhtin Meetings at the Frei Universität, Berlin, July 1999.

1. This influence is not acknowledged, and whether or not he was aware of the reference to Simmel's 1913 essay *Das Individuelle Gesetz* (The Indidividual Law) remains unknown. The essay was first published in German in *Logos* in 1913, and translated into Russian in *Logos,* 1914. I am working with the original German version reprinted as "Chapter 4: *Das Individuelle Gesetz*" (1968). See also Hans Joas's chapter on Simmel's essay, "The Immanence of Transcendence" (2001) for a reconstruction of the argument.

2. There seems to be little evidence that Bakhtin studied Kant except in a selective and usually secondary way. Young Bakhtin's lecture on Kant described in Pumpiansky's notes does not attempt to give any overview of his critical philosophy but focuses on his concept of peace (Pumpiansky 2001).

3. On the influence of the Marburg School, and on Ernst Cassirer in particular, see Craig Brandeis (1997) and Brian Poole (1998).

4. A point repeatedly stated in Mihailovic's study (1997, 51–69).

5. The German text here reads: *"Wiederum ist hier eine neue Scheidung und neue Synthese von Begriffen erforderlich: das Individuelle braucht nicht subjektiv zu sein, das Objektive nicht überindividuell. Der entscheidende Begriff ist vielmehr: die Objektivität des Individuellen."* (1968, 217). *"Das Entscheidende ist*

aber, dass individuelle Leben nichts Subjektives ist, sondern, ohne irgendwie seine Beschränkung auf dies Individuum zu verlieren, als ethisches Sollen schlechthin objevtiv ist. Die falsche Verwachsung zwischen Individualität und Subjektivität muss gelöst werden, wie die zwischen Allgemeinheit und Gesetzlichkeit. Dadurch werden die Begriffe frei, die neue Synthese zwischen Individualität und Gesetzlichkeit zu bilden" (1968, 220).

6. *"Darum ist ganze Leben für jede Tat und jede Tat für das Leben verantwortlich"* (1968, 237).

7. See especially his *Philosophy of Money* (1990).

8. The German text here reads: *"Freilich scheint seine Formel weit genug zu sein, um die Sittlichkeit eines Tuns auch dann an seiner 'möglichen Verallgemeinerung' zu bestimmen, wenn unser Tun so gefasst wird, wie es wirklich im Leben steht: mit dessen Ganzheit absatzlos verwebt, nur gerade beobachtete Welle in seiner kontinuierlichen Strömung. Tatsächlich aber ist das so erfasste Tun gar nicht zu verallgemeinern, denn dies hiesse nichts anderes, als das ganze Leben dieses Individuums als allgemeines Gesetz zu denken"* (Simmel 1968, 189–190).

9. See Vadim Liapunov's note 11 in Bakhtin's *Art and Answerability* (1990, 233).

Chapter 7. Citizenship and National Identity

1. While most commentators agree that Bakhtin remained apolitical across his life, this does not mean his approach cannot or should not be appropriated for political analysis. Ken Hirschkop (1999) gives a very broad outline of how Bakhtin's work can be thought of as an aesthetic approach to democracy, an outline that parallels Habermas's and Weber's approaches. Our contributions are complementary in the sense that we both look to a social theory situated between Bakhtin and Habermas even though my focus is not on Bakhtin's local contexts.

2. Although the tension between *ethnos* and *demos* is first theorized in Aristotle's *Politics*, one source of the more recent sociological treatment of these concepts appears to be an early book in the field of Canadian ethnic studies. See Emerich Francis, *In Search of Utopia: The Mennonites in Manitoba* (1955). The juxtaposition is further developed in the German context by Rainer Lepsius, *"Ethnos oder Demos"* (1991) and is couched in a critique of the tendency of the *demos* to ignore the needs of the *ethnos* in the context of the European Union. Habermas (1998b) refers to Lepsius's discussion but only in order to warn against any theoretical privileging of *ethnos* in developing the definition of the nation in the era of globalization. See also the special issue edited by Mabel Berezin and Jefferey Alexander of *International Sociology* on *Democratic Culture: Ethnos and Demos in Global Perspective* (1999).

3. Globalization also means contending with new forms of flexible capital accumulation, corporate media consolidations, and intensified transnational

flows of finance capital, information, goods, labor, refugees, and migrants (Sasan 1996; Habermas 1998b; Held and McGrew 1999).

4. I am indebted to Dominique Legros for this argument on non-state societies. On nations without states see Guiberneau (1999) and on definitions that draw the distinction between national and ethnic minorities around the world see Kymlicka (1995) and Brubaker (1999).

5. See his discussion of "Stage Six" in his postconventional theory of morality; Habermas (1990).

6. As David Hollinger points out, the modern usage of the concept of *ethnos* refers to a much narrower set of references than the more universal notion of a species-wide competence. On the other hand, its definition as "a particular solidarity rooted in history" (1995, 4) refers to a much wider range of meaning than the concept of ethnicity. My usage takes from Hollinger's definition without lamenting the loss of the universal referent and without falling into the deconstruction or relativism he also warns against.

7. For the largest part of Western history only some men, and only very rarely (if ever) some women, were considered citizens. Most were excluded either because they did not own property, because they were born enslaved, or because their existence was simply to far outside of the *ethnos* to be considered human. Beliefs regarding the superiority of one race or phenotype over another continued throughout the age of imperialism. Colonial subjects often took on the nationality of their colonizers but never enjoyed full citizenship rights. Today's postcolonial and postsocialist struggles against the "new racism"—the exclusion on the basis of "cultural incomparability" rather than phenotype—join new social movements as the forces that challenge the traditional definition of who is and who is not a citizen (Wieviorka 1991, 2000).

8. "The last set of rights are attached to a second major hurdle: naturalization, that is, induction into full membership or citizenship. For the latecomers, the migrants of the last decades, this last hurdle has, in many countries, come to be all but insurmountable" (in Barrbieri 1998, 173).

9. For more on the complexities of the question see the articles in Craig Calhoun (1994) and Rogers Brubaker and Frederick Cooper (2000).

10. The period of postnational euphoria was first blemished by little Denmark voting down the Maestricht treaty in the 1993 referendum. Paradoxically, little countries not only look to take advantage of new economic opportunities on the world scale but also press to secure new controls for their cultural protection. As the new Europe, along with its Western allies, were about to engage in its first bloodletting in Europe and between nations since 1945 with the bombing of Serbia, elsewhere, without a single shot being fired, the Scots received a provincial parliament in 1999; in 1997 the Puerto Ricans voted against all options (none of the five questions achieved any majority, including the question of maintaining the status quo) in their national referendum and in 1995 the Québécois remained locked in a stalemate after a

referendum for sovereignty and the negotiation of a new partnership with Canada was barely won by the no side. McCrone (1998) points out that these largely peaceful democratic neonationalist movements are driven by a combination of cultural and economic interests. Antinationalists, who in Canada and the United Kingdom echo each other in this regard, look for ways to diffuse the legitimacy of cultural, economic, and especially ethical identity claims in the name of the nation because it is assumed a priori that such claims can never stop from sliding down the slippery slope of exclusionary politics. Pro-nationalists champion *ethnos,* antinationalists *demos.* From the dialogical approach, it seems obvious that *ethnos* needs to be considered as a dimension of *demos* and conversely. Separating the two risks encouraging a wider variety of misunderstanding than thinking about them together as dialogic and and therefore open to transcultural exchange.

11. Here again, by postnationalism I mean that sovereignty gets exercised through international institutions and agreements rather than through the nation-state. (Kearney 1996; Ferry 2000; Habermas, 2001).

Chapter 8. A Dialogue on the Nation in Postnational Times

1. The following surveys are examples that cite the Quebec case in varying degrees of detail. David McCrone (1998); Craig Calhoun (1997); Michael Walzer (1997); Joycelyne Couture and Kai Nielsen (1996); Michel Seymor (1999b); John Hall (1998); and Alain Diekhoff (2000).

2. For a sample of other French language Quebec theorists who take up the question of contingency and postnationalism in Quebec see Gilles Bourque et Jules Duchastel (1995); Gilles Gagné (1995); Jacques Beauchemin (1998); Francois Rocher and Daniel Salée (1997).

3. Michel Seymor (1999a) comments on the linguistic interference regarding the different definitions of the English term *people* and the French *peuple.* The English definition can refer either to a nation as in the American "we the people" or an ethnic subgroup, Irish Americans. The French definition refers more to the idea of the nation as a nation-state. These definitions approximate my distinction between *ethnos* and *demos* as a reference to culture and politics. The idea of a community of citizens is closer to the definition of the *demos* as defined by a neutral state apparatus whereas the question of national identities falls under the sign of *ethnos;* i.e., as belonging to a nation or people (Schnapper 1994). In most federal multinational countries such as Switzerland, Belgium, and Canada (according to some definitions before 1982) the state is sometimes understood as distinct from the nation.

4. The discovery of North Sea oil created an economic boom in Scotland and the European Union created a new political arrangement that put pressure on central governments to develop more autonomy for national minorities such as those in Scotland and Wales and greater linguistic and, under

different circumstances, cultural autonomy for Catalonia (McCrone 1998; Keating 1996; Narin 1997).

5. See for example Kymlicka's (1998) and Gangnon's (2000) explanations of the difference between Canadian multiculturalist and Quebec interculturalist policies and the American "melting pot model."

6. Michel Seymor (1999a) challenges analyses of the Quebec case that presuppose a definition of its civil society as constituted in homogeneous ethnic terms as opposed to heterogeneous polycultural and modern terms. He counters that Quebec needs to be explained from the assumption that it has a fully modern heterogeneous civil society that has evolved alongside Canadian and American democratic patterns.

7. Canada is an officially bilingual (French-English) federation composed of several founding national societies (English, French, and Aboriginal) and regional cultures (Central, Western, Northern, and Maritime). In principal, the 1982 repatriation of the Canadian constitution from the British Privy Council (against the consent of the Province of Quebec) and the addition of the Canadian Charter of Rights and Freedoms provides legal definitions for the protection of the rights of all minority groups (Taylor 1993; Angus 1997). However, the amended constitution does not recognize Quebec as a nation within a nation as other federal constitutions do (Diekhoff 2000).

8. The traditional struggle of the Québécois French-speaking national minority against the hegemony of the majority English-speaking population of Canada has more recently been countered by new rights claims from minority immigrants, aboriginal nations, and a traditional English-speaking minority in protest against language laws that favor the usage of French as the public language in Quebec. See Simone Chambers's (1996) very interesting Habermasian analysis of English-French relations in Montreal.

9. Given the immense stakes Rioux attributed to the question of national liberation from the 1950s to the 1980s it is not surprising that he fell into deep despair at the end of his career. His last book, *Un peuple dans le Siècle* (1990), argued that time had in fact run out. Dumont's determination remained intact. He published his most impassioned plea for sovereignty association *(Raisons Communes)* during the year of the 1995 referendum, shortly before his death.

10. These data can be found in the 1996 census at the Statistics Canada web cite.

11. See G. Nielsen (1987) on the early context of Taylor's political activism. For Taylor the demands of neonationalsts differ only marginally from the traditional demands of the French Canadian ethnic or cultural nationalists as he put it in the 1960s: "The nation here was originally *la nation Canadien francais*. Now, without entirely abandoning the first formulation, it tends to be put as la nation Québécoise." (1993, 163) His position is much closer to the traditional dual nation accommodation denied by the Trudeau administrations compromise definition in the 1970s and 1980s of Canada as a mul-

ticultural and bilingual nation founded on a universal recognition of individual rather than collective rights and freedoms (McRoberts 1997).

12. The American ideal of assimilation into the melting pot of plural ethnicities heavily favors the procedural model of individual rights criticized by Taylor. Affirmative action is the main exception in the United States regarding the recognition of collective rights of minorities. But the burden of proof remains on individuals to demonstrate that they have been discriminated against. According to Alain Gagnon, the Canadian model of multiculturalism appears to challenge the American model but the model has two faults: 1) it had the historical effect of bypassing claims by aboriginals and Quebec neonationalists regarding constitutional rights for national minorities; and 2) it relativized the notion of culture to the point of folding the policy back into the same individualist model of procedural rights it sought to overcome (Gagnon 2000).

13. The 1993 Russian constitution, for example, guarantees internal political units ("twenty-one republics, six territories, ten autonomous territories, one autonomous region; two cities with federal status and forty-nine regions") the right to participate in the negotiation of international agreements. Even the United States allows some of its territories (the Marshall Islands, Palau, the Federated States of Micronesia) to make limited kinds of international agreements and sit at the United Nations (Dieckhoff 2000, 284).

BIBLIOGRAPHY

Adorno, Theodore. 1970. *Aesthetic Theory.* Translated from the German by C. Lenhardt. London: Routledge and Kegan Paul.

———. 1982. *Prisms.* Translated from the German by Samuel and Sherry Weber. Cambridge: MIT Press.

———. 1988. *Introduction to the Sociology of Music.* Translated from the German by E. B. Ashton. New York: Continuum Publishing.

———. 1995. *Negative Dialectics.* Translated from the German by E. B. Ashton. New York: Continuum Publishing.

Alexander, Jeffery. 1982. *Theoretical Logic in Sociology: Volume I: Positivism, Pressupositions and Current Controversies.* Berkeley: University of California Press.

———. 1998. *Neofunctionalism and After.* Cambridge: Blackwell Publishers.

Anderson, Benedict. 1983. *Imagined Communities.* London: Verso.

Angus, Ian. 1996. *A Border Within: National Identity, Cultural Plurality, and Wilderness.* Montreal and Kingston: McGill-Queens Press.

Bakhtin, Mikhaïl. 1990. *Art and Answerability: Early Philosophical Essays.* Edited by Michael Holquist. Translated from the Russian by Vadim Liapunov. Austin: University of Texas Press.

———. 1981. *The Dialogic Imagination.* Edited and translated from the Russian by Michael Holquist and Caryl Emerson. Austin: University of Texas Press.

———. 1984a. *Problems of Dostoevsky's Poetics.* Edited and translated from the Russian by Caryl Emerson. Introduction by Wayne Booth. Minneapolis: University of Minnesota Press.

———. 1984b. *Rabelais and His World.* Translated from the Russian by Hélène Iswolsky. Bloomington: Indiana University Press.

———. 1986. *Speech Genres and Other Late Essays.* Edited by Caryl Emerson and Michael Holquist. Translated from the Russian by Vern McGee. Austin: University of Texas Press.

————. 1993. *Toward a Philosophy of the Act*. Translated from the Russian and notes by Vadim Liapunov. Foreword and Edited by Michael Holquist. Austin: University of Texas Press.

Bariteau, Claude. 1998. *Québec: 18 septembre, 2001*. Montréal: Québec-Amérique.

Beauchemin, Jacques. 1998. "La question de la sovereignté. Rédéfinition des enjeux et nouveaux argumentaires," *Globe: Revue international d'études québécoises* 1: 53–76.

Bell, Michael, and Michael Gardiner, eds. 1998. *Bakhtin and the Human Sciences*. London: Sage Publications.

Benhabib, Seyla. 1990. "Afterward: Communicative Ethics and Current Controversies in Practical Philosophy." In *The Communicative Ethics Controversy*, edited by Seyla Benhabib and Fred Dallymayr. Cambridge: MIT Press, 330–369.

————. 1995. "The Debate over Women and Moral Theory Revisited." In *Feminists Read Habermas: Gendering the Subject of Discourse*, edited by Johanna Meehan. London: Routledge, 181–204.

————. 1992. *Situating the Self: Gender, Community, and Postmodernity*. New York: Routledge.

Benjamin, Walter. 1969. *Illuminations: Essays and Reflection*. Translated from the German by Harry Zohn. Edited by Hannah Arendt. New York: Schocken.

————. 1978. "The Author as Producer." In *The Essential Frankfort School Reader*, edited by Andrew Arato and Eike Gebhardt. New York: Urizen, 254–270.

Berezin, Mabel, and Jefferey Alexander, eds. 1999. *Democratic Culture: Ethnos and Demos in Global Perspective*, Special Issue of *International Sociology* 14, No. 3.

Bernard, Paul, Marcel Fournier, and Céline St Pierre, eds. 1998. *Le second souffle de la sociologie*. Special Issue of *Sociologie et Société* XXX.

Bernard-Donald, Michael. 1994. *Mikhail Bakhtin: Between Phenomenology and Marxism*. Cambridge: Cambridge University Press.

Bertrand, Pierre. 1989. "Le voyage immobile : Le Québec de l'an 2, 000 face au défis de la transculture," *Vice Versa* 2: 8.

Bloch, Ernst, et al. 1977. *Aesthetics and Politics*. Translated by Ronald Taylor. London: New Left Books.

Bourque, Gilles, and Jules Duchastel. 1995. "Pour une identité canadienne post-nationale, la souveraineté partagée et la pluralité des cultures politiques," *Cahiers de recherche sociologique* 25: 17–58.

Brandist, Craig. 1996. *Carnival Culture and the Soviet Modernist Novel*. London: MacMillan Press.

————. 1997. "Bakhtin, Cassirer, and Symbolic Forms," *Radical Philosophy* 85 (September–October): 20–27.

Brandist, Craig, and Gahlin Tihanov. 2000. *Materialising Bakhtin: The Bakhtin Circle and Social Theory.* London: MacMillan.

Brubaker, Rogers. 1998. "Myths and Misconceptions in the Study of Nationalism." In *The State of the Nation: Ernest Gellner and The Theory of Nationalism,* edited by John Hall. London: Cambridge University Press, 272–306.

———. 1999 [1996]. *Nationalism Reframed: Nationhood and the National Question in the New Europe.* Cambridge: Press Syndicate of the University of Cambridge.

Brubaker, Rogers, and Frederick Cooper. 2000. "Beyond Identity," *Theory and Society: Renewal and Critique in Social Theory* 29: 1–47.

Calhoun, Craig. 1997. *Nationalism.* Minneapolis: University of Minnesota Press.

Calhoun, Craig, ed. 1994. *Social Theory and the Politics of Identity.* Cambridge: Blackwell Publishers.

Calvino, Italo. 1981 [1979]. *If on a Winter's Night a Traveller.* Translated from the Italian by William Weaver. Toronto: Lester and Orpens Dennys Ltd.

Cicero. 1987. "On Ends." In *The Hellenistic Philosophers,* edited by A. A. Long and D. N. Sedley. Cambridge: Cambridge University Press.

Clark, Katerina, and Michael Holquist. 1984a. *Mikhail Bakhtin.* Cambridge: Harvard University Press.

Clark, Katerina, and Michel Holquist. 1984b. "The Influence of Kant in the Early Work of MM Bakhtin." In *Literary Theory and Criticism, Part I,* edited by Joseph P. Strelka. Berlin: Peter Lang, 304.

Clifford, James. 1997. "Diaspora." In *The Ethnicity Reader: Nationalism, Multiculturalism and Migration,* edited by Montserrat Guibernau and John Rex. Cambridge: Polity Press, 283–290.

Cohen, Jean, and Andrew Arato. 1992. *Civil Society and Political Theory.* Cambridge: MIT Press.

Cohen, Hermann. 1977. *Der Logique Reinen Erkenntnis.* Hildesheim: Olms (1902).

———. 1981. *Ethik des Reinen Willens.* Introduction by Steven S. Scharzschild. Hildesheim: Georg Olms (1904).

———. 1999. *Le principe de la methode infitesmale et son histoire.* Translated from the German and notes by Marc De Launy. Paris: Librairie Philosophique J. Vrin.

———. 1972. *The Religion of Reason: Out of the Sources of Judaism.* Introduction by Leo Strauss. Translated from the German by Simon Kaplan. New York: Ungar.

Cooke, Maeve. 1994. *Language and Reason: A Study of Habermas's Pragmatics.* Cambridge: MIT Press.

Côté, Jean-François. 2000. "Bakhtin's Dialogism Reconsidered through Hegel's 'Monologism':The Dialectical foundations of Aesthetics and

Ideology in Contemporary Human Sciences." In *Materialising Bakhtin: The Bakhtin Circle and Social Theory*, edited by C. Brandist and G. Tihanov. London: Macmillan, 20–43.

Couture, Joycelyne, Kai Nielsen, and Michel Seymor, eds. 1996. *Rethinking Nationalism: Canadian Journal of Philosophy*. Calgary: University of Calgary Press.

Cusson, Marie. 1998. "Un dialogue entre M. M. Bakhtine et H.-G. Gadamer?" *Recherches sémiotique* 18, Nos. 1–2: 137–152.

Diekhoff, Alain. 2000. *La nation dans tous ses États: Les identités nationales en movement*. Paris: Flamarion.

Dofny, Jaques, and Marcel Rioux. 1971. "Les classes sociales au Canada français." In *La Société canadienne-française*, edited by Marcel Rioux et Yves Martin. Montréal: Hurtubise, 315–325.

Dostoevsky, Fyodor O. 1991. *The Brothers Karamazov: A Novel in Four Parts With Epilogue*. Translated from the Russian by Richard Pevear and Larissa Volokhonsky. New York: Vintage Books.

Dubiel, Helmut. 1992. "Domination or Emancipation? The Debate over the Heritage of Critical Theory." In *Cultural-Political Interventions in the Unfinished Project of Enlightenment*, translated from the German by Barbara Fultner, edited by Axel Honneth et al. Cambridge: MIT Press.

Dumont, Fernand. 1981. *L'anthropologie dans l'absence de l'homme*. Paris: Presses universitaires de France.

———. 1993. *Genèse de la société québécoise*. Montréal: Boréal.

———. 1968. *Le lieu de l'homme*. Montréal: Éditions HMH.

———. 1981. *Le Sort de la culture*. Montréal: L'Hexagone.

———. 1996. *Raisons Communes*. Montréal: Boréal.

Durkheim, Émile. 1984 [1933]. *The Division of Labor in Society*. Translated from the French by W. D. Halls. New York: Free Press.

———. *The Rules of Sociological Method*. 1966 [1938]. Translated from the French by Sarah Solovay and John Mueller. New York: The Free Press.

Duvakin, V. D. 1996. *Besedy VD Duvakina's MM Bakhtinym*. Edited by V. B. Kuznetsova, M. V. Radzishevskii, and V. F. Teider. Moscow: Progress.

Emerson, Caryl. 1997. *The First Hundred Years of Mikhail Bakhtin*. Princeton: Princeton University Press.

———. 1993. "Preface to Mikhail K. Ryklin, 'Bodies of Terror,'" *New Literary History* 24: 45–49.

———. 2001. "Postface." In *Bakhtin and Religion: A Feeling of Faith*, edited by Susan M. Felch, Paul J Contino, and Gary Saul Morson. Evanston: Northwestern University Press.

Ferry, Jean-Marc. 2000. *La Question de l'État Européen*. Paris: Gallimard.

Fichte, Johann Gottlieb. 1992. *Fichte: Foundations of Transcendental Philosophy: (Wissenschaftslere) nova methodo (1796/99)*. Edited and translated from the German by Daniel Breazeale. Ithaca: Cornell University Press.

Francis, Emerich. 1955. *In Search of Utopia: The Mennonites in Manitoba.* Altona, Manitoba: D. W. Freisen.

Gagné, Gilles. 1995. "Dieu qui sauve tout: note sur le préambule," *Conjonctures* 22: 25–46.

Gardiner, Michael. 1992. *The Dialogics of Critique: M. M. Bakhtin and the Theory of Ideology.* Routledge: London.

———. 1993. "Ecology and Carnival: Traces of a 'Green' Social Theory in the Writings of M. M. Bakhtin," *Theory and Society* 22: 765–812.

Gagnon, Alain. 2000. "Plaidoyer pour l'interculturalisme." *Possibles,* 24: 4, 11–25.

Gellner, Ernst. 1983. *Nations and Nationalism.* London: Basil Blackwell.

Giddens, Anthony. 1998. *The Third Way: The Renewal of Social Democracy.* London: Polity Press.

Greenfield, L. 1992. *Nationalism: Five Roads to Modernity.* Cambridge: Harvard University Press.

Guiberneau, Montserrat. 1999. *Nations Without States: Political Communities in a Global Age.* Cambridge: Polity Press.

Habermas, Jürgen. 1970. *Toward a Rational Society: Student Protest, Science and Politics.* Translated from the German by J. J. Shapiro. Boston: Beacon Press.

———. 1984. *The Theory of Communicative Action Volume I: Reason and the Evolution of Society.* Translated from the German by Thomas McCarthy. Boston: Beacon Press.

———. 1985. *The Philosophical Discourse on Modernity: Twelve Lectures.* Translated from the German by Frederick Lawrence. Cambridge: MIT Press.

———. 1987. *The Theory communicative Action Volume II: Lifeworld and System: A Critique of Functionalist Reason.* Boston: Beacon Press.

———. 1989. "The Philosopher as a Diagnostician of His Time," *Vorposy filosofii* 9: 80–83.

———. 1990. *Moral consciousness and Communicative Action.* translated from the German by christian Lenhardt and Shierry Webber Nicholson. Cambridge: MIT Press.

———. 1991. "Justice and Solidarity: On the Discussion Concerning 'Stage' 6." In *Hermeneutics and Critical Theory in Ethics and Politics,* edited by Michael Kelly. Cambridge: MIT Press, 32–52.

———. 1992a. "Further Reflexions on the Public Sphere." *In Habermas and the Public Sphere,* edited by Craig Calhoun. Translated from the German by Thomas Burger. Cambridge: MIT Press, 421–461.

———. 1992b. *Postmetaphysical Thinking: Philosophical Essays,* translated from the German by William Mark Hohengarten. Cambridge: MIT Press.

———. 1993. *Justification and Application: Remarks on Discourse Ethics.* Translated from the German by Ciaran Cronin. Cambridge: MIT Press.

————. 1994a. *The Past as Future: Interviews with Michael Haller*. Translated from the German and edited by Peter Hohendahl. Lincoln: University of Nebraska Press.

————. 1994b. "Struggles for Recognition in the Democratic Constitutional State." In *Multiculturalism*, edited by Amy Gutmann. Princeton: Princeton University Press, 107–148.

————. 1996a. *Between Facts and Norms: Contribution to a Discourse Theory of Law and Democracy*. Translated by William Rehg. Cambridge: MIT Press.

————. 1996b. "National Reunification and Popular Sovereignty," *New Left Review* 219: 3–13.

————. 1996c. "Three Normative Theories of Democracy." In *Democracy and Difference: Contesting the Boundaries of the Political*. Edited by Seyla Benhabib. Princeton: Princeton University Press, 21–30.

————. 1998a. *Berlin Republic: Writings on Germany*. Translated from the German by Steven Rendall. Lincoln: University of Nebraska Press.

————. 1998b. *The Inclusion of the Other: Studies in Political Theory*. Edited by Ciaran Cronin and Pablo De Greiff. Cambridge: MIT Press.

————. 2001. *The Postnational Constellation: Political Essays*. Translated from the German by Max Pensky. Cambridge: MIT Press.

Hall, John, ed. 1998. *The State of the Nation: Ernest Gellner and The Theory of Nationalism*. London: Cambridge University Press.

Hartmann, Nicolas. 1926a. *Ethik*. Berlin: Leipzig.

————. 1926b. *Grundzug fur einer Metaphysik der Erkenntnis*. Berlin: Leipzig.

Hegel, G. W. F. 1991. *Elements of The Philosophy of Right*. Edited by Allen Wood. Translated from the German by H. B. Nisbet. Cambridge: Cambridge University Press.

Held, David, et al. 1999. *Global Transformations: Politics, Economics and Culture*. Stanford: Stanford University Press.

Heller, Agnes. 1990. *A Philosophy of Morals*. London: Basil Blackwell.

Hirschkop, Ken. 1986. "Bakhtin, Discourse, and Democracy," *New Left Review* 160: 92–113.

————. 1998 " Bakhtin Myths, or Why We All Need Alibis," *The South Atlantic Quarterly* 97, no. 3/4: 579–598.

————. 1999. *Mikhail Bakhtin: An Aestehic For Democracy*. London: Oxford University Press.

Hitchcock, Peter. 1998. "The Bakhtin Center and the State of the Archives: An Interview with David Shepherd," *The South Atlantic Quarterly* 97, no. 3/4: 753–772.

Hobsbaum, Eric. 1994. *Age of Extremes: The Short Twentieth Century*. London: Michael Joseph.

————. 1990. *Nations and Nationalism Since 1780: Programme, Myth, Reality*. New York: Cambridge University Press.

Hollinger, David A. 1995. *Postethnic America: Beyond Multiculturalism*. New York: Basic Books.

Holquist, Michael. 1990. *Dialogism: Bakhtin and His World*. London: Routledge.

———. 1998. "Afterword: A Two-Faced Hermes," *The South Atlantic Quarterly* 97, no. 3/4: 781–790.

Horster, Detlef, and Willem van Reijen. 1992. *Habermas an Introduction*. Translated from the German by Heidi Thompson. Philadelphia: Pennbridge Books.

Horton, John. 1998. "Charles Taylor: Selfhood, Community, and Democracy." In *Liberal Democracy and its Critics*, edited by April Carter and Geoffrey Stokes. London: Polity Press, 155–175.

Honneth, Axel. 1996. "Chapter 4: Recognition and Socialization: Mead's Naturalistic Transformation of Hegel's Idea." In *The Struggle for Recognition: The Moral Grammar of Social Conflicts*. Cambridge: MIT Press, 71–91.

Horkheimer, Max, and Theodore Adorno. 1972. *The Dialectic of Enlightenment*. Translated from the German by John Cumming. New York: Herder and Herder.

Horkheimer, Max. 1972. *Critical Theory*. Translated from the German by Matthew J. O. Connell. New York: Herder and Herder.

von Humbolt, Wilhelm. 1988. *On Language: The Diversity of Human Language Structure and Its Influence on the Mental Development of Mankind*. Translated from the German by Peter Heath. New York: Cambridge University Press.

Jaspers, Karl. 1957. *The Great Philosophers. (Kant). Vol. 1*. New York: Harvest Books.

Jay, Martin. 1993. *Force Fields*. New York: Routledge.

Joas, Hans. 1993. *Social Theory and Pragmatism*. Chicago: University of Chicago Press.

———. 1996. *The Creativity of Action*. Chicago: University of Chicago Press.

——— 1997 [1985]. *G. H. Mead: A Contemporary Re-examination of His Thought*. Cambridge: MIT Press.

———. 2000. *The Genesis of Values*. Translated from the German by G. Moore. Chicago: University of Chicago Press.

Joas, Hans, and Axel Honneth, eds. 1991. *Communicative Action: Essays on Jürgen Habermas's The Theory of Communicative Action*. Translated from the German by Jeremy Gaines and Doris L. Jones. London: Polity Press.

Kant, Immanuel. 1963. *Lectures on Ethics*. Translated by Louis Infield. Cambridge: Hackett Publishing Company.

———. 1973. *Critique of Judgement*. Translated by James Creed Meridith. Oxford: Oxford University Press.

————. 1978a. *Anthropology from a Pragmatic Point of View.* Translated by Victor Lyle Dowdwell. Carbondale and Edwardsville: Southern Illinois University Press.

————. 1978b. *Critique of Pure Reason.* Translated by Norman Kemp Smith. London: MacMillan.

————. 1990. *Foundations of the Metaphysics of Morals.* Translated by Lewis White Beck. New York: Macmillan Publishing Company.

————. 1993. *Critique of Practical Reason.* Translated by Lewis White Beck. Upper Saddle River, N. J.: Prentice Hall.

Kearney, Richard. 1996. *Postnational Ireland: Politics, Culture, Philosophy.* London: Routledge.

Keating, Michael. 1996. *Nations Against the State: The New Politics of Nationalism in Quebec, Catalonia, and Scotland.* London: MacMillan.

Kierkegaard, Søren. 1959. *Either/or. Vol. I.* Translated by David F. Swenson and Lillian Marvin Swenson, with revisions and a foreword by Howard A. Johnson. Garden City, N.Y.: Doubleday.

————. 1970. *Fear and Trembling.* Translated from the German by Walter Lowrie. New Jersey: Princeton University Press.

————. 1972. *Either/or. Vol. II.* Translated by Walter Lowrie, with revisions and a foreword by Howard A. Johnson. Princeton: Princeton University Press.

Koczanowicz, Leszek. 2000. "Freedom and Communication: The Concept of Human Self in Mead and Bakhtin," *Dialogism: An International Journal of Bakhtin Studies,* 4: 54–66.

Kymlicka, Will. 1998. *Finding Our Way: Rethinking Ethnocultural Relations in Canada.* Toronto: Oxford University Press.

————. 1995. *Multicultural Citizenship: A Liberal Theory of Minority Rights.* Oxford: Oxford University Press.

Layder, Derek. 1994. *Understanding Social Theory.* London: Sage Publications.

Leger, Francois. 1989. *La pensée de Georg Simmel: Contribution à l'histoire des idées au début du Xxe siècle.* Préface de Julien Freund. Paris: Éditions Kimé.

Lajoie, Mark. 1999. *On the Quebec Question.* Unpublished Manuscript.

De Launay, Marc. 1999. "Presentation." In Hermann Cohen. *Le principe de la methode infitesimale et son histoire.* Translated and notes by Marc De Launy. Paris: Librairie Philosophique J. Vrin.

Lemert, Charles. 1994. "Dark Thoughts About the Self." In *Social Theory and the Politics of Identity,* edited by Craig Calhoun. Cambridge: Blackwell Publishers, 103–131.

Lepsius, Rainer. 1991. "Ethnos oder Demo.s" In *Interesten, Ideen, und initiation.* Westdeutscher Verlag, 247–255.

Levine, Donald. 1995. *Visions of the Sociological Tradition.* Chicago: University of Chicago Press.

Lossky, N. O. 1951. *The History of Russian Philosophy.* New York: International Universities Press.

Lowenthal, Leo. 1961. *Literature, Popular Culture, and Society.* New Jersey: Prentice-Hall.

Luhmann, Niklas. 1995. *Social Systems.* Translated from the German by John Bednarz with Dirk Baeker. Stanford: Stanford University Press.

Lukács, György. 1971. *Theory of the Novel; a Historico-Philosophical Essay on the Forms of Great Epic Literature.* Translated from the German by Anna Bostock. Cambridge: MIT Press.

Maklin, Vitaly. 1998. "Questions and Answers: Bakhtin from the Beginning, at the End of the Century," *The South Atlantic Quarterly* 97, no. 3/4: 753–772.

Mannheim, Karl. 1936. *Ideology and Utopia; An Introduction to the Sociology of Knowledge.* Preface by Louis Wirth. New York: Harcourt, Brace and Co.

Marcuse, Herbert. 1977. *The Aesthetic Dimension : Toward a Critique of Marxist Esthetics.* Boston: Beacon Press.

———. 1964. *One Dimensional Man: Studies in the Ideology of Advanced Industrial Society.* Boston: Beacon Press.

Marshall, T. H. 1963 [1949]. "Citizenship and Social Class." In *Sociology at the Crossroads and Other Essays.* London: Heinemann, 67–128.

McArthy, Thomas. 1991. *Ideals and Illusions: On Reconstruction and Deconstruction in Contemporary Critical Theory.* Cambridge: MIT Press.

McCrone, David. 1998. *The Sociology of Nationalism: Tomorrow's Ancestors.* London: Routledge.

McRoberts, Kenneth. 1997. *Misrecognizing Canada: The Struggle for National Unity.* New York: Oxford Press.

Mead, George Herbert. 1903. "The Definition of the Psychical," *Decentenial Publications of the University of Chicago, First Series,* III: 72–112.

———. 1934. *Mind Self and Society from the Point of View of a Social Behaviorist.* Edited by Charles Morris. Chicago: University of Chicago Press.

———. 1956a. "Evolution Becomes a General Idea." In *George Herbert Mead: On Social Psychology,* edited by Anselm Strauss. Chicago: University of Chicago Press.

———. 1956b. "The Genesis of the Self and Social Control." In *George Herbert Mead Selected Writings,* edited by Andrew Reck. Indianapolis: The Bobbs-Merrill, Co., 290.

———. 1964. "The Social Self." In *George Herbert Mead Selected Writings,* edited by Andrew Reck. Indianapolis: The Bobbs-Merrill Co.

———. 1968a. "The Philosophical Basis of Ethics." In *George Herbert Mead: Essays on His Social Philosophy,* edited by John Petras. New York: Teachers College Press, Columbia University.

————. 1968b. "The Philosophies of Royce, James, and Dewey in the American Setting." In *George Herbert Mead: Essays on His Social Philosophy*, edited by John W. Petras. New York: Teachers College Press, Columbia University.

Medvedev, Pavel. 1985. *The Formal Method in Literary Scholarship: A Crirtical Introduction to Sociological Poetics*. Translated and Introduction by A. J. Wehrle. Cambridege: Harvard University Press.

de Michiel, Margherita. 1998. "Dostoïevski et Bakhtine: L'ecrivain et le lecteur. A propos de Problemy tvorchestva Dostoevskogo *[Problemes de l'oeuvre de Dostoievski.* 1929]," *Recherches sémiotiques*, 18, no. 1–2: 121–136.

Mihailovic, Alexander. 1997. *Corporeal Worlds: Mikhail Bakhtin's Theology of Discourse*. Evanston: Northwestern University Press.

Morris, Ray. 1995. *The Carnivalization of Politics: Quebec Cartoons on Relations with Canada, England, and France, 1960–1979*. Montreal: McGill-Queens Press.

Morson, Gary Saul. 1996. "Misanthropology," *New Literary History* 27: 57–72.

————. 1995. "Prosaic Bakhtin: Landmarks, Anti-Intelligentsialism, and the Russian Countertradition." In *Bakhtin in Contexts: Across the Disciplines*, edited by Amy Mankler, introduction by Caryl Emerson. Evanston: Northwestern University Press, 33–78.

Morson, Gary Saul, and Caryl Emerson, eds. 1989. *Rethinking Bakhtin: Extentions and Challenges*. Evanston: Northwestern University Press.

————. 1990. *Mikhail Bakhtin: Creation of a Prosaics*. Stanford: Stanford University Press.

Motyl, Alexander. 1999. *Revolutions, Nations, Empires: Conceptual Limits and Theoretical Possibilities*. New York: Columbia University Press.

Narin, Thom. 1997. *Faces of Nationalism: Janus Revisited*. London: Verso, 1997.

Nemeth, Thomas. 1996. "The Rise of Russian neo-Kantianism: Vvedenskij's Early 'Critical Philosophy,'" *Studies in East European Thought* 50, no. 2 (June): 119–151.

Nielsen, Kai. 1999. "Cosmopolitanism, Universalism and Particularism in an Age of Nationalism and Multiculturalism." In *Philosophical Exchange*, 3–38.

Nielsen, Greg Marc. 1987. "Reading the Quebec Imaginary: Marcel Rioux and Dialogical Form," *Canadian Journal of Sociology* 12, nos. 1–2: 134–150.

————. 1993. "The Frankfurt School." In *Encyclopedia of Contemporary Literary Theory*, edited by Irene Makaryk. Toronto: University of Toronto Press, 60–65

————. 1994. *Le Canada de Radio-Canada : Sociologie critique et dialogisme culturel.* Toronto: Éditions du GREF.

————. 1995. "Bakhtin and Habermas: Toward a Transcultural Ethics," *Theory and Society: Renewal and Critique* 24\6: 803–835.

————. 1997. "Culture and the Politics of Being Québécois: Identity and Communication." In *Critical Issues in Quebec Society*, edited by Marcel Fournier et al. Prentice Hall, 81–94.

————. 1998a. "The Norms of Answerability: Bakhtin and The Fourth Postulate." In *Bakhtin and the Human Sciences*, edited by Michael Gardiner and Michael Bell. London: Sage Publications, 214–230.

————. 1998b. "La Question du Quebec, le lien social et la théorie communicationelle de la démocratie." *Le Carrefour: Revue de reflexion interdsiciplinaire,*20–1: 109–131.

————. 2000a. "Action and Eros in the Creative Zone," *Dialogism: International Review of Bakhtin Studies* 4: 34–53.

————. 2000b. "Looking Back on the Subject: Mead and Bakhtin on Reflexivity and the Political." In *Materialising Bakhtin: The Bakhtin Circle and Social Theory*, edited by C. Brandist and G. Tihanov. London: Macmillan, 142–163.

Nikolaev, Nikoai. 1997. "Bakhtin's Second Discovery in Philosophy: 'Author' and 'Hero' with Reference to the Prototext of the Dostoevsky book." In *Dialogue and Culture: Eighth International Conference on Mikhail Bakhtin*, edited by Anthony Wal. Calgary. Unpublished Program.

————. 2000. "Publishing Bakhtin: A Philological Problem (Two Reviews)," *Dialogism: An International Journal of Bakhtin Studies* 4: 67–111.

————. 2001. "Appendix: M. M. Bakhtin's Lectures and Speeches of 1924–1925." Introduced and edited by N. I. Nicolaev. Translated by Leonid Livak and Alexandar Mihailovic. In *Bakhtin and Religion: A Feeling of Faith*, edited by Susan M. Felch, Paul J. Contino, and Gary Saul Morson. Evanston: Northwestern University Press.

Nussbaum, Martha. 1994. *The Theory of Desire: Theory and Practice in Hellenistic Ethics*. Princeton: Princeton University Press.

————. 1996. "Patriotism and Cosmopolitanism." In *For Love of Country: Debating the Limits of Patriotism*, edited by Joshua Cohen. Boston: Beacon Press.

————. 1999. *Sex and Social Justice*. New York: Oxford University Press.

Oquendo, Angel. 1999. "Defending National Culture in the Postnational State." Unpublished manuscript.

Ortiz, Fernando. 1978. *Contrapunto Cubano*. Caracas: Biblioteca Ayacucho.

Pan'kox, Nikolai. 1998. "Archival Material on Bakhtin's Nevel Period," *The South Atlantic Quarterly* 97, no. 3/4: 733–752.

Parsons, Talcott. 1954 [1950]. "The Prospects of Sociological Theory." In *Essays in Sociological Theory*. New York: The Free Press, 348–369.

Pfuetze, Paul. 1954. *The Social Self.* New York: Bookman Associates.

Pinter, Steve, and Greg Nielsen. 1991. "Intimacy and Cultural Crisis," *Canadian Journal of Political and Social Theory* 14, nos. 1–3: 69–87.

Poole, Brian. 1998. "Bakhtin and Casserir: The Philosophical Origins of Bakhtin's Carnival Messianism," *The South Atlantic Quarterly* 97, no. 3/4: 537–578.

———. 1997. "Bakhtin: From Phenomenology to Dialogue." Unpublished Manuscript.

Plato. 1963. "Meno." In *Plato: The Collected Dialogues, Including the Letters*. Translated by W. K. Guthrie. Princeton: Princeton University Press, 370-371.

Pumpiansky, L. V. 2001. Appendix: "M. M. Bakhtin's Lectures and Speeches of 1924–1925." Introduced and edited by N. I. Nicolaev. Translated from the Russian by Leonid Livak and Alexandar Mihailovic. In *Bakhtin and Religion: A Feeling of Faith*, edited by Susan M. Felch, Paul J. Contino, and Gary Saul Morson. Evanston: Northwestern University Press.

Radice, Martha. 2000. *Feeling Comfortable? The Urban Experience of Anglo-Montrealers*. Quebec: Les Presses de l'Université Laval.

Rawls, John. 1971. *A Theory of Juctice*. Cambridge: Harvard University Press.

———. 1996. *Political Liberalism*. New York: Columbia University Press.

———. 1991. *The Law of Peoples, With the Idea of Public Reason Revisited*. Cambridge: Harvard University Press.

Rehg, William. 1994. *Insight and Solidarity: The Discourse Ethics of Jürgen Habermas*. Cambridge: MIT Press.

Rioux, Marcel. 1950. "Remarques sur la notion de culture en anthropologie," *Revue d'histoire de l'Amérique française* IV, no. 3: 315.

———. 1955. "Idéologie et crise de conscience du Canada français," *Cité libre* 14.

———. 1978a. *Essai de sociologie critique*. Montreal: HMH.

———. 1978b [1969]. *Quebec in Question*. Translated from the French by James Boake. Toronto: J. Lewis and Samuel.

———. 1980. "La nouvelle culture: un effort de retotalisation des pouvoirs de l'homme." Interview with Edgar Morin, *Forces* 52: 4–15.

Ritzer, George. 1996. *Modern Sociological Theory*. New York: McGraw-Hill.

Rocher, Francois, and Daniel Salée. 1997. "Liberalisme et tensions identitaires: Éléments de réflexion sur le désarroi des sociétés modernes," *Politique et sociétés* 16, no. 2: 3–30.

Roschlitz, Rainer. 1993. "Kant et Darwin, le projet de Habermas," *Magazine littéraire* 309: 75.

Rosenthal, Sandra, and Patrick Bourgeois. 1980. *Pragmatism and Phenomenology: A Philosophic Encounter*. Amsterdam: B. R. Gruner Publishing Co.

Ryklin, Mikhaïl. 1993. "Bodies of Terror: Theses Toward a Logic of Violence," *New Literary History*. Translated from the Russian by Molly Wesling and Donald Wesling, Vol. 24: 51–74.

Rzhevsky, Nicholas. 1994. "Kozhinov on Bakhtin," *New Literary History* 25: 429–444.

Sabo, Kathy, and Greg Nielsen. 1984. "Critique dialogique et postmodernisme," *Etudes françaises*, 20, 1: 74–85.

Scharzschild, Steven S. 1981. "Introduction". In *Ethik des Reinen Willens*, edited by Herman Cohen. Hildesheim: Georg Olms, xii–xxxv.

Scheler, Max. 1973 [1916]. *Formalism in Ethics and Non-Formal Ethics of Values: A New Attempt toward the Foundation of an Ethical Personalism*. Translated from the German by Manfred S. Frings and Roger L. Funk. Evanston: Northwestern University Press.

———. 1970 [1914]. *The Nature of Sympathy*. Translated from the German by Peter Heath. Introduction by W. Stark. Hamden, Conn.: Arcon Books.

Schlucter, Wolfgang. 1996. *Paradoxes of Modernity: Culture and Conduct in the Theory of Max Weber*. Translated by Neil Solomon. Stanford: Stanford University Press.

Schnapper, Dominique. 1994. *La communauté des citoyens: Sur l'idée moderne de la nation*. Paris: Gallimard.

Seymor, Michel. 1999a. *La Nation en Question*. Montréal: Hexagone.

Seymor, Michel, ed. 1999b. *Nationalité, Citoynenneté, et solidarité*. Montreal: Liber.

Sidorkin, Alexander. 1999. *Beyond Discourse: Education, The Self, and Dialogue*. Albany: State University of New York Press.

Simmel, Georg. 1968. *Das Individuelle Gesetz*. Edited by Michael Landmann. Frankfurt am Main: 244–247. (First published in *Logos*. Moscow: Musaget'. 1913. Translated to the Russian in *Logos*. Moscow: Musaget'. 1914).

———. 1949. "The Sociology of Sociability." Translated by E. C. Hughes. *American Journal of Sociology* LV.

———. 1971. *Georg Simmel: On Individuality and Social Forms*. Introduced and edited by Donald Levine. Chicago: University of Chicago Press.

———. 1984. *On Women, Sexuality, and Love*. Edited by G. Oakes. New Haven: Yale University Press.

———. 1990. *Philosophy of Money*. Translated by Tom Bottomore and David Frisley. New York: Routledge.

Sini, Stefania. 1998. "Intonation, Tone, and Accent in Mikhaïl Bakhtin's Thought," *Recherches sémiotiques* 18, no. 1–2: 39–58.

Smith, Anthony. 1991. *National Identity*. London: Penguin Books.

Stallybrass, Peter, and Allon White. 1986. *The Politics and Poetics of Transgression*. New York: Cornell University Press.

Statistics Canada. http://www.statcan.ca.htm

Steinglas, Matt. 1998. "The International Man of Mystery: The Battle over Mikhaïl Bakhtin," *Linguafranca* 8, no. 3 (April): 3.

Tamir, Yael. 1993. *Liberal Nationalism*. Princeton: Princeton University Press.

Taylor, Charles . 1991. *The Malaise of Modernity*. Concord: Anansi.

———. 1998. "Nationalism and Modernity." In *The State of the Nation: Ernest Gellner and The Theory of Nationalism,* edited by John Hall . London: Cambridge University Press, 191–218.

———. 1994. "The Politics of Recognition." In *Multiculturalism,* edited by Amy Gutmann. Princeton: Princeton University Press, pp. 25–73.

———. 1993. *Reconciling the Solitudes: Essays on Canadian Federalism and Nationalism.* Edited by Guy Laforest. Montreal: McGill-Queens University Press.

Thériault, Yvon. 1998. "La nation orpheline," *Carrefour : Revue de réflexion interdisciplinaire* 19–20: 75–94.

Theunissen, Michael. 1984. *The Other: Studies in the Social Ontology of Husserl, Heidegger, Sartre, and Buber.* Translated from the German by Christopher Macaan. Cambridge: MIT Press.

Thompson, John. 1993. "The Theory of the Public Sphere," *Theory, Culture, and Society* 10.

Thomson, Clive, and Julia Kristeva. 1998. "Dialogisme, carnavalesque et psychanalyse: entretien avec Julia Kristeva sur la réception de l'œuvre de Mikhaïl Bakhtine en France," *Recherches sémiotique* 18, no. 1–2: 15–30.

Todorov, Tzvetan. 1979. "Préface." In *Esthétique de la création verbale* by Mikhail Bakhtin. Translated from the Russian by A. Aucouturier. Paris: Gallimard.

———. 1981. *Mikhail Bakhtine, le principe dialogique, suivi des écrits du cercle de Bakhtine.* Paris: Seuil.

———. 1998. "I, Thou, russia," *Times Literary Suppliment,* March 13: 6–8.

Trey, George A. 1992. "Communicative Ethics in the Face of Alterity: Habermas, Levinas, and the Problem of Post-conventional Universalism," *Praxis International* 11, no. 14: 412–427.

Tully, James. 1995. *Strange Multiplicities: Constitutionalism in an Age of Diversity.* Cambridge: Cambridge University Press.

Voloshinov, V. I. 1986. *Marxism and Philosophy of Language.* Cambridge: Harvard University Press.

———. 1976. *Freudianism: A Critical Sketch.* Translated from the Russian by I. R. Titunik and edited in collaboration with Neal Bruss. Bloomington: Indiana University Press.

Walzer, Michael. 1994. *Thick and Thin: Moral Argument at Home and Abroad.* Notre Dame: University of Notre Dame Press.

———. 1997. *On Toleration.* New Haven: Yale University Press.

Warnke, Georgia. 1987. *Gadamer: Hermeneutics, Tradition, and Reason.* Cambridge: Polity Press.

———. 1992. *Justice and Interpretation.* Cambridge: Polity Press.

———. 1999. *Legitimate Differences: Interpretation in the Abortion Controversy and Other Public Debates.* Berkeley: University of California Press.

Warren, Jean-Phillipe. 1998. *Un Supplément d'Âme: Les intentions primordiales de Fernand Dumont (1947–1970)*. Quebec: Les Presses de L'université de Laval.

Watchtel, Andrew. 2000. "Not Ready for Prime Time: The Prehistory of Bakhtin's Problems of Dostoevsky's Poetics in English," *Dialogism: An International Journal of Bakhtin Studies* 4: 112–126.

Weber, Max. 1946. "Science as a Vocation." In *From Max Weber*. Translated and edited by H. H. Gerth and C. Wright Mills. New York: Oxford University Press, 129–156.

———. 1949. *The Methodology of the Social Sciences*. Translated from German and edited by E. Schils and H. Finch. New York: The Free Press.

———. 1978. *Economy and Society: An Outline of Interpretive Sociology*. Translated by Ephraim Fischoff et al. Edited by Gunther Roth and Claus Wittich. Berkeley: University of California Press.

———. 1995a. "Freudianism." In *Weber: Selections in Translation*, edited by W. G. Runciman. Translated by Eric Mathews. Cambridge: Cambridge University Press.

———. 1995b. *The Russian Revolutions*. Translated from the German by Gordon Wells and Peter Baehr. Ithaca: Cornell University Press.

Weinstein, Michael. 1985. *Culture Critique: Fernand Dumont and New Quebec Sociology*. New York: St. Martin's Press.

Wieviorka, Michel. 1991. *L'espace du racisme*. Paris: Éditions Balland.

———. 2001. *La différence*. Paris: Éditions Balland.

Willey, Thomas. 1978. *Back to Kant: The Revival of Kantianism in German Social and Historical Thought, 1860–1914*. Detroit: Wayne State University.

Zac, Sylvain. 1984. *La philosophie religieuse de Hermann Cohen*. Avant propos de Paul Ricoeur. Paris: Librairie Philosophique de J. Vrin.

Zenkovsky, V. V. 1953. *A History of Russian Philosophy*. Translated by George L. Kline. 2 Vols. New York: Columbia University Press.

INDEX